# The Unseen Leader

Martin Gutmann

# The Unseen Leader

## How History Can Help Us Rethink Leadership

 Springer

Martin Gutmann [iD]
Lucerne School of Business
Lucerne University of Applied Sciences and Arts
Lucerne, Switzerland

ISBN 978-3-031-37828-7          ISBN 978-3-031-37829-4    (eBook)
https://doi.org/10.1007/978-3-031-37829-4

This Springer imprint is published by the registered company Springer Nature Switzerland AG
The registered company address is: Gewerbestrasse 11, 6330 Cham, Switzerland

Paper in this product is recyclable.

**Words of Appreciation for the Book**

"A provocative look at what history really teaches us about effective leadership. This book will challenge you to rethink some of your core assumptions about what it takes to align people around common goals."

—**Adam Grant**, #1 *New York Times* best-selling author of THINK AGAIN and host of the podcast Re:Thinking

"A delightful and powerful read. Through the simple act of profiling four of history's overlooked or misunderstood leaders, Gutmann challenges some of our most sacred leadership assumptions and lays the foundations for a new leadership story."

—**Erin Meyer**, Ph.D., *New York Times* best-selling author of No Rules Rules: Netflix and the Culture of Reinvention and Professor at INSEAD

"Deeply insightful and refreshingly unique! *The Unseen Leader* tells the profound tales of four leaders that teach and inspire us about the leadership that often doesn't make headlines, but rather quietly and purposefully instructs and guides teams to lasting success. This is a captivating read that will challenge you to see leadership in a new light and offer practical ways you can become the leader you strive to be today."

—**Dr. Marshall Goldsmith** is the Thinkers50 #1 Executive Coach and *New York Times* best-selling author of The Earned Life, Triggers, and What Got You Here Won't Get You There

"This book is a game-changer for anyone seeking to lead with purpose and impact. Gutmann challenges us to rethink our traditional notions of leadership by highlighting the often-overlooked, unseen leaders who make a lasting impact. Drawing on historical examples and his training as a historian, Gutmann portrays how these hidden leaders carefully analyze their surroundings, mitigate or diminish conflicts, and act in accordance with the forces of history to accomplish their goals. The book provides practical ways for aspiring leaders to become the kind of 'unseen leader' who can make a real difference in the world. At a time when leadership is increasingly synonymous with heroism, hubris, ego, and unfettered power, Gutmann offers a refreshing take on an alternative style that is effective and most importantly—needed—at this time. It's a must-read for anyone who wants to lead with vision, purpose, and lasting impact."

—**Fred Swaniker**, Founder of the African Leadership Group

"With one foot firmly planted in his training as a historian, Gutmann skillfully challenges readers to reexamine two fundamental assumptions often made about leaders and leadership. One provokes readers to critically examine the role that any one individual can have on the outcome of historical events. Great leaders, he suggests, may be the individuals who read the environment, minimize or de-escalate, act in alignment with historical forces, and know when the old rules, no longer apply. By moving away from our individualistic/heroic exemplars of history, we may uncover a vast array of others who deserve accolades for their unseen leadership."

—**Scott Allen**, Robert M. Ginn Institute Professor for Leadership & Social Responsibility at John Carroll University and host of podcast Phronesis

# Acknowledgments

I first conceived of this book nine years ago. In the near decade since, my children grew older, I changed jobs twice, and the various rhythms of life ebbed and flowed. But the idea behind this book was always there—all too rarely making it to the top of my to-do list but constantly occupying my thoughts. I am profoundly indebted to my wife, Dr. Djahane Salehabadi, for accompanying me on this journey, for enduring countless morning coffees during which another of the book's concepts was fine-tuned or abandoned, and for prodding me just to sit down and write. My three wonderful kids— Espen, Emil, and Ylva—were a source of inspiration and (necessary) distraction from the book. I would be remiss not to thank them, too, for sleeping in progressively longer each year, earning me precious time to write on weekend mornings.

Writing has never been a solo endeavor for me (at least not any time I've been happy with it). Ashley Curtis accompanied me on this project from the start (joined later by Sonia Curtis) as a trusted sparring partner, editor, co-researcher, and co-writer of critical sections of the book. I am deeply grateful to Ashley and Sonia for their dedication to this project.

I also benefited from a great number of beta readers and discussion partners at various stages of the project, whose feedback was vital in my sharpening the book: Dr. Scott Allen, Christopher Björk (who helped me fine-tune the very first sentences I penned for this project), Dr. Stefano Brusoni (whose encouragement over an espresso in his office convinced me to stick with this book), Paul French, Benriah Göldi, Dr. Adam Grant, Noah Gutmann (with whom a conversation in a London pub during the end-spurt of the writing process was particularly motivating), Patrick Gutmann, Rudi Gutmann, Rich Harvell (who gave me critical advice early on in the publication process), Markham

Heid, Chase Huff, Dr. Erin Meyer, Bridget Nurre Jennions, Dr. Djahane Salehabadi, Tim Steigert, Fred Swaniker, Dr. Paul Vanderbroeck, Dr. Reto Wegmann, and Christopher O. Williams. I could not have finished this book without the generous access to Jessie Griffith's beach house. Beth Houston and Jesse Foote helped me with a last-minute title tweaking, on a memorable day on the shore of beautiful Lake Brienz.

I am also grateful to my friends and colleagues who gave me moral support along the way: Guido Bieri, Jay Boynton, Will Decherd, Benriah Göldi, Lucas Iten, Dave O'Sullivan, Martin Oppferkuch, Jack Sasser, and Gabriel Torres-Brown, as well as my colleagues at the Lucerne University of Applied Sciences and Arts: in particular Dr. Richard Abplanalp, Dr. Vidya Alleman-Ravi, Jillain Farrar, Dr. Matthes Fleck, Dr. Joelle Loew, Dr. Ursina Kellerhals, Oliver Kessler, Douglas MacKevett, Richard Moist, Vinzenz Rast, Fabio Sandmeier, and Ingo Stolz.

I would also like to thank my agent at Writers House, New York, John Schline, for his efforts in finding a home for this somewhat quirky book and Prashanth Mahagaonkar, Ruth Milewski, and the team at Springer Nature for the smooth publication process.

# Contents

## Part III    Rethinking Leadership

# About the Author

**Martin Gutmann** Ph.D., is a Swiss-American historian, author, and professor at the Lucerne School of Business, Lucerne University of Applied Sciences and Arts in Switzerland. He has published three books, most recently (as co-editor with Dan Gorman) *Before the UN Sustainable Development Goals. A Historical Companion* (Oxford University Press). He lives in Freiburg-im-Breisgau, Germany, with his wife and their three children.

# Introduction: History and Leadership

Leadership is all the hype these days, and for good reason: the world has grown ever more complex and uncertain in the last two decades. The search for leaders and leadership secrets to help navigate this complexity has grown correspondingly. Organizations from Fortune 500 companies to local fire departments are keen to find or train individuals who can mobilize their peers and chart a course to success. In 2011, US companies spent $14 billion on leadership development[1]; by 2018, this figure had risen to $50 billion.[2] And leadership studies is not just serious business; it has become a major subject of academic inquiry. It is an established and thriving field in business schools and university psychology departments the world over.

I knew little of this when I was asked to teach a course on leadership some years ago. As with many things in life, I stumbled onto leadership studies quite by chance. I am a historian by training and found myself early in my career teaching political history at a small business school in Switzerland. Then, when the psychology professor who usually taught leadership fell out, I was asked to step in. In the weeks before the course began, I set to work reading everything I could get my hands on about leadership. What caught my attention early on in my reading was that among the great variety of approaches to studying leadership, there was one prominent trend: that of drawing inspiration and lessons from history's great leaders. Ernest Shackleton, Winston Churchill, Erwin Rommel, Napoleon, Lawrence of Arabia, JFK, and even Genghis Khan and Adolf Hitler made appearances in numerous books, articles, consulting pamphlets, and blogs. And this wasn't just my personal impression. A recent survey by a group of leadership scholars found 80,000

M. Gutmann, *The Unseen Leader*, https://doi.org/10.1007/978-3-031-37829-4_1

titles that seek to find leadership secrets in the examples of inspiring bio-graphical stories.[3]

The idea of extracting leadership lessons from the past is not in and of itself misguided. In fact, there are several advantages to this approach over studying contemporary scenarios.[4] Much like dietary advice and health fads, leadership truths have come and gone. Testing against a more diverse sample of data in highly variable contexts—such as the annals of history provides—is the best way to gauge applicability and durability.

More significantly, historical examples allow for a depth and neutrality of analysis that is difficult to impossible to achieve with contemporary examples. We have a far more profound understanding of the complex interplay of fac-tors that led to, say, the Second Boer War, fought between 1899 and 1902 in what would later become South Africa, than we do of the US invasion of Iraq, launched a century later in 2003. Most relevant sources for understanding the actual decision-making processes behind the 2003 war—such as the protocols of behind-closed-doors deliberations in the White House—are still classified material, inaccessible to writers. Moreover, for historical events such as the Boer War, we can lean on generations of scholarly scrutiny. The buffer of time allows us to entangle complexity and deliver sober judgments about the unfolding of events and the role individual leaders played therein.

However, as I delved into these texts on leadership in preparation for my teaching, I quickly noticed that the historical stories told in many of them were wholly disconnected from some of the most fundamental conclusions of contemporary historical scholarship (I later found out that other historians who stumbled onto management texts with a historical take came to similar conclusions).[5] In the many leadership blogs and articles about Churchill, for example, he is usually seated securely at the steering wheel of history, able to manipulate events at will through his words and actions. Moreover, the plot always features Churchill as a heroic protagonist, under threat from every conceivable danger, who, thanks to his tenacious grit and a superhuman exer-tion of energy, was eventually able to gain the upper hand. This corresponds remarkably little to the war that I had studied as a historian, in which human decisions and actions were consistently and gravely thwarted, diverted, com-plicated, or amplified by a complex set of interlinked technological, economic, and cultural drivers, not to mention the actions and decisions of countless other protagonists. Moreover, as a specialist in the Second World War, I knew that the secret to Churchill's successful handling of the war had nothing to do with his penchant for bold words and action.

The culprit in this gross misreading of history is what I came to call the Action Fallacy—the mistaken belief that the best leaders are those who generate the most noise and sensational activity in the most dramatic circumstances.

Armed with this realization, I set to craft a new leadership story, one that was rooted first and foremost in the insights from historical scholarship. Rather than beginning with a narrow focus on what one or another boisterous and energetic leader said or did, I wanted to start by looking more broadly at challenging episodes in history. I wanted to first understand how professional historians—unconcerned with contemporary leadership theories and fads—reconstructed these events. Only then did I identify those individuals who had been most influential in the event's outcome and sought to uncover their secrets.

History has all too often pitted men and women against challenging odds, circumstances in which time, information, and other resources were scarce and pitfalls awaited around the corner of every decision. In this book, I present four such episodes and the men and women who, more than anyone else, managed to master the moment: Roald Amundsen, easily the most successful polar explorer, but, paradoxically, one of the least well-known. Amundsen ticked off every notable achievement in polar exploration at a time when the available technology and knowledge were just advanced enough for Europeans to enter this hostile realm but fragile enough to offer scant assurance of a safe return. Toussaint Louverture navigated a political, military, and economic quagmire in leading the first successful revolution of an enslaved people—against the wishes of the most powerful European empires, including that of Napoleon. Gertrude Bell, mountain climber, desert explorer, and champion of Arab statehood in the aftermath of the First World War: a region rife with interregional and interreligious, not to mention great power, conflict. And, finally, Winston Churchill, undoubtedly the successful designer of the Allied victory (though not for the reasons usually cited) in what remains the single most complex—not to mention bloody—episode in human history: the Second World War.

What these stories reveal is that truly successful leadership has little to do with Hollywood stereotypes or heroic struggles. Instead, history's most effective leaders did not need to generate a lot of noise and activity because they often reduced dramatic circumstances to a minimum. For this reason, I must warn you, the four leadership tales recounted in this book do not sound like traditional leadership stories—they are more complex and less leader-focused. Rather than heroic protagonists boldly forging ahead, our leaders are at times mere side characters, barely hanging on to the coattails of history. But, I promise you this, it is a more honest retelling of how a few leaders were able to make history while most of their contemporaries were not.

This rethinking of the leadership story is, of course, more than an academic exercise. The Action Fallacy causes real problems. If we have been celebrating the wrong role models and leadership qualities and fundamentally misunderstood what made leaders effective *in the past*, the same is likely happening in your office, community, or sports team *today*. Because, after all, the biases and misconceptions we bring to our reading of the past are often one and the same with which we view the present. More likely than not, it is the loud, boisterous, self-promoting, and perpetually busy types—rather than the Amundsen and Bell—of your office who garner attention, who are promoted, and who serve as role models for the up-and-coming (in fact, as we will see later, several recent studies have confirmed just this fact).

We are, in other words, revering and promoting the wrong people for the wrong reasons. That's bad enough, but we are also—and this is the other side of the coin—systematically overlooking those with the greatest potential to make positive and lasting change simply because we don't recognize what they do as leadership. The Action Fallacy obscures the actual process through which effective leaders mobilize their peers and shape the outcome of events.

For this reason, rather than uncovering yet another leadership secret, this book proposes a different way of talking about leadership. Unhinged from the Action Fallacy, this book weaves a new leadership story, one that moves the perspective away from the granular details of what a leader said or did to an appreciation for how he or she understood and interacted with the larger forces at work in their particular time. It is a narrative that rewards leaders who avoid crisis rather than those who promote it. It is a story that privileges the subtle, often imperceptible ways in which effective leaders nudge events toward a favorable outcome rather than the spectacular but ineffective bulldozing tactics of many a famed leader. And it is a story that, more often than not, singles out and celebrates a new cast of leaders from the heroic ones we typically hear so much about. Such a story makes truly effective leaders of the past visible. And, it is my hope, it will make visible the truly effective leaders in our midst today as well.

It is time we craft a new leadership story. That is what this book sets out to do.

# Part I

## Toward a New Leadership Story

# The Polar Explorer, the Desert Fox, and the Action Fallacy

Few leadership parables are more compelling than that of Ernest Shackleton's fateful struggle for survival in the frozen wastelands of the Antarctic Ocean Shackleton and his crew of explorers set off aboard the Endurance in the summer of 1914, intent on being the first to cross Antarctica. Well before reaching the continent's shores, however, the ship became frozen in place in a vast sheet of ice. The men huddled within the captive hull for nearly a year until the ice crushed it and swallowed it up. Shackleton and his crew were now on their own, without a ship, far from the mainland and even farther from the nearest outpost of civilization. Over the course of the following half year, the men dragged their miserable possessions toward open water, camped on a shrinking ice floe, and braved the stormiest seas on earth in a tiny lifeboat. Finally, in May 1916, Shackleton and a small party reached the safety of St. Georgia. The rest of the crew, stuck on a guano-encrusted outcrop known as Elephant Island, was rescued soon afterward.[1]

The same month that Shackleton set off on his expedition a war erupted that would ravage Europe, fell four great empires, and kill millions of young men. During the opening skirmishes of the First World War, a young German officer named Erwin Rommel made a name for himself as a fearless and innovative leader. During the next World War, some two and a half decades later, Rommel emerged as a veritable military hero. In 1941, Hitler sent him to Libya to support the Italian army in its fight against British troops. The environment was harsh—sand and heat wore down men and machines alike. Rommel ignored the directive to remain on the defensive and instead led his small *Afrikakorps* to a series of spectacular victories across the vast expanses of the North African desert. Sporting a captured pair of British tank driver's

© The Author(s), under exclusive license to Springer Nature Switzerland AG 2023
M. Gutmann, *The Unseen Leader*, https://doi.org/10.1007/978-3-031-37829-4_2

goggles and his sand-encrusted battle tunic, Rommel looked nothing like his stuffy, aristocratic peers in the German officer corps. And for two long years, he gave a larger British force and its increasingly flabbergasted generals one unexpected beating after another. His exploits earned him the nickname "the Desert Fox."

Despite a breadth of approaches to studying leadership, drawing lessons from inspiring examples of the past is a prominent—not to mention best-selling—approach. This is why, despite their many differences, Shackleton and Rommel share a common legacy. Both have been canonized as leaders *par excellence*—the go-to examples for all the qualities a modern business executive, military officer, or football captain should emulate. In general accounts of the war that feature few commanders by name, Rommel's is the exception. He is the subject of dozens of books with titles that evoke a romantic and skillful leader, books like *Rommel: The Trail of the Fox*; *Maverick Military Leaders*; *Rommel: Leadership Lessons from the Desert Fox*. Reverence for Shackleton has been equally constant and jubilant. His epic journey has become the subject of a prodigious stream of writing canonizing his leadership qualities and a pillar of business school curricula. *Shackleton: Leadership Lessons from Antarctica; Leadership at the Extreme: Leadership Lessons from the Extraordinary Saga of Shackleton's Antarctic Expedition; Shackleton's Way: Leadership Lessons from the Great Antarctic Explorer; Forged in Crisis*—the list of books that commemorate Shackleton's journey and draw leadership lessons from it is long.

I don't mean to rain on Shackleton and Rommel's parade, nor to denigrate the passionate writing of their legions of fans. But before joining the chorus in celebrating these two reputedly great leaders, it is worth pausing to ask a basic question: were Shackleton and Rommel actually successful leaders? Surely their stories are inspirational and, if nothing else, make for gripping reading. But are they the right stories to learn about leadership from?

Of course, if we define leadership narrowly as responding to a crisis, then perhaps yes. Yet if we are curious, as I suspect most of us are, about why some individuals are able to *not only* respond to unexpected crises but to shape the outcome of events—whether that be leading a company to success or winning on the field of battle—then we need to cast our gaze wider. And then we are forced to ask some more challenging questions of Shackleton and Rommel. Did their actions and words lead to outcomes profoundly more remarkable than those of comparable leaders? Did they even achieve what they themselves had set their designs on. In light of these questions, Shackleton's and Rommel's accomplishments fail to impress because the answer is an unequivocal no.

That Shackleton was unsuccessful in achieving the goal he himself had set is obvious. During his expedition, he did not come anywhere near the South Pole, nor did he cross the continent. His advocates have frequently attributed his lack of achievement to unfavorable circumstances and "bad luck." This analysis is inaccurate. In reality, Shackleton disregarded indications that the pack ice was particularly hazardous in 1914, neglected to adequately train his team, and overlooked significant shortcomings in his selection of equipment. Once in trouble, of course, he worked admirably to get his men back to safety. But it was he above all who got them stuck in the ice in the first place. There is no doubt that his trip was beset by a crisis of epic proportions, but it was a crisis of his own making.

Compared to his peers, Shackleton's record looks even worse. During the so-called Heroic Age of Polar Exploration at the start of the twentieth century, four goals made up the *ne plus ultra* toward which all of the contenders were striving: the two geographic poles (South and North) and the two sea passages (Northwest and Northeast). One might expect that if Shackleton were as great a leader of polar expeditions as is so often maintained, he would have claimed at least one of the four prime goals. This was not the case. Instead, another man led the successful expeditions that first claimed three of the four objectives (and for good measure, the second crossing of the Northeast Passage as well). This man was a comparatively unknown Norwegian named Roald Amundsen.

A sober assessment of Rommel's exploits reveals a similarly semi-successful leader. While the peculiar composition of each battle—the terrain, the number and disposition of the enemy, the weather—makes comparisons between military leaders difficult, we can begin by judging Rommel by his own metric: he firmly believed that his troops would expel the British from Egypt, opening the doors to a German conquest of the Middle East. Instead, after his initial string of victories, he was himself driven off the continent by an inexperienced American army. Certainly, Rommel faced difficult circumstances; the ever more tenuous supply chain across the Mediterranean Sea, where the Royal Air Force waited to prey on German supply ships, was foremost among them. Such difficulties, however, were faced by all German generals as they fought against enemies with a vastly superior combined industrial output. These were realities that many other generals accepted as a fact and worked around.[2]

Contemporary military historians, working methodically through the historical sources and uninfluenced by the Rommel hype, have in fact come to the conclusion that the photogenic general was hardly as skilled as his legacy would suggest. His insistence on leading from the front made for brilliant photo ops and elevated his status at home, but left a serious gap in the command-and-control function of his headquarters. While he was dotting around in his staff car, doling out insults to soldiers he perceived to be slacking, his commanders yearned for clear directions. The numerical inferiority of his army vis-à-vis the enemy—a fact frequently trumpeted to elevate his stature—carries less weight when one considers that his opponents in the first year were equipped with barely battle-worthy light tanks, entirely useless against Rommel's panzers.[3]

Shackleton and Rommel exemplify an entire host of nominally great leaders whose exploits underpin contemporary notions of leadership. Yet when we take a step back, we are confronted by the sober but unequivocal fact that their statures today radiate far out of proportion with their accomplishments. And it gets worse—the same phenomenon is evident beyond the polar icefields and the desert battles of World War II. A careful reading of nearly any historical event that has produced leaders—the major wars, periods of exploration, revolutions, tense international stand-offs, particularly tricky business scenarios—reveals that the leaders who have emerged as the most prominent in posterity are not always the ones picked out by historians as having been most influential. Or the most influential are indeed commemorated, but for all the wrong reasons. Something must be wrong here.

## The Action Fallacy

I blame the Action Fallacy. The Action Fallacy is the term I use to describe our persistent belief that while accountants or engineers may accomplish their work through quiet reflection and in a modest manner, leadership is characterized by energy and movement in the face of harrowing odds. In any given crisis (the larger the better), the good leader is the one who moves and acts, while everyone around them is paralyzed by indecision. It is this lively action, so the Action Fallacy holds, that is the essential quality of a good leader, and the ultimate indicator of the leader's effectiveness.

Recent leadership and management studies have uncovered compelling evidence for various components of the Fallacy. Researchers working on the "babble hypothesis" have shown that those who talk more (regardless of what they say) are more likely to be perceived as leaders.[4] Other scholars have described the "busyness trap"—the tendency of aspiring managers to keep relentlessly busy, regardless of how valuable or useless this hyperactivity might be, because it leads to recognition and reward. Writing in the *Harvard Business Review*, Thomas DeLong soberly describes how this, "causes us to move with such mindless speed that we're like the proverbial chicken running around with his head cut off."[5] Erin Meyer, a Professor at INSEAD who has spent her career examining the styles and expectations of leaders in different cultures, has described the deep-seated disdain for inactivity and indecisiveness among American leaders coupled with "a belief that 'any decision is better than no decision.'"[6]

Beyond these and many other studies that collectively underpin the Action Fallacy lies a more fundamental pool of evidence, one that interests me as a historian much more: how we write and talk about leadership. Here too, evidence of the Action Fallacy is widespread and not only in the droves of popular leadership studies centered on the usual suspects: Napoleon, JFK, Churchill and, of course, Shackleton and Rommel. The Fallacy bleeds into how many of us define and talk about leadership today. In an often-quoted definition of leadership, Donald McGannon tells us that "leadership is action, not a position."[7] The experienced German politician Ralph Brinkhaus has said, "If you want to show leadership you don't consider the risk, you get on with the job."[8] Meanwhile, there is hardly a more severe indictment on the global political stage than that of the failure to act. A British diplomat reported dismissively of Bill Clinton that he "enjoys thinking about, discussing and talking issues to death," but that he "fail[s] to act."[9] Biographers and commentators who feel "their" leader's propensity for action has been given short shrift by qualities like intellectualism or deliberation have responded in strong terms to correct the record. Martin Luther King Junior's wife wrote of him, "If Martin Luther King, Jr., was an apostle of love, he was no less an apostle of action."[10]

At the same time, we don't have to dig deep into the catalog of leadership blogs and social media posts to find nuggets of similar wisdom, such as this one: "Take action! Take massive action toward your goals today! Don't wait! Jump in and get started."[11] Or the all-too-typical posts on LinkedIn that rake in likes by the thousands, such as this one, "extraordinary things require extraordinary effort."[12]

Despite the fact that academic leadership scholarship has, on the whole, become quite nuanced, some leadership scholars, too, fall prey to elements of the Action Fallacy. A quick survey of scholarly literature reveals that here, too, the ability to act fast or decisively is regularly at the top of qualities prescribed for leaders. A recent study published in the authoritative *Harvard Business Review* cites "deciding with speed and conviction" as one of four key qualities successful CEOs possess.[13] John Kotter, one of the preeminent business gurus of the last few decades, tells us in his best-selling book *A Sense of Urgency* that successful leaders have a "gut-level determination to move and win, now." Another leadership scholar cuts even more brazenly to the chase—she simply titled her book on leadership advice *A Bias for Action*.[14]

With this in mind, it is easy to see why Shackleton and Rommel, despite their objective failures, have fared so well in the public imagination. Both of them perfectly embodied the proclivity to act. Rommel set his troops in motion long before all their equipment had arrived from Germany, speculating that the British would be caught off guard. When his hapless Italian superior Garibaldi objected to his offensive posture, Rommel commented that "One cannot permit unique opportunities to slip by for the sake of trifles."[15] Rommel drove his men hard; he was known for darting between his army's multiple points of contact with the enemy in his mobile command vehicle.

The atmosphere was little different aboard the *Endurance*. When the ship first became trapped in the ice, Shackleton immediately ordered all hands on deck: two operating a giant saw, others bashing away at the offending ice with sledgehammers, while the machinists cranked everything they could out of the engine. If an observer could have zoomed in from above on the little ship, stuck in that endless white landscape, they would have been struck by how it buzzed with ceaseless activity. When crisis struck, neither Rommel nor Shackleton spent much time dwelling on it—instead, they set to work. Of course, this hyperactivity did not preserve them from failure.

Now, I am certainly not suggesting that acting quickly and decisively is never necessary for leaders. What I am suggesting instead is that the capacity for swift and effective action may not be the defining characteristic of good leadership. It may, in fact, be no more than a hurdle requirement (what managers like to call a "threshold capability") for effectively facing certain—but by no means all—leadership challenges. Just as good vision is a necessary condition for a pilot (if you don't have it, you need not apply), the willingness to act, even in the face of harrowing odds, may at times be a necessary condition for effective leadership. Yet just as it would be absurd to suggest that having good vision is the decisive factor in being a good pilot, so a proclivity to act is not a sufficient requirement for being a good leader.

Nor ought we to dismiss inactivity out of hand, absurd as this may at first sound. A striking feature of the pioneering expeditions of Roald Amundsen, Shackleton's lesser-known but immensely more successful competitor, is that they mostly make for dull reading. Amundsen, looking back on the successful navigation of the Northwest Passage, called it "more like a holiday trip of comrades" than a harrowing adventure.[16] Amundsen's expeditions were beset by little drama—just overwhelming success. In the next section, I will argue that it is precisely the "holiday trip" nature of Amundsen's expeditions that bears witness to the great effectiveness of his leadership.

The reason that we have so long overlooked Amundsen is that his leadership makes for a bad story. And stories are crucial for how we make sense of the past (and the present, for that matter). In fact, it is the power of stories that keeps the Action Fallacy so firmly anchored in our imagination.

## Keanu Reeves, Jesus, and the Power of Stories

Humans are narrative thinkers by nature and stories are vital to how we make sense of our world. Storytelling has been a central element of the human experience since our days in caves. In fact, many anthropologists see storytelling as fundamentally and uniquely human, "that separates us from other animals."[17] We are much more likely to remember details that are embedded in a story than those presented as cold facts. Our addiction to stories can even be seen on the biological level: studies show that listeners' brains undergo a series of powerful chemical changes accompanying the rhythms of tension and release in a typical adventure story.[18] Other studies have confirmed that, regardless of context or individual idiosyncrasies, we are naturally drawn to tales of an underdog.[19] Today, marketing students are taught to frame their products within a compelling story, and managers who want to convince their team to follow a new strategy are told to frame the change in a powerful narrative. We like to tell stories and we like to think in stories. This goes a long way toward explaining why we prefer to learn and study a complex phenomenon, such as leadership, through stories of the past.

This is all well and good, but our addiction to stories can also get us into trouble. When we are confronted by an overwhelming set of new facts and variables, we use stories to help us make sense of them. The stories we already know act as filters by focusing our attention on the elements of an event that we are already familiar with or by tricking us into interpreting events within the mold of the story we happen to like. And as it turns out, there are a few standard stories that we happen to like a lot. In one of our favorite stories, a leader (in the past, we usually told it of a "he") is called upon to deal with a harrowing crisis, one that would leave most people paralyzed by inactivity. The leader embarks on an inner journey of discovery in parallel to his battling the challenges of the outer world. When death, failure, and a complete collapse in morale among the leader and his followers loom, the leader taps into a final reservoir of strength. Through inspiring words and swift action, he captures the imagination of those around him and leads them to victory. When he succeeds, he transforms not only himself but all of his followers as well. The interesting thing is that this story is not exclusive to leadership tales; nor is it new. Well over 100 years ago, anthropologists surveyed the vast reservoir of human stories across time, culture, and regions and found that the same basic story dominates the human imagination. They called it the Hero's Journey.[20]

This is the story of Shackleton and Rommel; if you look below the surface—below the contrasting details of the freezing cold and the scorching desert sun—their stories are remarkably similar. And they are not just similar to each other but follow in the well-worn tracks of so many other versions of the Hero's Journey. Whether it be told of Shackleton or Rommel, Jesus or Luke Skywalker, or every character Keanu Reeves has ever played (think Neo in the Matrix), we are addicted to this same story. It is a story well suited to entertain, but there is a very big catch: it fails to capture the essence of what real leaders actually do.

Our addiction to this type of adventure story helps anchor the Action Fallacy in our interpretation of the past. Of course, we don't interpret every leader we see entirely and exclusively within this mold. Yet, this story exerts a gravitational pull on our perception. When scanning history, the exciting deeds of Shackleton, Rommel, and other action-prone leaders act as a magnet—drawing our undivided attention while obscuring both their own failures *and* the success of their less conspicuous contemporaries (some of whom we will meet later in this book). It can also facilitate a lazy handling of historical facts. Take, for example, the single best-known anecdote about Shackleton: his cool, no-nonsense recruitment text in the *Times*. This legendary ad is today a regular feature of leadership blogs and LinkedIn posts. It reads, "Men wanted for hazardous expedition. Small wages, bitter cold, long months of complete darkness, constant danger, safe return doubtful, honour and recognition in case of success."[21] This text, more than anything else, has come to succinctly highlight Shackleton's brazen and confident qualities.

There is just one problem with this text: Shackleton didn't write it. It is truly a legendary piece of writing, for it never existed.[22] At some point in the hundred years of celebrating Shackleton's greatness, an overenthusiastic writer took the liberty of inventing this element of the Shackleton story. Subsequent authors took the fiction as fact and slowly the mythical ad wove itself more firmly into established history. And because we are primed to view leadership through the lens of the Action Fallacy, we are willing not to ask too many questions.

The skewing caused by the Action Fallacy also affects our views of truly outstanding leaders. Winston Churchill, whom we will examine in a later chapter, presents the case of a man rightly celebrated as a brilliant leader, but for all the wrong reasons. The classic story of the Second World War has it that, at the dramatic low point of the summer of 1940, the British establishment and population were on the verge of caving in to Nazi pressure (incidentally, a near-death experience is a staple of the Hero's Journey). Only the newly appointed Prime Minister's rhetorical grace, stubborn grit, and consistently offensive spirit convinced a reluctant nation to fight on from this low point until it decisively defeated the Nazi Empire in 1945.

Rereading Churchill's words today, we can see the appeal of this interpretation. On the final day of the Dunkirk evacuation, when the British public was facing up to the startling fact that Hitler had brushed aside a coalition of Europe's most powerful armies in a matter of a few weeks, Churchill spoke to the nation. He called on Britons to "go on until the end" and decreed that, "We shall fight on the beaches, we shall fight on the landing grounds, we shall fight in the fields and in the streets, we shall fight in the hills; we shall never surrender." For a nation beset by doubt and fear, it is hard to imagine a better motivator than the brazen, tenacious, and ever-confident Churchill. Rather than surrender or succumb to a Nazi invasion, Britain clung on and emerged victorious.

Unfortunately, this reading of Churchill's leadership is poorly supported by the facts. For one, Britain was never in any danger of being invaded by Germany. Second, it was never truly alone. Third, if action-soaked rhetoric were indeed the key to victory, the crown might well have gone to Hitler, who electrified mass audiences at his rallies. Finally, and perhaps most importantly, Churchill was, by the metric of inspiration of his subordinates, a terrible leader. Working for him, as we shall see, was the dread of many a minister. How we tell his story—skewed by the Action Fallacy—leads to exactly the wrong conclusions about what in fact made him so successful. As we will see later in this book, his brilliant handling of the war had nothing to do with his proclivity to act or his rhetorical brilliance.

The secret to understanding Churchill's success lies in looking beyond his famous speeches, his brash personality, and his persistent haranguing of his generals to get a move on. In fact, the secret lies in turning the Action Fallacy on its head.

## The Currents of History

To craft a new story, we first have to uncover the implicit and faulty assumptions that underlie the old one. So what are the assumptions that underlie our privileging of Shackleton, Rommel, and the other leaders of the same ilk? I count two: The first assumption is that the outcomes of historical events are largely shaped by individual leaders. The second is that the need for leadership arises out of a crisis. The false conclusion that inevitably follows from these two assumptions is that successful leadership can be measured by how quickly, actively, and energetically a leader responds to the crisis he or she is faced with—the Action Fallacy in other words.

Let's begin with the first assumption that individuals shape history. One fundamental truth that will be laid bare through the stories in this book—a truth that historians have long since established—is that there is a real limit to the possible influence of any individual leader on the outcome of historical events. In all conceivable scenarios, from that of a manager in an office to that of the captain of a football team, there are countless forces beyond the control of the individual leader: organizational traditions and cultures, technological limitations, silent but persistent changes in the environment, decisions taken by persons or even groups far away.[23] These forces constrain and divert even the most energetic efforts and the most compelling rhetoric of a single person.

A simple example will help to visualize this point. Let's imagine our leader for one moment not as a hero bravely battling encroaching ice or a commander shouting orders at his troops but, instead, as a swimmer attempting to cross a river at peak flow. Regardless of how powerfully the swimmer moves her arms as she tries to make her way across the river, it will be the current, much more than the swimmer, that determines where she ends up. Historians and sociologists refer to such currents as structures. Economists and political scientists speak of drivers. I like to call them *currents*. Whatever you want to call them, they are essential for understanding effective leadership. As such, our goal in this book will be to understand where the swimmer ended up by examining not just the swimmer but the interaction between the swimming and the current. For it is only when a leader learns to make use of, take advantage of, and exploit to the full the far more powerful currents of her time that she is able to influence, to a greater or lesser extent, the outcome of her story. What makes this all the more challenging in real life, of course, is that there are multiple currents, few of which are visible and none of which flow in the same direction.

Because of my wish to understand the currents as much as the swimmer, the stories in this book have the peculiarity that they occasionally leave their human protagonists partially or entirely out of the picture for lengths of time a Hollywood director or leadership blogger might object to. Be that as it may, stories told like this come closer to capturing the essence of effective leadership and what it takes, ultimately, to make history.

The second assumption behind the Action Fallacy is that the need for leadership arises out of a crisis. But while a crisis may necessitate leadership, leadership does not necessitate a crisis. If a swimmer ventures haphazardly into the river and bravely and violently fights against the tug of the undercurrent as he forces his way across, is this a crisis of necessity? It makes for an exciting story, for sure, but not one suited to drawing leadership lessons. In studying leaders and leadership, we have developed a relatively narrow gaze, zeroing in on the leaders' characters, what they did and what they said. The unfortunate circumstances that precipitated their leadership sagas, the encroaching ice in Shackleton's case and the encroaching enemy tanks in Rommel's, are seen as an unquestioned backdrop. That's just how it was; that was the crisis they were required to overcome.

But what if we open our gaze to include the vast and complex space in which these leaders were operating? What if we suggest that the good leader is not the one who battles against a crisis, but rather the one who reads his environment so well that the crisis is minimized or avoided altogether? The swimmer who waits for the spring melt to pass, or who spies out and crosses a nearby—or far-away—footbridge? And when crisis and drama is unavoidable, what if the effective leader is not the one who makes the most noise and fights with herculean strength, but rather the one who accurately reads the circumstances of their times and carefully and painstakingly, and often over a long period of time, acts in alignment with the currents that they read, nudging them, perhaps diverting them, but always leveraging them to achieve their ends (while avoiding those currents that threaten to undo their efforts).

In the next chapters of this book, I will show how four leaders did just this. Other than Churchill, these leaders are notable because, outside of specialist history texts, they are relatively unknown; they demonstrate, among much else, that if we view leadership through a lens other than the Action Fallacy, we might discover a new cast of characters with which to people our narratives.

We have already been introduced to the Norwegian explorer Roald Amundsen. In his chapter, we will learn how he was able to achieve his outstanding record of success with next to no drama, despite having none of the institutional and financial support of his British rivals. We will then meet Toussaint Louverture, a former illiterate slave who led history's only successful slave revolt on the island that would later be known as Haiti. Whereas Amundsen's chapter features a leader deftly navigating environmental challenges, Toussaint was a master at understanding and leveraging complex human networks. The chapter tells the stories of the dozens of European men and rival revolutionaries, all of whom sought to maintain control over the extremely valuable plantation island. It follows Toussaint as he patiently and effectively built a campaign, both military and political, to win out over these many rivals and secure the independence of the island.

In the next chapter, we follow Gertrude Bell, a woman in a man's world—the post-World War One Middle East. More than anyone else, she facilitated

Arab independence and built a modern and capable Iraqi state that survived and thrived for the next two decades. The only woman in her milieu, Bell's influence made few headlines, and her work was generally fronted by that of powerful men, such as the much-celebrated Lawrence of Arabia. This chapter tells the story of how she was able to shape the perception of the men around her and an entire region in the midst of guerilla fighting, colonial squabbling, and political intrigue.

Finally, we pick up where we left Churchill in the earlier pages of this introduction. We will continue dismantling the persistent myth that Churchill's rhetoric and stubborn grit saved England from disaster at the hands of Hitler's army. Instead, the secret to Churchill's victory lay in his long and deliberate (but very much behind-the-scenes) campaign to draw the US into the war and to build the administrative structures necessary for managing a complex modern war.

Churchill has been, for good reasons, repeatedly touted as one of the greatest leaders of all time. Even so, I hesitated in profiling him. Though highly effective as a wartime leader, he cannot be considered great by other standards. An unabashed colonialist, Churchill spent much of his early career making the lives of Britain's subjects around the world miserable, and his comments and actions often revealed an imperialist and racist view of the world. I decided to include a chapter on him despite this. For one, it is important to illustrate not only how the Action Fallacy focuses our attention on the wrong leaders but also how it focuses our attention on the wrong qualities of effective leaders—and here Churchill serves as an excellent case in point. Furthermore, one of the most common sentiments that I hear from leadership buffs looking to the past is that "Hitler was an evil person but an effective leader" (a similar sentiment allows the same people to celebrate Rommel, who was far more complicit in the regime's crimes than many of his fans care to admit). I find this sentiment not only repulsive but simply wrong, and feel the need to counter it. Hitler, as we will see, can only be read as an effective leader when viewed through the lens of the Action Fallacy—a point that can best be made by comparing him to Churchill.

There is another, more fundamental reason for including Churchill. The Second World War is one of, if not the most complex leadership challenge in history. While no single individual deserves the credit for the Allied victory, no one deserves it more than Churchill. In this war, history's wild currents clashed in a confused torrent, far beyond the comprehension and control of most. This was true—in varied contexts—for our other three protagonists as well. While there is, of course, something fundamentally different about leading a nation in a global war than in navigating a small vessel through the perils

of the Arctic, uniting a disparate group of former slaves in a fight for independence, or battling patriarchy and clashing cultures in the Middle East, one
truth holds across them all. In each scenario, the odds were powerfully
weighted against any given individual seeing through the confusion, let alone
deliberately affecting a favorable outcome. Yet, remarkably, this is what each
of them managed to do without too much fuss or drama. In fact, they managed to do so in a way that has fully escaped the prying eyes of legions of
leadership enthusiasts. This book is, above all, an attempt to make these
unseen leaders visible again, to give them the credit that they deserve, and, by
extension, to cast light on what effective leadership actually looks like. To do
so, we must return to where we started this chapter: the far reaches of the
polar wastelands.

# Part II

## History's Unseen Leaders

# Holiday Trips in the Polar Wastelands. Roald Amundsen

Along the banks of one of the countless bends of the Yukon River, which snakes through the vast interior of Alaska, sits the small village of Eagle—an inhospitable and isolated outpost surrounded by vast forests, tundra, and unnamed waterways. The area around Eagle has always attracted adventurers, vagabonds, and eccentrics, so no one took much notice when, on a cold December day in 1905, a stranger on a dog sled approached on the frozen river from the North. The man, dressed in animal skins and speaking with a curious accent, dispensed with pleasantries and headed straight to the telegraph office.[1]

While Roald Amundsen arrived almost unnoticed in Eagle, the telegraph he sent caused a sensation around the world. This gaunt Norwegian explorer had just achieved, in a small herring vessel with a spartan crew, what the mighty British Navy had spent three-quarters of a century attempting without success: the first through-navigation of the fabled Northwest Passage.

Amundsen spent two months resting and recuperating in Eagle before returning to his crew and ship, frozen in place some 500 miles to the northeast. His rest was well deserved. The Northwest Passage had been a highly coveted prize, if not an obsession, among nineteenth-century explorers, and particularly among the British. This fabled route above the Canadian mainland harbored perils of every kind, from unpredictable ice floes to oppressive and unyielding cold and darkness. Dozens of British expeditions, though superbly funded and equipped, had retreated after probing no more than its outer perimeter. Others never returned.

For Amundsen, meanwhile, the Northwest Passage was just the beginning of a remarkable career. In the following two decades, he ticked off the remaining three great goals of polar exploration—the South and North Poles (both

M. Gutmann, *The Unseen Leader*, https://doi.org/10.1007/978-3-031-37829-4_3

firsts), and the Northeast Passage above Russia. By almost any measure, this modest Norwegian was the most successful polar explorer of all time. And a remarkable, though rarely acknowledged, leadership great.

## The Perfect Leadership Laboratory

Amundsen's adventures—and polar expeditions in general—present a perfect leadership laboratory. On such expeditions, a brutally hostile environment is a given, hardship and stress are certain, and all available assets—human, technical, and informational—are contained within the hull of a cramped ship or unceremoniously dragged along on sleds. If there was ever an undertaking that required good leadership, this was it.

In the 100-year heyday of polar exploration, from the 1800s through the early 1900s, droves of adventurers launched probes into the far reaches of the north and south. The approaches to preparation and execution varied from the nonchalant to the neurotic. Yet, the fate awaiting these adventurers was too often the same: slow death at the hands of the grinding cold, or a swift demise from an unexpected meeting with tons of ice inexorably driven across the water by strong winds. Three examples will suffice to give an idea of the realities faced by polar explorers in the nineteenth century.

In 1819, the Englishman John Franklin set off on an overland expedition to chart the coastline around the mouth of the Coppermine River on the northernmost tip of the Canadian mainland. Far from being the mere reconnaissance venture he had intended, the expedition became a three-year saga of suffering as the men—to the bewilderment of the Indigenous population—stumbled through the barren landscape, unable to find food and shelter. When a group of four stragglers became separated from the main party, one of them murdered his three companions and passed their flesh off as wolf meat to his famished colleagues in the main party. By the end of the trip, half the crew was dead and Franklin, remarkably, was a national hero.[2]

In 1897, a group of Swedish explorers set off from the island of Spitsbergen, an island in the northern reaches of Norway, in a hydrogen balloon. Their goal was to overfly the North Pole. Even before leaving the view of the small group of well-wishers gathered at the airfield, the balloon jerked earthwards, dipping the basket with the three hapless explorers into the frigid waters. It then rose again and set off uncontrollably toward the north. After two more days of near misses, the balloon crashed for good. The three men wandered south across the frozen sea before making camp on a deserted island, where their bodies were discovered some 30 years later.[3]

Travels like these by land and air were the exception. For the ship-bound explorer—and these were the vast majority—ice was the greatest threat. Waterways were completely frozen for months at a time; when they were not, sailors had to weave between free-floating bergs and extensive plates of impenetrable ice. British Navy expeditions at times resorted to hacking, sawing, and dynamiting this ice in order to advance. But ice posed other dangers as well. Island-sized ice plates, driven by strong winds, might careen toward unsuspecting ships like gargantuan freight trains. Ships could also become trapped in the ice, and this happened with astonishing regularity. In 1913 the Canadian ship *Karluk* set sail with a crew of 25 to explore the northern reaches of Alaska and the Canadian Arctic. Ice ensnared the ship and crushed it to pieces; eleven men died in the ensuing struggle for survival.[4] Shackleton's ship, of course, met a similar fate.

To those seeking the Northwest Passage, these "normal" hazards of polar exploration were exacerbated by navigational challenges. The Northwest Passage leads through a labyrinth of islands with a dizzying array of dead-end waterways. And, of course, no one knew exactly where the passage thread its way through the many ice-chocked channels and inlets. Or if there even was a passage to begin with.

## The Northwest Passage

Europeans had long speculated that there was a sea route above the American continent to Asia. In 1498, six years after Columbus came ashore in what he thought were islands off China (in reality, the West Indies in the Caribbean), his countryman John Cabot was commissioned by King Henry VII of England to find a northerly route to the Far East. Cabot was swallowed up by the hostile polar waters, and nothing was ever heard of him again. Many followed in his footsteps; the most successful leaders did no more than make it out alive.

By the 1800s, European monarchs no longer required a faster route to the riches of the East. Established shipping routes around the Horn of Africa and the steadily growing European presence in Asia meant a more secure supply of the spices for which early explorers had been willing to risk life and limb.[5] And while the nineteenth century was one of peace and prosperity in Europe, this absence of conflict was an inconvenience for John Barrow, Second Lord of the Admiralty in England. As the chief administrator of the mighty British Navy, Barrow needed a meaningful occupation for his great fleet and its restless officers. Polar exploration, Barrow saw, provided just the right kind of mission. It thus came about that in the 1800s, on Barrow's tireless initiative, the British Navy launched dozens of explorations in search of far-off goals. Barrow found in his ambitious captains a steady stream of willing participants, thirsty for glory and displaying an unshakeable confidence.

First on the list of Barrow's many goals was the elusive Northwest Passage. Neither the earlier explorers nor the hundreds of whalers who frequented the frozen waters up north had ever ventured farther than Spitsbergen or Greenland—which is not to say that their undertakings were for the faint of heart. The whalers at least had an economic incentive for their dangerous activities, while no one—not even Barrow—was under the illusion that anything of value would be gained by crossing the Passage. Amundsen later wrote quite pointedly that, "we may safely assume that even the most extravagant flight of imagination has never led anyone to penetrate the Arctic Regions in the hope of finding, 'gold, and green woods.'"[6] This was an era, however, in which men risked and frequently lost their lives in attempts to find the fabled city of Timbuktu or to march across the Gobi Desert. Navigating the ice and waters above the northern edge of Canada, therefore, did not seem an entirely unreasonable thing to do. In fact, it held an irresistible allure.[7]

But the Northwest Passage was a challenge like no other. A challenging leadership environment can take many forms: from a highly competitive market to a battlefield. In comparing the context of one challenge to another, we can differentiate along several dimensions: the variability, predictability, and seriousness of the hazards; the availability of external help; and the duration of exposure. It is rare to find a leadership environment in which all these variables are high. Fighting a fire is dangerous business, but to a trained firefighter, fire moves in predictable ways. Besides, the duration of exposure to its risks is relatively short. Launching a financial technology start-up involves facing a highly variable and unpredictable environment, but there is always the option of appealing for more investment. Navigating the Northwest Passage was a challenge along every dimension: the threats came in many forms, were of a highly unpredictable nature, and were all potentially lethal, while outside intervention was ruled out and exposure was long-term. Leading expeditions in this environment was truly a multi-dimensional challenge.

Strategic flexibility, meanwhile, was extremely limited once a ship had left its home port. From modern business executives to Roman generals, leaders have always taken on challenging projects with a strategy in mind, whether it was explicitly formulated or not. In most endeavors, this strategy can be revised. As planning turns to execution, the leader will continually adjust; a setback may spark a change in personnel or lead to new tools being employed. Amundsen and the others who attempted the Northwest Passage lacked these crucial options. Once an expedition had set off, it was impossible to fire a crew member, regardless of how incompatible he was with the group's social dynamic. The decision to bring a gasoline rather than a steam engine could not be reversed. Path dependency in polar expeditions was near total.

Isolation and duration also magnified the human leadership challenges, such as ensuring motivation and mitigating group conflict. After setting off from the already remote whaling outposts on the shores of Greenland, crews would be on their own until, in the best case, they reached the scattered outposts of Alaska, half a world away. Social conflict was a given in the cramped space of a ship's hull and was amplified by the fact that the small group of men would have no one else to interact with for years. This enforced intimacy doomed a number of ventures and could drive even the most robust characters to the brink of madness. Social cohesion was made all the more difficult by the fact that the nature of these expeditions eroded all distinctions between professional and private roles and spaces. With a project duration of years and daily interactions unavoidable, it was impossible for a captain to hide behind a false persona. For several years, Amundsen's men were not only his subordinates but his friends and family. Sooner or later, his true self was bound to come out; the challenge was to maintain the ability to inspire and influence men, even with his own weaknesses fully exposed. Long before the concept of authentic leadership became a fad, Amundsen embraced this model of leadership in the cramped space of his ship in the depths of the Northwest Passage.

Yet, Amundsen's success was still decades in the future as Barrow began dispatching expeditions to find the Passage, starting in the summer of 1818. Each of them followed a similar routine (with the difference that each was more sturdily outfitted and more confident than its predecessor). After crossing the Atlantic, the ships moved into position off the west coast of Greenland to await a loosening of the ice. When this happened, in late summer, they sailed north through waters strewn with ice, passing lone whalers along the way. Once at the upper edge of Baffin Bay, the explorers began the traverse across the northern tip of Canada, trying to find a navigable route through a bewildering array of islands, inlets, and ice. They never made it very far before winter set in. The ships that survived the winter intact then limped on toward the west for another short summer season. After two or three winters out, but with little progress made, even the most ambitious captains turned their ships back toward Greenland.

In 1845, however, Barrow felt the stage had been set for victory. He picked John Franklin, a polar veteran and experienced colonial administrator, to lead what he believed would be the culminating expedition through the Passage. It was the eight expedition Barrow had dispatched with the same goal and the third led by Franklin. This time nothing was left to chance. Franklin's ships, the *Erebus* and the *Terror,* were iron-plated beasts, propelled with formidable locomotive engines and outfitted with state-of-the-art internal heating and water filtration systems. The ships represented the cutting edge of naval technology and were stocked to the brim with the comforts of industrial society, including a library of 2400 books and stores of 8000 tins of canned food, including 97,000 pounds of meat. The crew was selected from the Navy's finest officers and sailors. The two ships were cheered on by a massive crowd as they glided out of port at Greenhithe in May 1845, the big white stripes painted on their black bodies swaying gently up and down in the Thames. Franklin and his crew of 128 never returned.[8] Their fate remained a mystery that would captivate Britain for years to come.

Roald Amundsen's successful voyage through the Northwest Passage differed from his British predecessors' expeditions along almost every metric. Amundsen lacked the institutional support enjoyed by the British endeavors, and this was reflected in the scale of his operation. Far smaller than Franklin's stout 370-ton *Erebus*, Amundsen's *Gjøa* weighed in at a petite 47 tons. Amundsen's team of seven would not have been sufficient to staff Franklin's kitchens. The British Navy and its network had built up an impressive arsenal of institutional knowledge and procedures. They were masters of the sea and knew how to maintain discipline and control under conditions of tremendous mental duress. They had access to state-of-the-art equipment tailor-made for their needs by specialist manufacturers. They had what is akin to a modern talent management system, which promoted and trained the lower ranks, tracked their past experience, and streamlined the process of staffing. Amundsen's endeavor, by contrast, resembled an entrepreneurial venture, small, scraggily, and severely underfunded. But it was one for which he had obsessively prepared for most of his life.

## Becoming an Explorer

Roald Engelbregt Gravning Amundsen was born on 16 July 1872. His father, Jens Amundsen, was a captain and merchant who managed to build up an impressive shipping business and a treasure chest of adventure tales from around the globe. He regaled his sons with stories of his experiences serving the British during the Crimean War or traveling to distant China. Roald spent his childhood exploring the woods and lakes behind the family house on the outskirts of Christiania—as Oslo was then known—with his three older brothers. Encouraged by his mother, he began reading books in English at an early age. He especially latched onto the tales of British explorers such as

Franklin, whom he first heard about at the age of eight or nine.[9] Franklin's books, "thrilled me as nothing I had ever read before," he recalled years later.[10]

His fascination with polar explorers transformed into an obsession on 30 May 1889. On that day, the great Norwegian explorer Fridtjof Nansen returned to Oslo from his successful Greenland expedition. The young Amundsen "wandered with the throbbing pulses amid the bunting and the cheers, and all my boyhood's dreams reawoke to tempestuous life." He imagined what it would be like to have such a celebration in his honor. And he knew just what polar endeavor he would have to undertake to turn this into reality. He thought to himself, "If *you* could make the Northwest Passage!"[11]

From that day on, Amundsen was singularly fixated. He slowly, painstakingly, and doggedly transformed himself into a world-class polar explorer.[12] Along with amassing whatever knowledge he could about the icy world above his native Norway from books and by questioning travelers, Amundsen perfected two vital skills: skiing and sailing. Skiing may seem like an obvious, must-have competency for anyone intent on exploring the far north or south, but many of the doomed British expeditions had neglected it altogether. Instead, the British initially preferred to haul sleds by foot; in the later phases of their attempts at the South Pole, they relied on temperamental, untested, and nearly always unsuited technologies such as snowmobiles. Meanwhile, like most Norwegians, Amundsen had learned to ski during his childhood. In his twenties, he set about perfecting this skill, especially in hostile environments.

Just a few months after his mother's death in 1893, Amundsen set off with a group of friends, intent on crossing the barren Hardangervidda plateau on skis. Though this mini-expedition was in their own Norwegian "backyard," it had never been undertaken in winter. The trip proved a reality check, and Amundsen came face to face with what he had yearned for since his childhood: suffering. Burdened by equipment failures and erratic temperatures, the men turned back, defeated, after covering only 50 kilometers. Three years later, Amundsen returned with his brother Leon to complete the 115-kilometer crossing, though not without meeting significant difficulties. Between these forays, Amundsen applied to join the crews of various expeditions and kept working on developing his physical strength. When he was examined by a military doctor in preparation for his obligatory service, Amundsen later recalled, the doctor blurted out in astonishment, "young man, how in the world did you ever develop such a splendid set of muscles?"[13]

Amundsen also set his mind to earning his qualification as a sea captain. This may seem a prerequisite for an explorer in the age of ships, but in fact it was not. Many expedition leaders did not captain their own ships (during its fateful voyage, the captain of the *Endurance* was not Shackleton himself but the cantankerous New Zealander Frank Worsley).[14] Amundsen described what inevitably followed when expedition leader and captain were two different persons:

> The fatal defect of this practice had been in every case, once embarked at sea, the expedition had not one leader but two. Invariably this resulted in a division of responsibility between the commander and the skipper, incessant friction, divided counsels and a lowered morale.[15]

Such double-leadership was not limited to maritime matters. Most British expeditions brought along doctors—"surgeons" in Navy jargon—whose primary responsibility was the wellbeing of the crew. (Amundsen's rivals Shackleton and Scott each brought two on their expeditions.) That this could lead to differences of opinion and strategy between the medical team and the expedition leader when the going got tough is self-evident. Especially given the fact that in the field, there was little the medical professionals of the day could undertake against the most typical polar mishap—frostbite—that anyone else could not master with a few hours of training.

Earning the master's certificate that would allow him to captain ships around the world was a tedious process that required logging hours at sea and passing written tests. Amundsen spent months on commercial vessels sailing around Iceland, Greenland, and farther afield before he finally earned his credentials in 1902.

With his extensive skiing and his initial ventures on commercial ships on the desolate seas around northern Norway, Iceland, and Greenland under his belt, Amundsen was ready to venture farther into the polar realms. But he still lacked the experience and credentials to launch his own endeavor. Instead, he sought to join an established expedition: the Belgian Adrien de Gerlache's journey aboard the *Belgica* to survey the waters, islands, and coastline of Antarctica. The trip set off in 1897 and was beset by problems from the start. To Amundsen, it served as a perfect example of how not to prepare for and lead a polar endeavor. Two of de Gerlache's haphazardly assembled crew bailed ship at Ostend (still in Belgian waters). In Montevideo, the cook was fired for getting into a brawl. One young sailor was swept overboard and drowned. Infighting and resentment were rampant. This notwithstanding, the trip did earn the distinction of being the first to winter in Antarctic waters. This was likely a distinction by circumstance rather than design. De Gerlache had failed to mention this part of the plan to anyone before departing. The winter was miserable. One crew member died of scurvy; the others all suffered horribly. With one exception: Amundsen. Unafraid to experiment with Antarctic foods, such as penguin meat ("[tastes] excellent, not unlike beef"), he put on weight during the winter and, in the words of biographer Borman-Larsen, "frolicked in the pack ice like a child in a playground."[16]

Amundsen returned home from the trip having learned invaluable lessons and with polar credentials that he could leverage in planning his own expedition. On the basis of his *Belgica* experience, he managed to secure an audience with Nansen, the best-versed and most well-known Norwegian explorer of the day. Things were coming full circle: it was Nansen who had inspired him a decade earlier to dedicate his life to becoming an explorer. Now, it would be his blessing that would seal Amundsen's fate. For without it, it would be next to impossible to secure the financial backing from wealthy Norwegian families and companies. When finally invited into Nansen's study, "I stood face to face with the man who for years had loomed before me as something almost superhuman—the man who had achieved exploits which stirred every fibre of my being."[17] Amundsen nervously laid out his unconventional plans for the Northwest Passage. Nansen approved. He would remain a mentor and supporter for the rest of Amundsen's life.

Fresh off this success, Amundsen spent the winter of 1900–1901 in the northern Norwegian fishing town of Tromsø. Lacking the institutional knowledge and resources exploited by the large British expeditions, Amundsen sought help where he could find it. He talked to as many whalers and arctic seamen as he could. "Many of these old chaps are interesting and informative," he wrote to his brother Leon.[18] He worked incessantly on his skiing. And he read profusely.

Amundsen was also keen to find a suitable and—equally importantly—affordable ship. Finally, he came upon an old fishing vessel called the *Gjøa*. It was far from state-of-the-art—in fact, it was exactly as old as Amundsen himself. He made up for the ship's deficiencies with ingenuity and hard work. Unlike the British, he could not afford to use steam-powered engines—nor did he desire to. His was a sailboat and a small one at that, but he had gasoline tanks designed to fit snugly into the hull to fuel a small 13-horsepower engine. This was a daring move: gasoline engines were new and had the distinct disadvantage that their fuel was flammable. However, the engine saved both weight and space and, unlike steam-powered engines, had no lag—it could be engaged in an instant. Amundsen packed five years' worth of food into ergonomic wooden containers, each meticulously labeled and stacked. These containers, when unpacked, could be reassembled into a wooden hut. The food he chose was also a mix between the new and the old—it was dried using a technique he had observed among Indigenous Arctic peoples (In an age in which a European sense of superiority to Indigenous peoples was rampant, Amundsen stood out for his willingness to learn as much as he could about Sami and Inuit customs and survival techniques). A six-month trip to the north of Norway tested his system.

The final two pieces of the puzzle were the crew and the financing. Unlike the other explorers of his day, Amundsen himself—not a government or a Geographic Society—footed much of his own bills. The advantage of this setup was that he was beholden to no one in selecting his men. The disadvantage was that even after he sank all of his inheritance into the venture, he was still short. Nansen appreciated this hidden burden on explorers outside the established British circle. Years later, when Amundsen returned successfully from the South Pole, Nansen wrote, "When the explorer comes home victorious, everyone goes out to cheer him. We are all proud of his achievement—proud on behalf of the nation and of humanity. How many of those who join in the cheering were there when the expedition was fitting out, when it was short of bare necessities?"[19] With Nansen's support, Amundsen began what would always be his least favorite part of being an explorer: fundraising. He reviled it and for good reason. "No one but a penniless explorer can realize the frightful handicap from which nearly all explorers suffer in having to waste time and nervous energy in their efforts to raise the money to equip their expeditions. The heartbreaking discouragements, the endless delays, the blows to pride, if not to self-respect, involved in this search for funds, are a tragedy of the explorer's life."[20] He was, as would be true for most of his endeavors, only marginally successful and was forced to take out loans. He would leave for the Northwest Passage heavily in debt.[21]

## Into the Northwest Passage

As Amundsen busied himself with final preparations in the summer of 1903, his bills were raking up and his creditors becoming increasingly restless. On 16 June, with rumors rife that a group of frustrated creditors would seek to impound his ship, Amundsen and his crew set off surreptitiously under the cover of darkness and a relentless rain.[22] Following the Atlantic crossing, the journey continued in the well-worn tracks of its British predecessors. After a brief stopover in Greenland to resupply, the *Gjøa* sailed north through Baffin Bay, the wide channel between Greenland's western shore and Baffin Island. It continued northward well past the Arctic Circle, where icebergs became more frequent and whalers less so. Near the top of Baffin Bay, Amundsen, like the explorers before him, turned into Lancaster Sound, a narrow waterway that leads into the labyrinth of islands that forms the Canadian archipelago. By 22 August, the *Gjøa* had reached Beechey Island, the site of Franklin's first wintering. Here, the crew came upon three graves—the first of the many victims of Franklin's misadventure.

The *Gjøa* spent the night in a little cove amid a nondescript rocky landscape. Amundsen sat up on deck long after his crew had gone to sleep. He envisioned, "the splendidly equipped Franklin Expedition heading into harbour...the English colours flying at the masthead and the two fine vessels full of bussle."[23] He also reflected on the whirlwind decade and a half that had brought him to this point in his life and to this desolate spot on earth. Nansen had been a formative mentor in his journey. But so too, he owed a certain debt to Franklin. He later wrote that, "Strangely enough the thing in Sir John's narrative that appealed to me most strongly was the sufferings he and his men endured. A strange ambition burned within me to endure those same sufferings."[24] He would be spared the level of suffering that inflicted Franklin's men—he was already too good of an explorer for that. But surprises did lay ahead.

A few days later the *Gjøa* continued in the tracks of the *Erebus* and *Terror* through inlets and islands named for the brave captains who had come before him or their patrons in London: Barrow Straight, Peel Sound, Prince of Whales Land. The ship was fully loaded and resembled, "a moving-van afloat," in Amundsen's later words. As it slid slowly through the waters, the men performed their duties while their many sled dogs lumbered around the deck, looking for scraps of leftover food to supplement their meager rations. The dogs would be instrumental in facilitating the expedition's mobility during the long winter months, especially after Amundsen sought out Inuit to train his crew in their proper use. For now, however, the dogs had little to do.

From Peel Sound, Amundsen steered his ship southeast in a long, clockwise traverse of the southern shore of King William Island. The string of good weather and frictionless sailing was bound to end eventually. At the end of August, it did. Strong squalls pummeled the tiny ship and a thick layer of fog hid the various perils. In the morning of 1 September, the *Gjøa* briefly ran aground in shallow waters. That same night a fire broke out in the engine room—as Amundsen later dryly pointed out, "right among the tanks holding 2200 gallons of petroleum." The crew put it out with fire retardant and buckets of water.[25] The next day, the ship ran aground again. It remained lodged on shallow rocks as winds and waves battered it about. For a moment, Amundsen considered abandoning the *Gjøa*; throwing some supplies overboard, however, allowed a large wave to wash the little ship off its perch and back into deeper waters. "It was a rare thing to see any frantic enthusiasm on board the Gjøa[…]but this time the jubilation could not be controlled and it burst out unrestrained."[26]

Amundsen blamed himself for the mishap. What had he done wrong that they had come so close to disaster? He could think of nothing concrete he should have done differently. In fact, in reexamining the episode, we find that Amundsen's unusually brisk action and sharp orders earlier that day had saved the crew from a fiery end. When a day earlier, Ristvedt had reported a small leak in one of the petroleum tanks, Amundsen had immediately ordered the gas transferred to the second tank. "On clearing up the engine-room after the fire," Amundsen later recalled, "we found that the tap of the emptied tank had been wrenched right off during the struggle with the fire. Had my order not been carried out promptly over 100 gallons of petroleum would have spurted into the burning engine room."[27] Yet, the episode continued to weigh on him. His crew was of a different opinion. One of them later wrote, "no praise could be too much for Amundsen's conduct during these trials. It was his first expedition, but he was just a natural born leader."[28]

After these intense days, Amundsen settled his ship and crew in for the winter on the southern tip of King William Island. It was 9 September 1903. He named the spot Gjøa Harbor; today it is called Uqsuqtuuq. Like droves of explorers before him, including Franklin and Ross, Amundsen would spend two winters in the same location. There is an important difference, however. In Amundsen's case, staying in place for two winters was by choice. He had raised some of his funding by giving the trip the scientific objective of making proper measurements of the nearby Magnetic North Pole. Rather than continuing the journey when the ice melted the following summer, Amundsen kept his crew in place for a second winter to assure that his measurements were accurate. For anyone familiar with previous expeditions to the Passage, the decision to winter twice without being forced to would hardly have been comprehensible. Wintering was, for good reason, the dread of most polar explorers.

## Amundsen's Winters in the Arctic

No challenge in the polar landscape tested leaders more than wintering. The success or failure of many an expedition rested on how the leaders prepared for and managed this seemingly mundane aspect of their trips. The term itself undersells the full burden of this inescapable element in polar travel. When we imagine the expeditions of explorers such as Ross, Franklin, and Amundsen, we invariably see movement: the ships weaving their way between ice floes, the crew frantically adjusting sails to the whim of the winds, the captains trekking to higher ground on nearby islands to spy out a view of the way ahead and hurriedly shouting instructions to their industrious crews. These moments of action and movement were the exception, however. Depending on where an expedition was underway, it could expect to be frozen in place for nine to eleven months of the year. For much of this time, darkness was absolute and temperatures in the lower reaches of the imaginable.

Darkness, cold, and confined space were one thing; the complete absence of any meaningful activity was another. Wintering in the Arctic was as mentally taxing as it was physically demanding. Apart from short forays outside, wintering crews were forced to stay within the hull of their ship, which was completely immobilized in one of the most isolated locations in the world, surrounded by hundreds if not thousands of miles of frozen wilderness. Keeping ennui from spilling over into madness was the primary occupation of leaders in this environment.

Mixed in with boredom was the ever-present threat of death. In 1553, three ships were dispatched from England to find a northeastern route for the lucrative spice trade with Asia. They turned back after reaching 72 degrees north, a notable achievement for the day, but were forced to winter on the Kola Peninsula, near today's Murmansk, Russia. The following spring, Russian fishermen found 63 men cramped inside the two ships, frozen in place, "some of them seated in the act of writing, pen still in hand, and the paper before them; others at table, platters in hand and spoon in mouth; others opening a locker, and others in various postures, like statues."[29] Whether due to carbon monoxide poisoning or cold, death had crept up on the worn-down crew in the midst of their dreary existence. It could also arrive quickly. Crews needed fuel to heat their living space, melt snow for water, cook, and provide lighting, and this meant that fire was a constant threat. Flames could rip through a wooden ship in the dry polar air as through a desiccated matchbox, spelling a swift end for those trapped onboard and a slightly more protracted death for any who managed to escape into the Arctic wilderness.

The series of British expeditions that Barrow had dispatched in search of the Northwest Passage had made small but steady improvements as one expedition learned from another. William Parry became the first to spend the winter north of the Arctic Circle during his 1819 attempt at the Passage. Settling into a cove on Melville Bay, Parry and his men were able to look back on an already successful venture. Behind them lay over a thousand miles of coastline they had been the first to chart, and they were optimistic about what the spring would bring. In preparation for the winter ahead, they hammered a large canvas over the ship's deck as a tent of sorts. Candles were rationed at one per officer per week. Then the crew hunkered down to wait for summer.[30]

Parry tried to maintain routine and military discipline during the long wait. The sailors—who in their captain's opinion "resemble[d] children"—were chased out of bed at 5:45 each morning to scrub the deck. During the day, they were forced to practice marching. When not meting out punishment, officers had a series of scientific duties to fulfill. Had anyone from outside stumbled upon this frosty camp, the sight would have been truly comical. Here, in the highest latitudes Europeans had ever trodden, a restless captain was forcing his frozen crewmen to march, day in and day out, to the rhythm of an organ. Despite the small relief of an occasional theater production, it was the dreariest of existences.[31]

The most challenging aspect of wintering was psychological. Stuck in a landscape of never-ending snows over which the sun never rose, life was void of any meaningful inputs. Outside of their cramped confinement, there were no sounds and no colors. Only darkness, interrupted occasionally by the eerie Northern Lights. This proved a doubly tricky nut for the British officers to crack. They had to convince their crews not only that they would survive to see the sun again, but also that once they did, they should continue pushing further into the unknown. For Parry this proved too much. When the ice finally retreated enough to allow continued passage, it was already August. Parry's ships tentatively limped westward. But by the end of the month, the men began to spot winter ice forming again. Winter, it seemed, was beginning in the very same month in which it had ended. They turned around and headed home.

Wintering would continue to be the bane of polar expeditions. On an exploration launched by John Ross in 1829, the second winter brought some good news when the captain's nephew James Ross—an officer on the expedition—successfully located and claimed for Britain, the Magnetic North Pole on the shores of the island he named after King William. This was in June. With this discovery in hand, John Ross decided to cut his losses and return home as soon as possible. He and his crew waited throughout the rest of June, all of July, and most of August. Finally, at the end of August, the ice loosened its grip on his ship, and after the long "winter" of immobility, the team began heading back to Greenland. The ship wove its way through the broken ice for a heartbreakingly fleeting *two days* (and a mere 6.4 kilometers) before being frozen in place again. A third winter loomed. Ross vented his frustration, "The sameness of everything weighed on the spirits, and the mind itself flagged under the want of excitement; while even such as there was, proved but a wearisome iteration of what had often occurred before."[32]

Ross eventually managed to extract his stricken crew from their Arctic internment, but not before abandoning their ship, trudging across endless ice, and pillaging the stores left behind by Parry—after he had been forced to abandon one of his ships on Somerset Island during his second attempt at the Passage—where Ross's crew was forced to spend a miserable fourth winter out. Their epic, which puts Shackleton's later trials to shame, ended in 1834 when the crew was rescued by the *Isabella*, a ship that Ross had commanded on Arctic voyages earlier in his career.

By the time Franklin set off in 1845, the British Navy was determined to solve the wintering problem by technological force. The ships had internal heating systems, copious stores of preserved foods, two organs, and a pet monkey. The *Erebus* and *Terror* had a rich record of Polar service to boot— James Clark Ross, nephew of John, had used them during his survey of the waters of Antarctica in between 1839 and 1843. In fact, when Ross stopped over in Tasmania (then known as Van Diemen's Land) in November of 1840, Franklin, who was the island colony's lieutenant governor, joined him aboard the *Erebus* as it slipped out of port. This quirk of history was pointed out years later by none other than Amundsen, who wrote, "Strange are the ways of life! There stood Franklin on the deck of the ship which a few years later was to be his deathbed."[33] Because unbeknownst to Franklin on that carefree day under the warm rays of the South Pacific, when he would set foot on the ship again, fate had a nasty surprise in store.

Things had started off well for Franklin and his intrepid crew. After traversing Lancaster Sound, Franklin chartered a course north around the western edge of Cornwallis Island—either in the hopes of finding an ice-free channel to the west or to make a quick dash to the North Pole. With neither an option, Franklin returned south via the eastern shore of the island and set his crew up for the first winter at Beechey Island. When they set off again the next summer, Franklin made a fatal miscalculation. Unlike Amundsen, who would weave delicately around the southern shore of King William Island half a century later, Franklin charted a course due west across the top end of the island. In doing so, Franklin exposed his ships to the ice pack—the continent-sized plate of ice that expands and contracts around the Pole each year. Once it ensnared the *Terror* and the *Erebus*, it never let go.[1] Summer came and went, twice, without the ice loosening its grip on the stricken ships. We can only imagine the increasingly tense officers' conferences, rising restlessness among

---

[1] The ships were found in 2014 and 2016. There is some evidence that the *Terror* had been freed from the ice, recrewed by some of the survivors and sailed into a small inlet before being abandoned again. See, https://www.nationalgeographic.com/adventure/article/sir-john-franklin-searched-for-northwest-passage-then-vanished-feature.

the crew, and ever harsher enforcement of naval discipline as the realization set in that the expedition was doomed.

There are gaps in our knowledge of what happened next. What we know is as tragic as it is harrowing. When no word arrived from Franklin, several rescue missions were dispatched. A few clues were found quickly, such as a clay pipe left behind on Beechey Island.[34] Eventually John Rae, an employee of the Hudson's Bay Company, was able to piece together snippets of the fate Franklin and his men had suffered. A few Inuit told Rae they had met a group of scraggly white men pulling a small boat across the ice near King William Island. They indicated that the men had abandoned their ships after two winters spent encased in sea ice. Dozens of the crew, including Franklin, had been killed off by cold, starvation, scurvy, or other disease. In fact, for reasons unknown but rife with speculation, death had been an early and consistent companion on Franklin's trip long before their copious supplies of food would have run out. Three sailors had died in the first winter on Beechey Island. By April 1848, when the ships were abandoned, another 21 had died (according to a note from the surviving crew found under a cairn on King William Island in 1859).[35] Poisoning from the lead soldering that "dripped like melted candle wax down the inside surface" of the cans of food is just one theory, proposed by the Canadian anthropologist Owen Beattie (who exhumed the Beechey Island bodies in the 1980s).[36] Another is that a neurotoxin, Botulism Type E, doomed the men.[37]

With Franklin dead, the survivors were making a desperate scramble toward the mainland of Canada. They never made it. Later in the season, the Inuit found the remains of a camp at which bodies lay scattered about, some sporting visible hack marks; human remains were found in cooking pots. One officer was sitting up, dead, still clutching a rifle. When pressed for details by Rae, the Inuit produced trinkets to validate their story including pristine Victorian silverware with the initials of the officers—a distant reminder of the Victorian pride and pomp with which the crew had set sail.

Amundsen did not wish to repeat the mistakes of his predecessors, and therefore planned the wintering during his Northwest Passage expedition carefully. With such a short summer, there was a great temptation to push ahead as far as possible until literally frozen in place. But with the way ahead unknown and the exact date at which one would become icebound uncertain, Amundsen reasoned that a few days of lost mobility were less costly than foregoing a choice spot for wintering. Amundsen was far from a leader prone to squeezing the last out of himself and his weary crew, and soberly admitted, "I confess that I wanted breathing time."[38] It was with this in mind that he set up camp in September 1903 in Gjøa Harbor, facing the mainland of Canada, with King William Island effectively blocking out the worst of the ice.

Despite being underway decades after Ross and Franklin, Amundsen and his crew enjoyed few of the luxurious amenities of the British expeditions. There was no library to speak of, and an organ would have been impossible to squeeze into the tight quarters of the small herring boat. Yet, Amundsen and his men, unlike every other expedition to winter before them, seem to have enjoyed their stay. Amundsen had chosen his small crew with the full knowledge that they would be spending years together and had attempted to select compatible personalities. Nonetheless, they gave each other space: two of his crew lived on shore in a small hut they built out of the wooden storage containers, Amundsen and his second-in-command lived in the ship's cabin, while the remaining three in the ship's forecastle. Just as importantly, he had chosen crewmen from the far north of Norway—men who were already used to living for months without sunlight. The eerie darkness interrupted only by northern lights was not new to these men. Although they reported that they were beginning to get on each other's nerves by the end of the second winter, they were spared the psychological torture experienced by so many before them.

Amundsen, unlike most other explorers of his day, also set out to deliberately befriend the local Inuit. His motivations were manifold. He knew that a broader sphere of social interaction would make the winter more bearable. As news of the strangers camped out in the harbor spread, Inuit bands from far and wide made the trip to visit them. The *Gjøa* became something of a congregating point, even a center of social drama: a place of dancing, practical jokes, misunderstandings, friendship, shared meals and, most likely, sex. Amundsen's men were not always pleased at having so many visitors. But they were not filled with the hopeless dread that all the other wintering expeditions had experienced—the feeling of waiting in a lifeless twilight zone. There was life, and plenty of it.

Amundsen also took advantage of the opportunity to learn as much as he could about the skills the Inuit had developed for living in this harsh climate—knowledge that would be important on future journeys. One of the photographs from the winters in Gjøa Harbor shows a series of igloos Amundsen's crew constructed under the careful eye of an Inuit, each one clearly sturdier than the last. His treatment of the Inuit, though not free of the influence of European stereotypes, was considerably more open and respectful than that of nearly all the polar explorers before him.[39]

Unlike the British leaders, Amundsen imposed little discipline on his men. Each man had a job to do, but beyond this, they were left largely to their own devices. Their captain did insist on their staying physically fit and to this end the crew went skiing. In fact, two crewmen built a ski jump; they later fondly recalled that on Amundsen's first go, he approached it at full speed. "He jumped like a hero but landed on his back and was hit on the forehead by one of his skis." The crew also embarked on regular hunting expeditions, often in the company of Inuit friends. The steady supply of fresh meat held scurvy at bay and kept the five-year supply of dried foods in the *Gjøa*'s pantry from being depleted.

After spending two winters in Gjøa Harbor, Amundsen and his crew continued along the narrow strip of water between the Canadian mainland and Victoria Island. Much of this area was known, thanks to a series of overland expeditions and the extensive search for Franklin. Nonetheless, traversing it by sea and thus completing the Passage was an unprecedented undertaking. At the end of August 1905, the little ship and its crew spotted another vessel, a whaler from San Francisco. "I am exceedingly pleased to be the first to welcome you on getting through the Northwest Passage," the captain said as he shook hands with Amundsen on deck. After a final winter spent with American whalers at King Point—during which Amundsen undertook his solo round trip to the telegraph office in Eagle—the crew sailed down around Alaska and ended the journey in San Francisco.[2]

Amundsen's success caused a sensation, especially in the US and, of course, in Norway. In Great Britain, it caused consternation.

## The Other British Obsession

While it is true that Amundsen benefitted from far better maps and charts than his predecessors—many of them created during the fruitless searches for Franklin—his advantages should not be overstated. Amundsen tended to adopt old rather than new technologies, in particular regarding clothing. And attributing his success to an unfair advantage is out of place in any case: during the rest of his career, Amundsen competed directly with contemporaries. This was especially the case during his expedition to reach the South Pole, the objective he set himself after returning from the Northwest Passage. In this attempt, he competed with two of the most celebrated explorers of all time.

In 1879, a Swedish team had completed the Northeast Passage across the northern tip of the Eurasian landmass—a challenge Amundsen would successfully take on in 1920. The North and South Poles, however, remained unclaimed on Amundsen's return from the Northwest Passage. Of the two,

---

[2] One of Amundsen's crew members died during this final winter, most likely of appendicitis.

the South was the more formidable challenge. First, ships had to approach the icy continent by crossing the stormiest and most desolate seas on earth. Then, once a team had anchored securely, the real task began: trekking across the icy desert in the coldest temperatures on earth toward the nondescript geographic pole. The passage to the North Pole, which is located in the midst of an ice sheet, presents no great topographical obstacles to an explorer. Antarctica, where the South Pole is located, however, is a continental landmass with mountain ranges higher than the Alps. Reaching the South Pole required a nuanced interplay of skillsets and modes of travel. Up to this point in his career, Amundsen had focused solely on waterborne exploration. Overland travel was new to him—though he had learned a lot from the Inuit at Gjøa Harbor. Further, in attempting the South Pole, he had to compete with two skilled explorers who had spent their entire careers focused on that single goal. If persistence and experience had been the determining factors, it would have been one of these men who first reached the Pole.

In 1901, the English explorer Robert Falcon Scott mounted the first serious expedition to the South Pole.[40] Scott and a small party managed to reach 82 degrees south, the farthest point anyone had yet attained. The expedition nearly ended in disaster, however. Scott and his party were underdressed and underfed. Among the many problems that beset them was scurvy, the dread of seafarers. One of Scott's crewmen suffered severely enough that he had to leave the expedition prematurely. This man was Ernest Shackleton, a young and ambitious Irishman. Shackleton saw Scott as an incompetent leader whose emphasis on naval discipline had undercut the expedition's chances of success. Scott, in turn, blamed Shackleton for the failure. A bitter rivalry was born.

Shackleton mounted his own expedition in 1907 aboard the *Nimrod*. To Scott's dismay, Shackleton bested his record, coming within 100 miles of the Pole (if we want to commemorate Shackleton, it should really be for this achievement rather than his expedition on the *Endurance*—Amundsen called it "the most brilliant incident in the history of Antarctic exploration."[41]). While he was more successful this time than he would be a few years later on the *Endurance*, Shackleton skirted disaster by inches. Scurvy and hunger ravaged the crew as they made their way back on foot across the icy plains. (Shackleton himself admitted later that skis might have been a better choice than slogging across the ice on foot.) Scott meanwhile set off again in 1910. He had made adjustments based on his nearly fatal trek ten years earlier. In order to ensure his team's mobility, whatever the conditions, Scott this time brought along skis, sled dogs, Siberian ponies and two motorized snowmobiles. Spirits were high when, in January 1911, he established a base camp at

McMurdo Sound—today the site of the US Arctic mission. From there, he established supply depots at 70-mile intervals. These would enable a small party to make the final trek to the Pole and back without having to carry too much weight.

In November, Scott and 15 others set off for the final leg of the journey. While spirits ran high, Scott made a series of last-minute adjustments that would ultimately doom his venture. The plan was to establish a final food depot, "One Ton Depot," from which a team of four would embark on a final push to the Pole. This camp, however, was set up far short of its planned location. The final assault team would have to cover more ground than they originally thought to get to the Pole and back. At the last moment, Scott also decided to embark on the last stretch with a team of five rather than four, without adequately adjusting the food supply carried by the group. The group ground on, pushing themselves to their physical limit. Food began to run low and the men's physical condition deteriorate. They finally did reach the Pole on 17 January 1912. To their dismay, they found it marked by a Norwegian flag. Amundsen had beat them to it.[42]

## Amundsen's Pivot to the South Pole

In 1908, in between speaking tours and the editing of his Northwest Passage diary, Amundsen purchased a chalet, set in rocky woodlands on a fjord outside of Christiania. It was here that he set to work planning his next adventure. With the fame and recognition, he had gained from his expedition through the Northwest Passage, Amundsen had fewer financial limitations in preparing his next trip—at least to begin with. Nonetheless, he chose a relatively small crew: 19 men and 97 sled dogs. His selection of both the human and canine members of the team was meticulous, bearing in mind both the qualities of the individuals and their potential for working together as a team. Skiing was once again a central requirement, but Amundsen also looked for other niche competencies. While one of his crew was a professional skier, another was an experienced ice pilot and a third an experienced dogsled driver.

Remarkably, Amundsen's goal was initially not the South but the North Pole. His childhood hero and mentor Nansen had pioneered what he called the drift strategy for reaching this icebound, landless North Pole. Nansen had rammed a specially designed ship, the *Fram*, into the pack ice, with the expectation that the moving ice would bring his vessel close enough to the Pole to allow for a quick ski to his goal. The idea worked in principle—Nansen spent some three years in the pack ice above Siberia before being spat out again in

1896. He failed to make the final push to the Pole, however. Amundsen was optimistic that, with some adjustments to Nansen's strategy, he would meet with success. He petitioned the Norwegian government to allow him the use of Nansen's old ship the *Fram* (which was now the property of the state).

While Amundsen was preparing to attempt the North Pole, however, news broke that Dr. Frederick Cook—whom Amundsen had befriended on the *Belgica* expedition—and another American explorer leading a separate party had reached the Pole. Both claims were questioned at the time; today, most experts agree that they were entirely bogus.[43] But Amundsen could not have known this, and so, working on the assumption that the North Pole had been bagged, he quickly set his sights to the south. He kept his intention secret, even from most of his crew. His discretion is understandable. It was not clear whether his creditors would support his changed objective, especially since a well-known British team under Scott had already announced its intention of tackling the South Pole by the time Amundsen and his crew set off.

Some Amundsen detractors have accused him of engineering a "Race to the Pole" by keeping his plan secret and only revealing it dramatically once under way. Some even suggest that this race led to Scott's demise. This is, however, a gross misreading. If anyone was engaged in a war of psychological manipulation, it was Scott; Stephen Bown writes of him that his "tactics were to use publicity to clear the field, to cause any potential rivals to back down, and in effect to lay claim to the pole as his and Britain's property."[44] With only one of the four goals of polar exploration left to achieve, Scott and the British establishment agreed, the South Pole had to be Britain's. But, as Bown points out, Amundsen was already planning his trip to the South at the time Scott announced his own.

## Success via the Butcher's Shop

Amundsen set sail on 9 August 1910. His men still did not know of their true destination, though some had begun to suspect that something was awry. The fact that Amundsen was bringing dogs from Norway, rather than more sensibly purchasing them along the way to the Pole, was only one of several objects of curiosity.

But Amundsen was harboring more than one secret. He was, once again, financially strung out. When the news had broken of the two North Pole "successes," the Norwegian state had canceled a large grant for Amundsen's expedition, and private investors were also pulling out. Amundsen was forced to mortgage his house and take on as much debt as he could bear. His brother and business manager Leon wrote that, "the position is no better, and maybe worse, than when the *Gjøa* sailed." And here lies one of the major but rarely discussed distinctions between Amundsen and his competitors. When Shackleton returned from his failed *Nimrod* expedition in 1909, and once again in 1916 from the attempt with the *Endurance*, he was given a hero's welcome. Amundsen knew that he was in a completely different position: if he returned unsuccessful from his South Pole expedition, regardless of any tales of derring-do, he would face utter financial ruin. The strain on Amundsen in the lead-up to the trip must have been enormous. We must keep this fact in mind, especially when we examine the decisions involving deliberate restraint that he repeatedly made on his final advance to the Pole, instances when a more action-prone leader may have pushed on anyway for fear of losing out to Scott.

On 6 September, the *Fram* arrived at the island of Madeira to take on supplies. Leon Amundsen, who had taken a steamer there, greeted the crew. A few hours before setting off again three days later, Amundsen and his brother broke the news of their new destination to the crew. They were offered free passage by steamer back to Norway if they preferred not to go on. None took Amundsen up on the offer. While the ship sailed south, Leon returned to Norway to break the news to the world. After delivering letters to the King and Nansen, he released the story to the press. The race to the Pole was on.

Amundsen and his team arrived on the Antarctic continent in January 1911—high summer in Antarctica—and began preparing for a dash to the Pole the following summer. One of the first obstacles on the way to the Pole was the Ross Ice Shelf. Originally discovered by the British captain James Ross, this immense sheet of ice covers an area the size of France and, along its edge, drops precipitously down to the water below. Ross called it "the Barrier." Deciding that landing in the same place as Scott would be inadvisable—not to mention awkward—Amundsen had scoured all the texts he had been able to find from previous explorers. (He himself had never set eyes on the ice shelf.) Several explorers, writing decades apart, mentioned a Bay of Whales in which the sheer wall of ice was broken down into manageable steps. Amundsen surmised, correctly, that he would be able to land his ship there and scamper up onto the shelf proper with his men. It worked out exactly as planned. Once on top of the Shelf, the nine men of the "Polar Party" assembled a prefab wooden hut and a series of tents connected by snow tunnels, and set about establishing food depots along the planned route, while the other nine returned with the *Fram* to Argentina to resupply and make repairs.

Amundsen was meticulous in his calculations. Before departing for the Pole, he and his team built three depots along the route, with a total of 3400 kg of food and supplies. They were marked with rows of 20 two-meter-high flag posts that fanned out at right angles. The final depot was 800 kilometers from the Pole. Amundsen calculated that most of the final five-man team's supplies would be consumed getting to the Pole; finding the depots on the way back would thus be a matter of life and death.

As the Antarctic winter began to fade toward the end of August, temperatures remained unforgiving and violent storms were frequent. Amundsen grew nervous—what if Scott's party, encamped on the other end of the Ross Ice Shelf, had already set off? While the original departure date for the small ski party had been set for 1 November, Amundsen now advocated leaving immediately. His was not a military expedition, and he had no way of compelling his men to venture out in the still-brutal temperatures. Yet, he managed to convince them, and on 8 September, they set off. This proved to be a mistake. After two days of reasonable weather, the temperature dropped precipitously to −56 degrees Celsius. "This was undeniably bitter," Amundsen recalled.[45] One of his men, Bjaaland, was more direct. "God help me it was just shit and best forgotten."[46] But the dogs suffered most of all, who shivered miserably during the nights and had to be lifted into their harnesses in the mornings. The group decided to press on to the first depot and then return to their winter camp at Framheim. "To risk men and animals out of sheer obstinacy and continue, just because we have started on our way—that would never occur to me," he later wrote. "If we are to win this game, the pieces must be moved carefully."[47]

On 20 October, Amundsen and four men set out again, accompanied by fifty-two dogs pulling four sleds. With the assurance that there was plenty of food waiting for them at each depot, they moved with deliberate calm, covering an average of 22 ½ miles per day, less at the start of the trip.[48] Remarking on the slower pace at the start, Amundsen later wrote, "We could easily have done twice this, but as it was more important to arrive than to show great speed, we limited the distance."[49] This was no exaggeration. During a trial run the year before, the team had managed sixty-two miles in a single day.[50]

In mid-November, the group reached the end of the Ross Ice Shelf and crossed onto land. Both mentally and physically, the party was in good shape. In fact, Amundsen and one of the men, Olav Bjaaland, took a detour up the first prominent peak they encountered, Mount Betty, simply for the sake of "having real bare ground under our feet," and to enjoy some telemark ski turns on the way down. Bjaaland, a former ski champion, executed the turns in "fine style." Amundsen did not, and took an ungraceful tumble.[51]

With the flat shelf behind them, the men had to chart a course up the steep and sharp peaks that span the Antarctic continent. This entailed hair-raising ascents up steep glaciers, weaving on skis between gaping crevasses. Even a minor accident or equipment failure could have doomed the party. "The wilderness of the landscape seen from this point is not to be described; chasm after chasm, crevasse after crevasse, with great blocks of ice scattered promiscuously about, gave one the impression that here Nature was too powerful for us."[52] But his choice of skis and sled dogs as his primary mode of transportation paid off. The team reached the top of the mountain pass four days after beginning the treacherous climb, and the way to the Pole now lay open before them. With the mountains behind them, they set up camp, and Amundsen ordered 23 of the dogs slaughtered to bolster food supplies. "The holiday humour that ought to have prevailed in the tent that evening—our first on the plateau—did not make its appearance; there was depression and sadness in the air—we had grown so fond of our dogs."[53] Indeed, one of the most striking features of Amundsen's writing is the rich stories of his beloved dogs and their individual behavioral quirks. Yet, as he also regularly pointed out, he had learned from the Inuit to see dogs as working animals and not as pets.[3]

After a few days' rest at this camp, which the team called the "Butcher's Shop," the party set off for the Pole. At three in the afternoon of 14 December the sled drivers called out a "simultaneous 'Halt.'" The five men had reached their goal. They celebrated, shook hands, and together planted the Norwegian flag—"five weather-beaten, frost-bitten fists they were that grasped the pole." Amundsen reasoned that, "it was not for one man to do this; it was for all of us who had staked their lives in the struggle, and held together through thick and thin."[54] They ate a hearty meal, took stock of their remaining supplies and took measurements for a full 24 hours. Finally, they set up a tent, in which they left a note for Scott and a letter to the Norwegian King (with the request that Scott deliver the letter, should Amundsen and his party fail to return home). They then turned around and spent 39 days skiing and sledding back to their base, where they arrived only one day behind Amundsen's original schedule.

While Amundsen's success with the Passage had owed a debt to the many explorers who had charted much of the terrain before him, the South Pole was different. His route from the Bay of Whales had been entirely unknown, unlike the well-worn tracks that Shackleton and Scott frequented from McMurdo Sound. While Amundsen did not make much of this point—indeed, he consistently spoke highly of Scott—it was not lost on Nansen. He

---

[3] Amundsen was never called out for this calculated cruelty. From today's perspective, this may be one of his most questionable acts.

pointed out a few months after Amundsen's success that, "From first to last he and his companions have traversed entirely unknown regions on their ski, and there are not many expeditions in history that have brought under the foot of man so long a range of country hitherto unseen by human eye." To hammer the point home, he continued, "not at any point does his route touch that of the Englishmen—except by the Pole itself." Nansen was assuming—correctly—that Scott had reached the Pole too, and that he would shortly return to tell the world about it. "When, in a year's time we have Captain Scott back safe and sound with all his discoveries and conditions, on the other route, Amundsen's results will greatly increase in value."[55] In this later assumption, he was mistaken. Scott and his party did reach the Pole shortly after Amundsen. But he and his men were exhausted, and their food supplies were running out. They all died on the way back to their ship.

## Escaping the Escalation Spiral

Preparing for an expedition into a hostile environment requires research, route selection, and the proper selection and training of a crew. The packing list is equally fundamental. Unforgiving weather, the need for complete self-sufficiency, and the possibility of getting stuck for an indeterminate period of time led most captains to favor large teams and massive reserves. Perhaps no expedition's buffer topped Franklin's in his attempt on the Northwest Passage. The *Erebus* and *Terror* boasted stores of several thousand cans of food and nearly 100,000 pounds of flour. The crew of 129 covered nearly every conceivably useful skill—from carpentry to navigation—save two: Arctic hunting and skiing. The safety gained from such a buffer, however, is imaginary. A larger crew necessitates more food, which necessitates a larger hold, which necessitates a larger engine, which necessitates more fuel. The quest for added safety through excess thus leads to an escalating spiral. Each British expedition was larger than the previous one, a result of the mistaken belief that the Passage or Pole would yield to the application of a little more force.

A case in point is Scott's attempt to guarantee his group's mobility on the Antarctic ice. His snowmobiles were a relatively new product and had not been properly tested; they soon broke down. His ponies required huge supplies of feed but were ineffective in the Antarctic terrain, which was wholly unfamiliar to them. The number of dogs he brought along was too small to make a substantial contribution. The team did bring a small number of skis but didn't know how to use them. Scott himself did not know how to ski, nor was it a skill he looked for in hiring his crew. In fact, Scott was something of a novice in snow, having little experience with the medium except that gained on his two failed expeditions. In the end, his expedition's mode of travel consisted almost entirely of brute human slogging. His was a neither-here-nor-there approach, trying to bring a little bit of everything in the misguided hope that one of the tools would do the trick.

None other than Amundsen had warned Scott's expedition that the choice of transportation might doom their venture. While Amundsen had been setting up camp for the first winter by the Bay of Whales, a party from Scott's expedition stopped by for a visit. Amundsen invited them to try out his dogs. "They refused," he recalled. "Scott, on the other hand," Amundsen continued, "had come South equipped with motor sledges, which had immediately demonstrated their impracticability over the surface of ice and snow. He had brought also—and to these he pinned his fate finally—a number of Shetland ponies. I was confident that this was a fatal mistake, and much to my sorrow it was in part the cause of Scott's tragic end."[56]

In both of his expeditions treated in this chapter, Amundsen approached the question of reserves and technology with far more nuance than his competitors. While his food supplies were copious, he took few other creature comforts. He privileged nimble mobility over quantity and power. He insisted that his men be expert skiers. His outlook on technology was neither conservative nor dogmatically forward-looking. He took whatever tools were most suited to maintain the flexibility and speed he sought. Adding a gasoline engine to the *Gjøa*, for example, was bold; this was very much the age of steam, and gasoline engines were a novelty and considered too dangerous by many—including the crew that installed it for him.[57] Yet, no available fuel packed as much energy per volume—thus freeing up room on the ship for food—nor allowed an engine to be started in an instant.

Amundsen stuck with this strategy in his preparation for the South Pole. The *Gjøa* had been the right choice for the Northwest Passage. Its petite size and shallow draft had allowed it to nimbly maneuver through the tight spaces of the Canadian Archipelago. To reach the South Pole (or the North, which he had initially planned for), however, involved contending with stormy open seas and, worse yet, aggressive and unpredictable pack ice. Southern winds could loosen up the ice plates and chunks, allowing ships plenty of room to wiggle their way through to the continent, but northern winds jammed the ice together and compressed it—and anything caught in between. The *Fram's* eggshell bottom was ideally suited for tough ice—whether in the north or the south. Its design was completely in keeping with Amundsen's inclination to avoid rather than overpower the forces that nature would inevitably throw at him. When the *Fram* was squeezed by encroaching ice, the pressure would lift the hull rather than pinch it together. Amundsen also doubled down on his use of new marine engines. Rather than sticking with the gasoline engine he knew from the Northwest passage, he had a brand-new Swedish marine diesel motor built into the *Fram,* which boasted fifteen times the power of the *Gjøa's* engine.

The wisdom of these two choices is evident when we compare the experience of the British, most notably Shackleton. Shackleton, to be fair, took more care in selecting equipment than many of his compatriots. The *Endurance*, despite its Royal Navy-esque name, was originally a Norwegian ship designed for travels in icy waters.[4] Shackleton had the ship refurbished; unlike Amundsen, however, he prioritized the ship's ability to punch through ice rather than its survivability under compression. He also fell in line with the British logic of steam power. This choice would prove disastrous.

Already a few days after leaving South Georgia in early December 1914, Shackleton and the *Endurance* crew spotted particularly thick pack ice. Nonetheless, Shackleton decided to push on. For the following weeks, the ship weaved and ground its way slowly through the maze of icebergs and plates, inching toward the continent. By the end of January, however, Shackleton had sailed into a trap. Strong winds had compressed the ice, and the ship was stuck. Over the next few weeks, the crew made several herculean efforts to break the ship free. It was to no avail. On the morning of 14 February, the ship was again floating freely in a small pool surrounded by thick ice. Salvation loomed some 400 meters away, where a small channel of open water had appeared. If they could make it there, they might yet have escaped with their ship intact. Shackleton set his men to work hacking and sawing their way at the ice while the ship rammed into it under full steam. Over a day and a half's work, they made painstaking progress of some 180 meters. At that point, however, Shackleton was forced to call the effort off. Coal takes up much more room than diesel and was consequently at a premium on ships. Shackleton felt he could not risk using up any more of his precious supply in the attempt to break the ship free. The ship thus remained ensnared in the ice, slowly drifting south for the next several months, creaking and groaning under the steady pressure.

In October 1915, Shackleton and his men once again had a brief opportunity to escape. On the 14th, the ice loosened, and the ship was again afloat in a small pool. Two days later, the men spotted open water just outside their encasement. A diesel engine could have been engaged in an instant, and its

---

[4] In fact, it had been built for Adrien De Gerlache to take tourists on polar bear hunting excursions, though it never served this purpose.

full power immediately leveraged. Instead, Shackleton had to order his men to run up steam. It took four hours alone to get sufficient meltwater channeled into the boilers, at which point a leak was discovered. The boilers had to be completely drained before they could be repaired, and the chance at escape slipped away. The next day the crew spotted open water again but did not have sufficient time to build up enough steam to make a dash for it. Under sail alone, the *Endurance* could not dent the narrow line of ice that stood between it and freedom.

That was it. By the end of October, bitterly cold temperatures and ceaseless winds compacted the ice around the ship. Over the following weeks, the *Endurance* began to buckle and deform as the pressure of the ice grew too great. "She quivered and groaned as rudder and stern post were torn off," recalled Captain Worsley. "To me, the sounds was so terribly human that I felt like groaning in sympathy…it gave me the horrible feeling that the ship was gasping for breath."[58] The engine room flooded. By the end of October, Shackleton had moved his men onto the ice. By the end of November, the ship had been crushed to pieces and disappeared.

It is impossible to be sure how Shackleton would have fared with a ship like the *Fram* and its diesel engine. No doubt it would have given him an ace up his sleeve when it mattered most. What we do know is that Amundsen obsessed over collecting as many such aces as possible. In the end, this particular one did not have to be played; another rendered it redundant. For Amundsen had selected as one of his crew an experienced "ice pilot," Andreas Beck, who boasted a lifetime of experience guiding ships in Norway's upper reaches. Amundsen dutifully relinquished control to Beck in the ice-chocked passages, and the *Fram*'s journey proved uneventful.

While Amundsen was on the cutting edge of innovation in his choice of engine, he had no qualms about abandoning modern European technologies in other areas. He and his men wore Inuit fur suits—superior to the best European textiles in warmth, breathability, and comfort. Like the Inuit, they ate raw seal meat—a practice many explorers eschewed—whenever the opportunity presented itself, because doing so prevented scurvy.

Amundsen was the first to fully escape the escalation spiral. Because he tapped into the knowledge and existing trade network of the Inuit during his Northwest Passage expedition, it did not need to be self-sufficient. The contrast to the British example is striking. After two winters on the ice, Franklin's men had had no choice but to make a run for civilization. By contrast, after two winters on King William Island, Amundsen and his men could easily have remained for another two. Restlessness and the wish to complete the Passage motivated them to move on, not the depletion of their resources.

# Leading Men: The British and the Norwegian Way

In 2001, a century after Scott embarked on the first attempt at the Pole, Harvard Business School Professor John Kotter published his classic article "What leaders really do." Kotter proposed that whereas management is about "dealing with complexity," leadership is about "dealing with change."[59] Put differently, management is the process of imposing structure, of planning, of writing budgets, and of hiring. Leadership is about putting this into practice, about dealing with unforeseen issues, about overcoming setbacks, and about motivating teams. While it is beneficial for academics to keep the two competencies apart, real life rarely affords such a neat distinction. All the planning in the world will not suffice to get you to the Pole or through the Northwest Passage. Amundsen, as with most truly successful leaders, was able to combine his prowess in planning with an innate sense of how to relate to his men and handle unforeseen circumstances. Indeed, in this area, too, he stands out—especially when we compare him with the major British explorers.

Already in 1574, the English explorer Martin Frobischer set off to attempt the Northwest Passage. Some of his best men disappeared off the coast of Greenland. Frobischer suspected foul play by the Inuit who had been accompanying the party. More likely is that Frobischer's mercurial nature motivated his men to abscond, reasoning that, as one historian has written, "even desertion on the Baffin coast may have been preferable to suffering [Frobischer's] displeasure." The expedition returned to London. A century later Henry Hudson, who shared with Frobischer a penchant for mistreating his crew, was not as lucky. Having grown tired of the torments Hudson inflicted on them, his crew set him and his son afloat in a small rowboat without food or water in the desolate and frigid bay that bears his name today. While such abuse was unique, other captains, including Franklin, imposed strict behavioral rules and banned swearing and excessive drinking.[60]

Frobischer and Hudson could not help that they lacked the knowledge and technology that would allow later explorers, such as Franklin and Amundsen, to penetrate the inner reaches of the Passage. Another driver of their failures, however, was very much in their hands. Both captains exemplified the British Navy's culture of harsh military discipline. Trying to motivate crews by doubling down on naval discipline became a British tradition. Richard Collinson, one of the captains sent to on the fruitless search for Franklin, returned from the Arctic with nearly all of his officers confined to their quarters under arrest. Another would-be Franklin rescuer, Robert McClure—who also ended up trapped in the pack ice and forced to abandon ship in 1853—liberally doled out dozens of lashes for swearing and flew into "terrible, positively inhuman" temper tantrums at the slightest infractions of his crew (though having approached the Passage from the West, and walking East after abandoning their ship, McClure did become the first to traverse the Passage on foot).[61]

Even private expeditions, such as Scott's attempts on the South Pole, relied on the military mode. As former officers, men like Scott knew no other way to lead. Before his *Discovery* expedition, he insisted to the Royal Geographic Society—one of his main sponsors—that "I must have complete command of the ship and landing parties." It is noteworthy that the only British captain to lead through vision and inspiration rather than orders and threats was Shackleton.[62] This might be in no small part because Shackleton had been on the receiving end of Scott's martial discipline during the 1901 expedition.

While most polar captains were transactional leaders—rewarding men for precisely following orders and punishing them when they did not—Amundsen was a transformational leader. Aboard the *Gjøa* there were no rules. He wrote after the trip that, "I know myself how irksome this strict discipline is," and that he had been determined to apply "a system of freedom on board as far as possible, to let everyone feel that he was independent in his own sphere." To Amundsen, it was critical to treat each member as a "thinking being and not as a wound-up machine."[63] During their successful bid to reach the South Pole, meanwhile, Amundsen and his men spent much of their time sleeping. Amundsen saw that whenever they were not moving on their skis and sleds, they could best use their time by resting rather than engaging in some calorie-consuming military drill. At the same time, important decisions, such as which route to pick up the mountain barrier in November 1911, were made jointly.[64] One of his crewmen, Helmer Hansen, recalled that this style of leadership did not diminish Amundsen's ability to direct. "The discipline was instinctive…[I]n the daily life there were not distinctions of rank, and yet no one was ever in doubt about who was in command."[65]

It was not just Amundsen's own attitudes that allowed him to successfully inspire and influence his crew. He selected his men with great care. We have already seen that all his men knew how to ski and had had previous exposure to a polar environment; Amundsen also took care, however, to build a group in which each member's temperament complemented those of the others. One of his crew of six on the *Gjøa,* and again on the *Fram,* was a full-time cook, Adolf Lindstrom. Lindstrom was no sailor and no athlete; he was overweight and directly contributed little to the actual process of achieving the expeditions' ends. Yet, he was an immensely jolly and uncomplicated person, "always happy and in a good mood, in spite of having every reason to be bad-tempered," as one crewmember recalled, who took great pleasure in cooking.

His temperament and the specialty Norwegian pies he made became the social glue in the men's daily existence.

Amundsen made his technological decisions not only with the outcome of the expedition in mind but also with their effect on his leadership capabilities. While the diesel engine on the *Fram* was brand new, Amundsen deliberately left another new technology off his packing list on his expedition to the Pole: the wireless radio. This is all the more surprising because being the first to break the news of a successful expedition was almost as important as actually being the first to realize the success. Amundsen knew that, without a radio, he might have reached his objective but would be prevented from sharing the news with the world for months before the *Fram* arrived back at a port. The possibility of calling for a rescue via radio was another obvious element of the new technology's appeal. Yet, despite these potential benefits, Amundsen decided that there was more value in sealing his group off from the world. In his excellent biography, Stephen Bown writes of this decision that, "He claimed to reject the wireless not because of its weight or expense or doubts about its functionality, but because of its potential effects on his leadership." Foregoing a radio allowed Amundsen and his crew to focus solely on the mission at hand, to be neither distracted nor tempted by goings-on back in civilization. Amundsen explained his logic to a group at the Royal Geographic Society before his trip (when his stated objective was still the North Pole), "Imagine that we have spent two years in the drifting pack, and still have three more years to spend—imagine that we suddenly get a dispatch stating that some of our dears are seriously ill or dying, or whatever it may be. What would then be the result?"[66]

## The Unseen Explorer

Amundsen was not free of faults, and he did suffer his share of misfortunes. During the final winter of the Northwest Passage expedition, which was spent with whalers above the Yukon after completing the Passage itself, one of his crewmen developed appendicitis and died. Amundsen was later heavily criticized by the British for excluding a doctor from his crew, though it is unlikely a doctor could have done anything to alter the poor man's fate. While wintering on the Ross Ice Shelf on the South Pole Expedition, one of the crew grew disruptive, and Amundsen had to formally reprimand him. (Incidentally, this man was the only expedition member Amundsen had picked as a favor to his mentor Nansen, against his own better judgment.) During his later expedition through the Northeast Passage, as the ship and crew sat out the winter, one of the young crewmen grew weary of the enterprise and decided to walk to the nearest Russian settlement, some 650 km away. Another crewman volunteered to accompany him. Amundsen gave them his blessing, six sled dogs and a year's worth of supplies. The two men perished. Amundsen would second-guess this decision for the rest of his life, calling it, "the one real tragedy in all my polar work."[67]

Still, Amundsen remains the outlier among polar captains. Unlike his competitors, he had no institutional support. Franklin's expedition was an official undertaking of the British Navy. Scott's trips to the South Pole, though private, operated within the context of the British establishment, with sponsorship and assistance from the Royal Geographic Society (in the case of the Discovery trip), among other institutions. Amundsen was an entrepreneur, and much like today's start-up founders, his own money was on the line during his trips. Like many of today's successful entrepreneurs, Amundsen was involved in every detail of the planning and execution of his expeditions. Much of the vernacular used to describe successful start-ups could be applied to Amundsen as well. In constructing his system for each expedition—the combination of ship, supplies, storage, and transportation technologies, and so on—he took an iterative approach by testing early and adjusting accordingly. In his bestseller *The Lean Startup*, Eric Ries describes how successful Silicon Valley ventures have mastered the art of the "pivot"—building on a successful component of a business model toward a new and perhaps previously unplanned goal.[68] Amundsen embodied this spirit too, his last-minute switch from the North Pole to the South being a case in point.

Given his indisputable track-record, it is a curiosity that Amundsen is so little known. That failed explorers like Scott and Shackleton are far better-known than him is at first difficult to comprehend. There are, however, many explanations. For one, Amundsen was not a natural self-promoter like Franklin, Scott, Shackleton, and the other boisterous, self-aggrandizing British captains. Nor was he entirely comfortable speaking English—and in the age in which he lived, as now, being known in London or New York was the path to global fame. Amundsen did learn, over time, to present his trips in compelling ways, and much of the fundraising he did for his later trips was accomplished via public speaking and writing books. In the US, he even managed to gain celebrity status in the late 1920s. But it was clear to many that his heart was not in this aspect of his work. Nansen wrote that in contrast to Scott and his British contemporaries' penchant for *promoting* their expeditions, Amundsen, "was a man of deeds, one of those silent men who gets things done."[69]

Finally, we must bear in mind that the presentation of the past as we see it today has been curated by generations of commentators. Studying history is really an archaeological activity that consists of peeling away the interpretative layers laid down by many successive observers. What becomes immediately noticeable about Amundsen in this regard is that, though he enjoyed a brief spell of fame, a cabal of powerful British men worked tirelessly to deflate his image (and to elevate that of other British men). This was quite simply because Amundsen had the "misfortune" of not being British. In the first decades of the 1900s, the British Empire was at its zenith; it encompassed one-fourth of the globe's inhabitable surface and one-fifth of the world's population. This imperial structure was propped up by feelings of superiority and entitlement from which even polar expeditions were not exempt. Notables of the British Navy and the Royal Geographic Society barely concealed their disgust that Amundsen had—unfairly, as they insisted—nabbed one "British" prize after another. Amundsen consistently received less attention—and for his part, accepted fewer speaking engagements—in Great Britain than in the US or closer to home in Norway. In fact, his stature was so low that when the bomb-shell news that he was heading south rather than north—and therefore directly competing with Scott—broke around the world on 2 October 1910, the British press hardly took note of it.

Making matters worse, Amundsen was a commoner. He did not have the upper-class pedigree expected of notable men who moved in circles of influence in London. His mentor, Nansen, provides a contrast. Nansen was respectable in the eyes of the British; he had earned a doctorate and displayed a clear interest in worthy causes beyond exploration. He became the Norwegian ambassador to London and was one of the initiators of the League of Nations. He was, or at least came to play the part of, a gentleman explorer. For Franklin, Scott, and to some extent even Nansen, putting up with the hostile environment of an expedition was a necessary sacrifice made to achieve a worthy goal. They tolerated the discomfort but truly reveled in life back home. With Amundsen, it was the other way around. His only passion was exploration; it was on expeditions that he felt his best; he rather "tolerated" being at home. In fact, Amundsen's biographer Stephen Bown points out that Amundsen spent very little time at home, preferring to be "on the road" in the US or elsewhere when not on expeditions. He had no inclination to learn to dress and speak differently for the sake of impressing a group of armchair explorers in London.

For this reason, despite his superior record, Amundsen was written off by the British establishment as a second-rate explorer. On one of the rare occasions when Amundsen gave a presentation in London, Lord Curzon, the head of the Royal Geographic Society, introduced Amundsen by referred to the latter's "remarkable luck" in terms of weather and ice conditions on his expedition to the South Pole. Of course, Amundsen's string of successful ventures had little to do with luck. His success stemmed from his ability to properly gauge the challenges and opportunities of polar travel and build technological and human systems accordingly. While he displayed the calm and steady hand of a stereotypical leader—when the *Gjøa's* engine room caught fire during the Northwest Passage trip, he responded in the same no-nonsense, all-hands-on-deck manner that we celebrate in Shackleton—he was far less charismatic than the other polar explorers. He made up for this, however, with his ability to understand the true drivers of success and failure in the polar environment. He understood the fact that any attempt at moving fast and with force—the hallmarks of the heroic leader—was bound to lead to disaster. Amundsen prepared himself, his men, and his equipment to an extent—and related to them in a humane way—that they could conceive of voluntarily staying an extra winter—or more—in the hostile confines of the Northwest Passage. His handling of men and mission on a day-to-day basis only reinforced this sentiment. This is the true hallmark of a successful polar explorer.

Amundsen recognized his own recipe for success. In response to the insistence of Curzon and many other British detractors that the failures of Franklin, Scott, and other heroic British captains were due to misfortune, while Amundsen's successes were due to luck, Amundsen wrote, "Victory awaits him who has everything in order—luck, people call it. Defeat is certain for [he] who has neglected to take the necessary precautions in time; this is called bad luck." What to the uncritical viewer looks like "luck" is, in fact, this very alignment of the planning, intentions, and actions of a leader with the external circumstances with which he or she is faced. When this occurs, success quite simply looks too easy to have been the result of human design. Amundsen's success, however, was very much by design: a design that understood and leveraged the cold facts of polar exploration rather than trying to outflank them by brute force.

This is the ultimate reason why Amundsen has failed to make an appearance in leadership literature and the reason that it is essential that he should. His method of leading, of reducing the various forms of friction that inevitably grind a venture down to the utmost, of ensuring that he was equipped and staffed to handle whatever uncertainties he nonetheless encountered, is less spectacular than the stories we like to retell. They do not conform to the

Action Fallacy. This goes a long way toward explaining his absence from the leadership section of bookstores. The methods of Shackleton and others, who at times brazenly stumbled into difficulties only to persistently hack their way back out of them, of course very much do conform to our expectations of leaders. In fact, even Amundsen himself could not help but admire Shackleton's unrivaled penchant for action. He wrote in 1912 (that is, *before* the epic *Endurance* adventure), "Sir Ernest Shackleton!—the name has a brisk sound. At its mere mention we see before us a man of indomitable will and boundless courage. He has shown us what the will and energy of a single man can perform."[70] And while Amundsen's flutter of fame in the US and beyond began to fade in the years following his death (with the obvious exception of his native Norway), Shackleton's stature was ascendant. In 1959, the American journalist Alfred Lansing published what would become a best-selling account of Shackleton's ordeal: *Endurance. Shackleton's Incredible Journey.* The rest, as they say, is history.

Sadly, though not altogether surprisingly, Amundsen died on an expedition he neither led nor had planned for. In the spring of 1928 one of his colleagues, the Italian explorer Umberto Nobile, set up shop on the Norwegian islands of Svalbard, halfway between Norway and the North Pole. From there he mounted a series of flights to the Pole in the airship *Italia*. While flying across vast uninhabited spaces, whether by airplane or dirigible, was risky business at the time—Charles Lindberg's famed solo flight from New York to Paris had been completed just the year before—Nobile's endeavor was not truly novel. In fact, in 1926, Amundsen, Nobile, and a crew of 16 had successfully reached the Pole in an airship and then continued on to Alaska. When Nobile set off on the *Italia* in 1928, then, the exercise seemed routine. His third flight to the North Pole that season took a mere 18 hours, thanks to strong winds. On the way back to Svalbard, however, the airship struggled with these same winds and, in circumstances that remain unclear, slammed into some ice floes northeast of Svalbard. The impact tore a gash in the passenger cabin. Nobile and eight crewmen were left stranded on the ice, while the remnants of the airship and six crew members were blown away, never to be seen again.

Luckily for Nobile and his earthbound men, one of the doomed crew members had thrown whatever equipment was close at hand out of the hole in the airship as the wind jerked the airship away in the chaotic seconds after impact. With this equipment, Nobile and his men were able to construct a makeshift radio antenna and send word that they needed help. A disordered and no less dramatic rescue effort ensued involving ships, planes and crews from eight countries, which gave rise to further crash landings on the ice. By the middle of July, the men had all been rescued. Umberto Nobile received a hero's welcome in Italy.

In Norway, however, there was only mourning. Roald Amundsen had been at a luncheon in Oslo when he heard of Nobile's plight. He stood up and declared his intention to help out his friend in need. On 18 June 1928, he boarded a twin-propeller French Navy plane from the mainland toward Spitsbergen. The plane disappeared. With it, the world lost one of its greatest explorers and one of its most outstanding leaders.

# Napoleon's Thorn. Toussaint Louverture

## The Retreat

In the autumn of 1795, in the French colony of Saint-Domingue—modern-day Haiti—a group of retreating troops congregated along the banks of the overflowing Artibonite River in the mountainous interior of the island.[1] The water was brown with the freshly eroded mud of the long rainy season, and the battle-weary men, most of whom were Black former slaves, were carrying very little—by this point, munitions and even clothes were scarce.[2] Most of these soldiers had been emancipated when French administrators outlawed slavery in the colony two years earlier and had spent the last year defending France's claim to the colonial territory against invasion by competing European powers. These powers—allied England and Spain—wished to reimpose slavery in order to harness the significant economic potential of the sugar and coffee plantations of Saint-Domingue, the so-called pearl of the Antilles, which, just four years earlier, had been producing half of the sugar and coffee in the world.

The troops had successfully defeated Spanish forces and were now fighting valiantly against Spain's British allies. But the British were proving a difficult adversary and the arrival of two large reinforcements had facilitated the English capture of the city of Port-au-Prince in June 1794. After a failed attempt at taking on the British in the open field on the city's outskirts, the troops' commander, Toussaint Louverture, had ordered the retreat.[3] Toussaint was a thin, seemingly unimposing man. He frequently made his troops laugh by recounting that his childhood nickname had been "Fatras-Bâton"—skinny stick—and at just five feet two inches he was by no means the typical picture of a martial hero.[4]

But retreating was no act of desperation. Instead, Toussaint was holding true to one of his most frequently repeated maxims, "slowly goes far and patience beats force."[5] He understood that by buying himself time in the island's mountainous backcountry, which was especially difficult to access during the long rainy season, and whose dense forests and steep slopes were unfamiliar to his British opponents—at the time only a third of the island had been mapped—he would be able to wait in relative safety while the British numbers were decimated by one of the island's most effective natural repellents: yellow fever. Living in close quarters in the mosquito-infested coastal regions over which they had control, the British forces were losing a staggering 15 percent of their troops each month to the illness.[6] For the next two years, while disease was wearing down the British ranks, his army would hold its defensive position in the interior of the island, staging strategic attacks and then disappearing back into the steep slopes, long grasses, and forests of the hinterland.

Nor was disease the only natural force that Toussaint leveraged to achieve his ends. Among the men who would fight against Toussaint's forces was Lieutenant Thomas Phipps Howard of the York Hussars, who served in the British contingent in Saint-Domingue from 1796 until 1798. In his diaries, Howard recounted how Toussaint's troops used the cover of a violent tropical storm to draw close to a British encampment and launch a six-hour-long attack, which Howard later described as "one of the grandest effects of horror I have ever experienced."[7]

In fact, Toussaint and his generals made a habit of exploiting the noise and distraction of tropical storms in their attacks. This strategic alignment with the island's climate served a psychological as well as a camouflaging purpose, for while the noise of pounding rain and crashing thunder sometimes did drown out the sounds of approaching soldiers and horses, in most cases there was nothing there to drown out. But who was to know? The Pavlovian association of thunderstorms with Toussaint's ambushes led to a widespread, almost superstitious dread of storms among the British troops. Whether there were actually Republican soldiers approaching under the cover of the flashing sky, pelting rain, and roaring winds or not, Toussaint had harnessed the buildup of dark storm clouds to inspire perpetual fear in his opponents. His enemies waited restlessly as every storm approached, listening to the cracks of breaking branches and trying to discern voices amidst the howling Caribbean winds.

The British also knew that Toussaint and his generals were almost constantly aware of their position, thanks to an extensive network of spies and informers. This allowed Toussaint's forces to ambush the British at the most inopportune junctures and unexpected moments. One of Toussaint's later adversaries described his team of messengers as being able to "guide themselves through tracks which only they knew of and were able to find even in the darkest of nights by relying on natural starlight."[8] On a number of occasions, his men snuck up to a British camp at night, fired shots to rouse the sleeping British, and then disappeared without a trace—only to repeat the exercise a few hours later. Howard reported that while in Saint-Domingue he lived in a state of perpetual terror that he would be "murdered from behind the bushes."[9]

Toussaint Louverture was an expert in leveraging the forces of nature to multiply the effect of his own forces. Employing these tactics, his army eventually forced a vastly diminished British force to negotiate an exit from the island in 1798. Yet, his victory against the British was only one chapter in his long and convoluted struggle to gain independence for his island and freedom for his people. The Haitian Revolution— the only successful slave revolution in history—lasted from a slave insurrection of 1791 until the declaration of an independent Haiti in 1804. The Revolution put a permanent end to systemic slavery on Haitian territory, politically dispossessed the oppressor class on the island, and ended European imperial rule over a territory that, as the world's most prolific producer of sugar and coffee in the late eighteenth century, had been France's most lucrative colony. This chapter examines how Toussaint Louverture achieved this remarkable feat with an army of the dispossessed.

## The Forgotten Revolution

Toussaint Louverture was born as human property on the Bréda sugar plantation in Haut-du-Cap in the late 1730s or the early 1740s (we don't know for sure) and lived most of his life as a slave. He was the leading force behind the one of the most remarkable events in what was a remarkable period of history—what British historian Eric Hobsbawm termed The Age of Revolution.[10] But the Haitian revolution remains fundamentally different from the more well-known and more celebrated American and French revolutions. These were led by well-educated, wealthy white elites who were fighting for their economic interests and political freedom. The leaders of the Haitian rebels were fighting racialized enslavement and were not themselves established men with money. Born without even ownership of their own bodies, their room to maneuver and their available resources were far more restricted, while the stakes for which they were fighting were far higher than their French and American counterparts'. But, so too, their eventual success was all the more remarkable.

Despite this, Toussaint is not among the ranks of celebrated revolutionary greats. Quite the contrary—while Napoleon, George Washington, Thomas Jefferson, and Simón Bolívar, make frequent appearances in popular culture, Toussaint is noticeably absent. The racial prejudices that pervade the pages of history and management books go a long way toward explaining this fact. That former slaves led by a Black man had successfully defeated the most powerful empires of the age was a fact that white writers through the ages would rather ignore than acknowledge—let alone celebrate. In fact, "many statesmen of the nineteenth century simply refused to admit that [the Haitian Revolution] had taken place," notes the introductory pages to one of the period's archival collections somberly.[11] Toussaint was and has largely remained an unseen leader.

But there may be more behind Toussaint's absence from our collective record than racism. The Haitian Revolution does conform to the Hollywoodesque stories we so desperately crave, in which friend and foe, and progress and setback are clearly demarcated. From the initial insurrection in 1791 to the wresting of ultimate control from France over a decade later, the revolution followed a complex and circuitous path. Allegiances and alliances shifted as events unfolded, colonists and metropole often disagreed violently, and factions of the same "side" fought fierce battles against one another. Moreover, the island's complex social structures defy the simple generalizations that snappy stories require.

Then there is the role of Toussaint, which also fails to fit the mold of the Action Fallacy. At the start of the slave insurrection, Toussaint was not to be found at the head of the groups of angry insurrectionists that roamed the island. Instead, he was biding his time and opaquely pulling strings from his plantation home. And, at the far end of the Haitian story, when the revolutionaries finally vanquished their enemy and gained their independence, Toussaint was already dead. It is hard to imagine a Hollywood movie or bestselling book in which the main protagonist fails to make an appearance in the opening scene and is dead by the time of the plot's climactic end. With Toussaint and his revolution, however, that is exactly what we have. Yet, this fact in no way diminishes the extraordinary work of this leader. Though Toussaint Louverture did not live to see its end or aftermath, the Haitian Revolution was more his work than that of any other actor. He created an army and a political strategy that defeated the Spanish (twice), the British, and finally, the French Imperial forces, overthrew a centuries-old system of enslavement, and wrenched the most lucrative colony out of France's hands at the height of its imperial power. Despite not fitting into our preferred story-telling mold, it remains one of the most astonishing leadership tales in history.

## The Land of the High Mountains

Originally the home of indigenous Taíno Arawak people who called it Ayti, "the land of high mountains," the island that today is home to Haiti and the Dominican Republic was first colonized in 1492 by Christopher Columbus. In his report to the Spanish King, Columbus wrote that, "[the island] is a miracle. Mountains and hills, plains and pastures, are both fertile and beauti-ful."[12] He renamed it "La Espanola"—the Spanish Island—a name that morphed over time into "Hispaniola." The eastern part of the island became the Spanish colony of Santo Domingo, but the western part began to be used as a base by French pirates. As the French settlement grew, it developed into a colony called Saint-Domingue, which was formally ceded to the French by the Spanish in a 1697 treaty.

The native Taíno population had already perished before Toussaint's birth, as a result of their enslavement by Spanish colonizers who exploited them on the burgeoning plantations of the island. The majority of them succumbed to European diseases, while others died from excessive labor and maltreatment. Subsequently, the colonizers resorted to recruiting white European inden-tured servants to toil on the lucrative sugar plantations of Saint-Domingue. Over the following decades and centuries, Black African slaves were forcibly transported to the island by both Spanish and French forces. In 1574, Hispaniola's populace consisted of approximately 1000 individuals of European descent, including landowners, indentured servants, sailors, and the descendants of original buccaneers, contrasted with 12,000 Black slaves.[13] As the economic potential of the plantations became apparent, the ghastly trade in human lives only pick up. By the end of the 1880s there were 500,000 slaves in the French colony.[14]

While the number of Black slaves in the colony skyrocketed, the white population remained relatively small. At the onset of the slave insurgency of 1791, white people made up just five percent of the colony's population. Meanwhile, Saint-Domingue had become by far the largest exporter of sugar in the Caribbean, with an annual export economy worth 137 million livres in 1788—more than three times the output of second-place Jamaica, which was under British control.[15]

The white population of Saint-Domingue was hardly homogeneous. The descendants of the buccaneers whose settlements had initially justified the French claim to the western third of the island still lived there. They, as well as descendants of indentured servants and criminals exiled to the island in the 1720s, were known as "Little Whites." Over the course of the eighteenth century, a wealthy class of white French landowners, lawyers, and government administrators also formed on Saint-Domingue. These were widely referred to as "Big Whites."

The enslaved population was characterized by an intricate social structure, reflecting a complex hierarchy. The cruel and demeaning treatment slaves were forced to endure, coupled with diseases, led to an extremely high death rate. On the Bréda sugar estate where Toussaint was raised and lived for most of his life, the life expectancy of a slave was only 37 years. Newly trafficked African men and women, primarily originating from the kingdoms of Kongo, Yoruba, and Allada in present-day Republic of the Congo, Nigeria, and Benin, respectively, replaced those killed off. These new arrivals often spoke only their native languages and were unfamiliar with the subjugation and demeaning realities of enslavement. This ghastly cycle created a social division between the African-born slaves, known as *bossale*s, and the Creoles of African heritage who were born in the colony and often assumed influential roles on plantations, working as *commandeurs*—supervisors—as coachmen, or in other "elite" positions. These men were frequently given significant responsibilities by their white managers and owners, with whom they were in close contact.

Many slaves, not having been born into conditions of servitude and maltreatment, ran away from the plantations and formed independent communities in the island's mountainous hinterland. This phenomenon was known as *marronage*. Elite slaves, meanwhile, came to wield considerable influence on the plantations and were frequently viewed as leaders by their fellow slaves, or, in some cases, as allies by managers and plantation owners.[16] The slave insurgency of 1791 was masterminded by a group of these elite slaves, in whose circles Toussaint had been moving since the late 1780s. An onlooker observed that during the early days of the revolt it was "the valets and the coachmen, and those who were closest to their masters, who generally struck the first blows."[17]

# Walking on Barrels of Gunpowder

White landowners frequently raped Black women slaves. In some cases, there were consensual relationships between slaves or freed Blacks and whites. This resulted in a growing class of mixed-race people of color on the island, many of whom were freed by their white landowning fathers. They tended to be relatively wealthy and often owned slaves themselves and were the second-most-affluent group on the island after the "Big Whites." While this mixed-race population advocated for greater racial equality, its members were generally not in favor of abolishing slavery, an institution from which many of them benefited. These free people of color also included a small number of Black former slaves who had been granted *manumission*—emancipation—by their owners. Toussaint was one such man; he was granted free status in the 1770s by the manager of the Bréda plantation, Bayon de Libertat, after successfully negotiating the return of a group of *marron* slaves to the plantation.

Bayon de Libertat relied on Toussaint for much more than mediation on the plantation; having recognized his superior intellect, he frequently consulted him on business matters relating both to the plantation and to his own private affairs. This ability to make himself indispensable to important European figures and to garner influence, "through his talents as a conciliator," as one historian phrased it, would define the trajectory of Toussaint's political and military career.[18]

In the lead-up to the insurrection of 1791, both the relations between Saint-Domingue's white landowning class and the French monarchy and those between the white landowning class and free people of color were growing increasingly tense. Limited protections for Black slaves—such as the provision of sufficient food and shelter and the prohibition of rape, murder, and extreme cruelty—had already been enshrined in French law by the Black Code of 1685, but they were expanded by King Louis XVI in the 1780s in a series of reforms that sought to improve working conditions for the slaves on Saint-Domingue.[19] The white planters deeply resented this development. Bayon de Libertat wrote "soon we will no longer be the masters of our own [slaves] anymore."[20] And while the lives of slaves were nominally improved by these ordinances, the rights of free people of color were increasingly restricted over the course of the second half of the eighteenth century. Legislation was introduced in Paris that barred free people of color from entering the French civil service and the medical profession, and from dressing like and eating at the same table as whites.

The Caribbean was not the only place in which the age's injustices bred discontentment. The burgeoning middle class in Paris was growing increasingly resentful of the fact that they were taxed to cover the King's extravagant spending, while the Nobility and Clergy were not. On 20 June 1789, the representatives of this Third Estate swore an oath to wrest a constitution from the King. Locked out of their assembly hall, the group did so in the next-best-place: one of Versailles's lavish indoor tennis courts. A few days later, on 14 July 1789, the storming of the Bastille in Paris marked the beginning of the French Revolution. Despite the ideals of "Liberté, Egalité, Fraternité" that drove the French people to take up arms against their King, however, the protections and rights afforded Saint-Domingue's slaves in 1784 were rolled back by the French national revolutionary legislature, the Constituent Assembly. On 8 March 1790, the Assembly decreed that criticizing slavery was a criminal offense and that slaves were the property of settlers. On 15 May 1791, white settlers were given a veto over any French reforms that might apply to "non-free" inhabitants.

On the island itself, colonial assemblies were quick to form in the wake of the French Revolution. The most treasonous of these was the Saint-Marc Assembly, composed mostly of mid-level white planters, which was active between April and July 1790. The assembly declared its right to self-government and firmly decreed that free Black and mixed-race people had no political rights at all in the colony. In response to this apparently treasonous declaration of legislative independence, the French Governor of Saint-Domingue at the time, Antoine de Peynier, sent troops to disband the legislature, whose members were subsequently sent to France and tried for sedition. When Peynier left the colony shortly thereafter, however, his successor was lynched by white rebels, and Port-au-Prince became an independent white republic outside of the scope of French administrators.

At the same time as slaves and free people of color were seeing the few rights that had previously been granted them under French monarchical rule stripped away by colonial assemblies, rumors spread that the King of France had decreed the end of slavery, but that white landowners were refusing to accept his decree. This rumor would help stoke the already furious resentment on the part of the enslaved men and women of Saint-Domingue. Tensions reached an all-time high, and the French colonial administration was in disarray. Landowners felt that they were "walking on barrels of gunpowder."[21] They would continue to do so for another two years as tensions simmered.

# The Index Card at the Center of It all

On 14 August 1791, slave foremen from over 200 plantations met at the Lenomard de Mézy plantation, where they agreed to take control of the island from its white population on 25 August. On that day, the colonial assembly was scheduled to meet in the northern administrative capitol of Cap-Français.[22] If uprisings occurred simultaneously in both the plains and the city, the insurgents could take out the island's most powerful figures—in government, commerce, and agriculture—in one blow.

Many did not have the patience to wait that long. One group of slaves rose up three days later, followed by another two days after that. The colonial administration and plantation owners quickly quashed them. Then on 22 August another group led by the vodou priest and one of the most important faces of the revolutionary movement, Dutty Boukman, attacked the Clément plantation in Acul county, where he had been enslaved before his escape into *marronage*. The rebels under his command killed the white plantation staff, the refiner, and the plantation's attorney. This time, the spark of insurrection caught on. Soon fires were blazing all across the northern plain; within weeks, 1400 estates had been burned to the ground. Hundreds of columns of dark smoke rose from the northern plains and were visible all the way from Cap-Français.[23]

Toussaint did not leap into action when the insurgency began—in fact, his initial reaction was to remain on the Bréda plantation in order to ensure the safety of Bayon de Libertat's wife. When attempts were made to set fire to the sugar cane fields, Toussaint had the blazes put out and instructed the plantation's slaves, including members of his own family, to cut and press the cane as usual. In a letter published in 1799 in the French *Le Moniteur*, Bayon de Libertat noted that when he returned to his plantation after the uprising everything was in order, and Toussaint informed him that the damage had been minimal. Ostensibly, then, Toussaint was not an active instigator or even participant of the revolt. But this view is deceptive. For it is not the violent punch of a revolution that determines its staying power, but, more often than not, the level of organization behind the scenes. And it is here, in the subtle networking and scheming, that Toussaint played a critical role.

Ostensibly, Toussaint served as secretary to Georges Biassou, one of the insurgent movement's four main leaders. This minor function does not do justice to the scale of his involvement. There is, first of all, scattered documentary evidence that Toussaint was heavily involved in the planning of the insurrection (in which he made it appear as if he played no part). A letter addressed to Biassou in October 1791 and signed "Médecin Général"—Toussaint used a number of pseudonyms in this early period, this one likely in reference to Toussaint's talents as a healer in the Allada tradition—speaks of contact with a Spanish emissary who was probably providing the rebels with weaponry and food. Later on, Joaquin Garcia, the governor of Spanish-controlled Santo Domingo, received a letter asking him for logistical support in fighting the French forces. Garcia believed that "other hands and heads" than Biassou's, "with more intellectual ability," had been involved and wondered who it was that really held, "the reins of their government."[24] A French general stated things more bluntly: "hidden behind a curtain, it was Toussaint who directed all the strands of the plot, and he was the one who organized the revolt and prepared the explosion."

Toussaint's apparent subordination to Biassou was likely illusory and is indicative of his political pragmatism. By hiding his involvement, he could shield his reputation, ensuring that his name did not become synonymous with positions or policies he did not agree with and preventing European powers from forming an impression of him before he had the time and space to curate that impression. Working in Biassou's shadow meant that he could gain influence, status, and authority in the rebel movement without needing to outwardly associate himself with it. He later wrote to Garcia that, "I reported and accounted for my operations to General Biassou, not at all because I considered myself to be his subordinate, but for love of the good, being familiar with his impetuous, muddle-headed, thoughtless character, likely to do more harm than good."[25] This policy of pragmatic deference was one Toussaint would employ over and over again throughout his political career. He was, in other words, an unseen leader by choice.

More significantly, Toussaint is the only known connection between the four central figures of the slave revolt that resulted from the meeting on 14 August. Dutty Boukman, Jean-Francois, and Georges Biassou—three of the insurgency's four primary public actors—were all coachmen, like Toussaint, and were well-known to him. Jeannot Bullet, the fourth, worked on Bayon de Libertat's brother-in-law's plantation and was a close acquaintance of Toussaint. Toussaint's *manumission* and his employment as a coachman for Bayon de Libertat from the 1770s onward allowed him to expand his network of contacts in and around the city of Cap-Français. He likely met Biassou because Biassou's mother was a slave at the La Charité hospital, where Bayon de Libertat often ate.

Historian Phillipe Girard has used church and notary records from the time and has been able to reconstruct this network. He writes of his own work—in a scene reminiscent of the detective finally identifying the mastermind on a crowded board of mugshots and reports—that, "When all the index cards are pinned to the wall, they converge on one man who seems to appear, as if by magic, at the centre of it all."[26] It was Toussaint who connected the dots between the scattered flickers of insurrection, flickers that grew into a revolution.

## Learning to Compromise

Months of revolutionary violence, skirmishes, and bloodshed followed. Then, in September 1792, the revolutionary leaders Jean-Francois and Georges Biassou opened negotiations with the colony's French civil commissioners. They proposed that they would persuade their soldiers to return to plantation work in exchange for the French administration granting clemency to the rebel leaders. Toussaint, then supposedly serving as Biassou's secretary, was heavily involved in the matter and counseled lowering the number of leaders for whom amnesty was being sought from 300 down to 50, as this was more likely to result in a deal. While some subsequent writers are critical of what they see as a self-interested moral compromise, Sudhir Hazareesingh asserts that, "it was unlikely that [Toussaint] saw this ceasefire as an endgame . . . the offer was plainly an attempt to divide the more pragmatic white colonists in Cap-Français from the hardliners."[27] Toussaint was a complex political strategist, and a move that was on the face of it a step backward often turned out to be a temporary measure in a larger plan. He himself later said that "as soon as unrest began in Saint-Domingue...I saw that the whites could not last because they were divided and heavily outnumbered."[28]

Toussaint's ability to navigate compromises in the short term, and thereby securing safety and resources for the sake of long-term progress, constituted a defining trait of his character. He demonstrated a pragmatic and utilitarian approach, comprehending the significance of the rebels' accomplishments thus far. However, he also possessed a keen awareness that the continuation of their struggle relied heavily on a steady provision of weapons and sustenance. And indeed, this would later become a serious problem for them.

Had the proposal been accepted by the French, the rebels would have substantially improved their earlier position. Notably, 50 influential Black rebel leaders would have been granted amnesty, enabling them to exert enhanced influence within the colony, leveraging their newfound prominence. But the colonial assembly refused the deal. Despite the arrival of fresh French troops, the situation evolved into a stalemate, characterized by the insurgents' control over a significant portion of the northern plain and the mountains to the south and east, while the coastal cities remained firmly under French control.

This willingness to compromise has led to the mistaken interpretation that Toussaint was not philosophically motivated. In July 1792, a remarkable text, the *Lettre originale des chefs des negres revoltes,* was published in *Le Créole Patriote,* a paper based in Paris and run by the Jacobin abolitionist Claude Milscent, a former planter in Saint-Domingue. The *Lettre* pointed out the philosophical contradictions between the 1789 Declaration of the Rights of Man and the slavery practiced in French colonies, and argued for *liberté generale.* It stated in no uncertain terms that without equal rights for members of all races, Saint-Domingue would not have a prosperous future. But it also promised that free slaves would recognize the white colonists' right to "full enjoyment" of their property and revenue. There has been much speculation about who the author of the *Lettre* was, but the most recent research strongly suggests that it was Toussaint.[29]

If we assume that Toussaint is its author, the *Lettre* provides a remarkable insight into his long-term vision as it stood not even a year into the revolution. It shows Toussaint playing a long game, motivated by an ideology of emancipation and equality. Unlike Dutty Boukman and contemporary *marron* leaders who advocated expelling or killing members of the white population in order to achieve freedom for the Blacks, already in 1792 Toussaint was laying out his vision for a society that was not only multiracial and meritocratic, but that also kept intact as much of the island's economic infrastructure and potential for trade relationships with European allies as possible. He wanted more than the overthrow of white supremacy on the island: he wanted the permanent abolition of slavery and the building up of the economic resources that would be required to safeguard the Black population's liberties.[1]

## Switching Allegiance; and Then Again

In September of 1792, King Louis XVI was deposed, and France became a republic. On 4 April, the new government abolished racial discrimination in the colony—meaning that free people of color would now be allowed to vote and hold political office. This angered many white colonists, who formed

---

[1] In addition to setting out a vision for the future of Saint-Domingue, the *Lettre* was also a succinct philosophical treatise denouncing the entrenched, systemic racism developed to justify and facilitate the slave economy. Therefore, in 1792, while still battling French forces from the rebel stronghold in the northeast of the colony, Toussaint may well have also been instigating a philosophical debate about racial equality in Paris.

their own assemblies and were on the verge of declaring independence. At this point, the French National Assembly dispatched Commissioner Léger-Félicité Sonthonax, a Jacobin activist who had written articles advocating the abolition of slavery, to St. Domingue, tasking him with ensuring that Saint-Domingue remain in French hands. His first act, astonishingly, was to appeal to the white *colons* by publicly declaring his belief in the necessity of slavery. His goal in making this declaration was to prevent a white counterrevolution.

In January 1793, Sonthonax launched a military campaign against the Black insurgents, driving them out of their long-held headquarters in Grande-Rivière and backing them up against the border of Spanish Santo Domingo. But Sonthonax's French troops soon faltered, and it became clear they did not have sufficient resources to defeat the surprisingly disciplined rebel movement. Precisely at this moment, the colony also became involved in another, more pressing conflict.

Back in France, at 10:00 in the morning of 21 January, King Louis XVI arrived in a green carriage at the *Place de la Révolution* (formerly the Place Louis XV) in Paris. His hands were tied behind his back with a handkerchief, his hair was cut, and his collar removed. The condemned king said a few words to the large crowd, but they were quickly drowned out by a drumroll. Then, after securing the King at the base of the guillotine, the executioner jerked the rope, and the blade slid down the rails, severing the King's head in one swift cut.

Spain, whose king belonged to the same Bourbon dynasty as Louis, declared war on France the same day—leading to a war now known as the War of the Pyrenees. France then promptly declared war on Spain's ally, Britain. One result of this was that many French *colons* treacherously jumped ship, clandestinely sending representatives to London to sign an agreement with the British to help them take control of the island. At this point, Sonthonax and his fellow commissioner, Étienne Polverel, performed an about-face; instead of courting the treacherous *colons*, they sought to appease the Black leaders and end the Black rebellion by reissuing the Black Code and ordering it read aloud on all plantations.

The Spanish, meanwhile, who had been covertly providing the Black rebel armies on Saint-Domingue with weaponry and rations in order to stir up trouble for the French, now formalized their alliance with Black rebel leaders, including Toussaint. The Spanish forces had been under orders from Madrid to form an alliance with one of the military factions in Saint-Domingue—either the rebelling Black former slaves or the rebelling white *colons*—and the disciplined, well-trained troops under Toussaint's command seemed to them a far better bet than the changeable and disorganized white rebels. They thus made overtures to the Black rebel leaders, and in March 1793, "a Black man sent by Biassou," presumably Toussaint, approached the Spanish to negotiate the formal allegiance of the rebel troops. By June, he had negotiated, "the immediate emancipation of all slave combatants and their incorporation as auxiliaries in the Spanish forces." Now in command of 4000 troops and fighting on behalf of the Spanish, Toussaint rapidly took back the French territories of Dondon, Marmelade, Verrettes, Petite-Riviere, and Plaisance within just a few months—"more often by ruse rather than by dint of military force," as Hazareesingh writes.[30] Toussaint's incredible effectiveness as a military commander did not go unnoticed, and it earned him the praise of the Spanish Governor.

Not only was Sonthonax now dealing with the fact that Jean-Francois, Biassou and Toussaint were rapidly capturing French towns for the Spanish crown, but he also faced a threat on an entirely different front. The new Governor of Saint-Domingue, General Francois-Thomas Galbaud, arrived in Cap-Français on 7 May 1793. Galbaud himself owned plantations on Saint-Domingue, and he immediately began instituting reforms to increase the rights of white plantation owners. Having already warned him to cease and desist to no avail, on 10 June 1793 Sonthonax returned to Cap-Français to remove Galbaud from power and send him back to France. Galbaud initially resigned himself to his fate and allowed himself to be escorted onto one of the warships in the Cap harbor. He joined a fleet of sailors who had been impatiently awaiting permission to set sail for France ever since Britain had declared war. (The French administration had banned wartime travel to France for fear of British interception.) The sailors, whose racism often expressed itself in physical confrontations with free men of color when they went out into the city, now rallied to Galbaud's cause: on the night of 20 June 1793, they stormed the city's arsenal and attempted to take control of the commissioners' headquarters in the administrative capital. At this point, the commissioners, realizing that they and their mixed-race allies were about to lose control of Cap-Français to Galbaud and the white rebels, offered emancipation to all enslaved men of military age who agreed to fight for them. On 21 June, they were forced to flee to the nearby town of Haut-du-Cap. Just when their fate seemed sealed, however, their attempts to reach out to the Black insurgents met with success. Pierrot and Macaya, two rebel leaders operating in the hills around Haut-du-Cap, arrived in the town with 2000 men in tow. Three thousand people lost their lives in what one historian has called, "the worst episode of urban violence in the entire history of the Americas." The result was that Sonthonax remained in power.[31]

Despite the fact that they were now emancipated in the eyes of the French, many of the rebels who had fought in the conflict were reluctant to formally pledge their loyalty to the French side while the rebel movement's leaders, Jean-Francois, Biassou, and Toussaint, were fighting in the service of the Spanish King. French attempts to lure Jean-Francois and Biassou to France's side were unsuccessful. Sonthonax thus came under increasing pressure to go further than his original offer of emancipation, and on 11 July 1793, he declared that the wives and children of Black men who joined the army would also be emancipated.

It is evident that Sonthonax was no longer really in control; the plantation economy had ceased functioning, and he needed to do everything in his power to retain what support he had among the northern Black population. On 29 August 1793, having issued repeated orders for slaves to return to plantations to no avail, and thus effectively having no other choice, he declared all the slaves of the colony emancipated.[32] Slavery on Saint-Domingue was now a thing of the past, and though the danger of re-enslavement became very real on a number of occasions over the course of the next decade—and was briefly instituted again in individual regions under Spanish or British control—the practice would never be systematically realized again.

On the very same day that Sonthonax announced the emancipation of all the slaves on Saint-Domingue, 29 August 1793, Toussaint released a public proclamation in which, in no uncertain terms, he made sure that credit went where credit was due—to the Black rebel leaders and armies. He stressed that the rebellion was ongoing, and that equality, though achievable, had not yet been achieved. He appealed to the men and women of Saint-Domingue to join him in its pursuit.[33] This was the first recorded instance of his use of the surname Louverture. Up until this point, he had used the last name of his owners, Bréda, and then, once he had begun serving as a Spanish auxiliary, had gone simply by Monsieur Toussaint.[34] The strategic telling of a political story and the symbolic curation of his image—which was so important to Toussaint that he had gone for years under a series of pseudonyms to prevent having his name soiled by the inopportune words and actions of others—would return like a *leitmotif* throughout his leadership.

By the spring of 1794, Spanish forces, largely thanks to Toussaint, had taken control of almost all of Saint-Domingue. In May, however, following the proclamation of the *liberté générale,* Toussaint struck a deal with the French governor Etienne de Laveaux and defected to the French side. He swiftly won back for France all the regions he had previously conquered for the Spanish, with the result that the Spanish were forced entirely out of Saint-Domingue in July 1795 and even ceded Santo Domingo to France in the

Treaty of Basel—though they left the actual date of the handover undetermined. The next several years would see him battling the British on behalf of the French. This was because the British were now determined to keep up the fight. Abandoned by their Spanish allies, they enlisted the help of royalist French *colons* who were unhappy about the abolition of slavery and preferred the British in control so they could return to business as usual. A year and a half after their arrival on the island, British forces had captured Port-au-Prince, Saint-Marc, and Leogane, as well as the area around Jeremie. It was around this time that Toussaint and his troops withdrew to establish their defensive positions on the banks of the Artibonite River where we met them at the beginning of this chapter.

## Toussaint the Military Leader

Toussaint's meticulous and calculating strategic capabilities and his logistical organization were nowhere more clearly evident than in his military leadership. Despite having no formal military training and being in his fifties by the time he participated in his first military operation, he developed unique and creative tactics that drew on both the discipline of the European military tradition and the guerrilla tactics of the *marron* runaway slaves, whose subversive methods were especially well suited to the island's mountainous terrain. Toussaint himself had begun training in the art of battle after the 1791 revolt; he began receiving daily instruction in fencing and military strategy from a former officer in Cap-Français and later received theoretical instruction from several French officers. Much of what he learned, however, was self-taught. He read Herodotus' history of the wars between the Persians and the Greeks, Vegetius' *Scriptores de re militari*, and Caesar's *Commentaries*, among many other works. He requested a copy of the governor's military training manual from Laveaux in 1794 and also took an instruction manual from a royalist officer in 1795.[35] He was nothing if not thorough.

Toussaint relied on more than the European military tradition, however; he was exceptionally creative in its adaptation to circumstances on Saint-Domingue. The elements of *marron* guerrilla resistance techniques he incorporated in his tactics included, in the words of Hazareesingh, "the systematic exploitation of the advantages of terrain, the entrapment of the enemy and capture of his equipment; camouflage; the psychological intimidation of the adversary by a variety of means; the use of deceptions such as false ceasefires and surrenders."[36] Toussaint's style of combat was a harbinger of the fluid tactics that would characterize many successful guerilla campaigns across the world in the centuries to come.

The discipline Toussaint instilled in his forces was designed to prevent the use of any undue violence against civilians and even, remarkably, against enemy combatants—as far as was possible. He prohibited his officers from pillaging, the punishment for which was execution. He also insisted that homes and plantations not be burned, a further indication that his long-term goal—an egalitarian society that would not have to battle impossible odds to regain its former economic prosperity—was always on his mind.

Toussaint's non-violent morality was supported by his soldiers. In July 1795, Toussaint captured the town of Mirebalais without the use of force by negotiating with the townspeople. In another episode, Toussaint diverted scarce clothing and food from his own troops for a group of white women and children left behind in a Spanish-controlled camp. When Republican troops took back Port-au-Prince from the British in 1798 without pillaging the city, despite the fact that they were forced to go without food for two days, a local inhabitant asked, "What European troops would have maintained such tight discipline under the same conditions?"[37]

A French general who fought against Toussaint's forces declared that the unity of his racially diverse troops was his "most remarkable accomplishment."[38] As this statement suggests, Toussaint's army was by no means an entirely Black one: it included the mixed-race officer Augustin Clervaux and the mixed-race Colonels Morisset and Gabart, among many others; white Europeans also featured in Toussaint's upper military ranks, among them his long-time Chief of Staff General Pierre Agé and Barada, a former military commander in Cap-Français.

Toussaint sought to exemplify in his own armed forces the multiracial cooperation that he foresaw as Saint-Domingue's future, and the very existence of his army was a rebuke to anyone who though a multiracial society impossible. Not only was it possible, in fact, but it was proving highly effective. And this was not just a show: there is no doubt that Toussaint's success as a military leader could not have been realized if there had not been a real sense of brotherhood within his military ranks. His ability to recognize those with the potential to be influential leaders of a social and military movement in the people around him, regardless of their rank or status at the time, constituted the meritocratic foundation of his military culture.

# Orchestrating the Governor's Removal

In the early months of 1798, when the British had been effectively defeated by Toussaint's troops based near the Artibonite and were actively seeking to withdraw from Saint-Domingue, a new French governor, Gabriel de Hédouville, arrived in the colony, along with several hundred civil servants. Hédouville had been tasked with reinstating administrative order and reducing Toussaint's considerable influence in all walks of civilian life. Even before his arrival, Toussaint was aware of Hédouville's reputation as a conservative who believed the revolutionaries had come down too hard on the planters.

Hédouville was wary of the power that Toussaint, who had been appointed Commander-in-Chief of the armed forces of Saint-Domingue by Sonthonax in 1797, exercised in civil administration, and particularly in local governments. The relationship between Toussaint and Hédouville, which started on a friendly footing, began to suffer as Hédouville increasingly questioned Toussaint's authority. He instigated an investigation into one of the civil administrators appointed by Toussaint for alleged financial mismanagement, and rebuked Toussaint for imprisoning a planter over a dispute involving animal theft, which, he pointed out, was clearly a matter for the judiciary and not the military. Hédouville reminded Toussaint that the army did not have the same authority to act in areas that were under France's control as it did in areas that were not. He also sought to restrict the rations and clothing provided to Toussaint's army. These disputes set the course for a power struggle between the two men.

The two also clashed over how to deal with white émigrés, almost exclusively counterrevolutionary royalists, who had left Saint-Domingue for Philadelphia and elsewhere on the North American continent and were now seeking to return. Hédouville advocated strict adherence to Article 373 of the 1795 French constitution, which prohibited pardons for anyone who had fought against the Republic or had supported those who had, while Toussaint was far more lenient, seeking to foster an atmosphere of forgiveness and unity. When Hédouville published a proclamation stating that no émigré would be pardoned, Toussaint openly declared that he would pardon anyone in the coastal towns under British control who had sided with the occupiers. Hédouville responded by issuing a decree restating French policy on the matter. But Toussaint continued to brashly ignore Hédouville's position.

It was around this time that the British General Thomas Maitland, tasked with negotiating the withdrawal of his country from Saint-Domingue, arrived on the island. He reached out to both Hédouville and Toussaint and informed them that he would like to conduct the negotiation of Britain's departure exclusively with the two of them. Hédouville wrote to Toussaint, pointing out that the move was clearly an effort to sow division between them and that he thought it best if neither responded. By the time Toussaint wrote back to Hédouville, professing complete agreement, he had, in fact, already met with Maitland to discuss a cease-fire, British withdrawal, and the possibility of future trade. These discussions were the precursor to a "secret convention" signed by Toussaint and Maitland and approved by the US Consul Edward Stevens in August 1798, in which the British agreed not to prevent the arrival of provisions to Saint-Domingue and not to interfere in the politics of the French colony, while Toussaint agreed not to make any attempt to invade Jamaica or incite a rebellion among its slaves. Toussaint was also able to nego-tiate for military supplies from Jamaica, including 100 barrels of gunpowder, 200 stands of arms, and 7000 flints. The convention also made clear that Black troops and slaves who had served in the British forces could not be brought back to Jamaica, but were to remain on Saint-Domingue to work as free *cultivateurs*. It further specified that the areas of the island still under British control were to be left to Toussaint and the army, and not to Hédouville's administration.

At this point it is likely that Toussaint had long decided to try to rid himself of the nuisance of Hédouville's presence. In July 1798, he began encouraging Hédouville to make the *cultivateur* system more stringent by forcing laborers into binding contractual agreements with their employers. The *Arrêté concernant la police des habitations* enacted in 1798 was the work of both men, but Toussaint was careful not to associate his name with it. It is likely that he intentionally encouraged Hédouville to adopt harsh measures in order to foment discontent and foster ill will toward the governor.[39] Toussaint went on to stoke fears that the new measures, which included punishments for run-ning away and introduced minimum contractual periods of three years' labor on plantations, were a precursor to further restrictions of laborers' freedom and potentially even foreshadowed the end of the *liberté generale*. Yet at the same time as he was actively inciting revolts and formal complaints in protest at the new legislation, Toussaint, in his other role as dutiful servant of the French Republic, was encouraging municipalities to carefully document the workers' demands and put them to Hédouville.[40]

In October 1798, Toussaint finally expelled Hédouville from Saint-Domingue. In the explanation for the Governor's departure that he sent to Paris Toussaint stressed that Hédouville's removal was taking place according to constitutional procedure. He took great care not to appear to be removing Hédouville because of any personal dislike: the well-documented grievances of the people of Saint-Domingue and the resulting assessments of the municipal authorities that Hédouville was a problem were given as the sole reasons that Toussaint was sending the Governor back to France.

In the course of this six-month episode, then, Toussaint orchestrated the non-violent ejection of his rival from the colony by encouraging him to pass inflammatory legislation, acting as the secret instigator of strikes and a popular uprising in response to this legislation, appearing to arrive to restore the peace when unrest broke out, encouraging those who were unhappy with the governor to make use of established procedures to voice their complaints to the regional authorities, and ultimately positioning himself as the most reasonable and reliable authority in the colony. He had the clear (and now well-documented) support of the people, and also appeared to have been committed to the use of the proper, constitutional Republican channels to deal with the difficult situation. In order to stage this *coup de theatre*, he relied on the fears existing in the general population of the dispossession of their Black protectors in the army and their own subsequent re-enslavement.

But while Toussaint clearly played on these fears to achieve his political ends, he himself was genuinely worried about the perpetual threat of re-enslavement. Toward the end of the decade, a shift began to take place in French views on emancipation and civil rights for Black people and people of color in the colonies. Arguments for the restoration of slavery in Saint-Domingue began finding expression in a variety of pamphlets that claimed the former system had provided slaves with food, lodgings, and medical treatment to a standard higher than that expected by French peasants.

In 1797, Toussaint, whose contacts in the USA and France kept him informed of political goings-on, received the text of a speech given by the Count of Vaublanc, Vincent-Marie Viénot, a prominent figure in the counterrevolutionary movement whose family had lost its wealth when it lost the right to own slaves on Saint-Domingue. Viénot alleged that the colony had fallen into anarchy and that Europeans were being massacred by mixed-race southerners and Black northerners who had an unquenchable "predilection for violence." He claimed that Saint-Domingue was now ruled by a military government "made up of ignorant and uncouth" Blacks and that Toussaint aimed to incite local rebellions and "systematically massacre all the whites." For good measure, Viénot also stated that the economic situation was dire because of the indolence of the former slaves, who, in a vein characteristic of their race, would not work unless forced to, and had abandoned the plantations.[41]

Toussaint understood immediately what this manifesto heralded: a serious threat to the emancipation he had been working so hard to protect and by an important member of the French legislature. He was quick to respond with a pamphlet that he sent to the Directory in Paris, in which he argued against the racist tropes of Viénot's speech and defended his politics and his record. He also clearly set out a new ideal of citizenship—one based not on skin color or social class, but rather on acceptance of the principles of the Republic and service to the community. In doing so, he was creating a narrative that validated his Black troops' rights to their citizenship: they had put themselves at risk to defend French ideals and thereby actively demonstrated the qualities that define true citizenship.[42]

Particularly revealing in Toussaint's pamphlet was his acknowledgment of the harm caused to white planters during the initial insurrection in 1791. He took the position that it had been the whites who had pushed the Black population to the violence they committed and claimed that the Blacks had had no other choice—a fact which did not, however, diminish some of the horrors committed. This genuine remorse for regrettable damage frequently appears in Toussaint's own political statements. For example, in May 1794, when Toussaint was still ostensibly in the Spanish service but had likely already declared his intention to defect to the French, he was in Gonaïves when a violent episode broke out between his forces and the Spanish garrison. The outcome was the killing of 150 extremist, counterrevolutionary white *colons*. Toussaint wrote to the vicar to apologize for the loss of life—legend has it, however, that he had ordered the violence himself just after attending Mass. It is likely, therefore, that he saw the move as necessary but deeply regrettable.

## Political Storytelling

As he demonstrated in his proclamation of 29 August 1793, in his successful obscuring of his early involvement in rebel activity, and in the *Lettre* of 1792, Toussaint had a keen knack for political storytelling, and was highly aware of how his actions were perceived. He liked to point out both the broader significance of events and their specific ironies as they were occurring. The fact that so many accounts of near-theatrical point-proving survive from a life whose details are otherwise relatively obscure is evidence of the extent to which Toussaint was effective in intentionally shaping his image, both by spreading rumors and stories among Saint-Domingue's largely illiterate but well-networked population and through the precise and exacting philosophical proclamations and detailed letters he sent abroad.

Santo Domingo, though officially ceded to the French by the 1795 Treaty of Basel, had remained under Spanish oversight even after the signing of the treaty. In January 1801, following months of disagreements with Hédouville's successor Philippe-Rose Roume about whether to attack Santo Domingo, Toussaint invaded it anyway and, as the result of a brilliant military campaign, claimed for France the formerly Spanish-held colony that made up the eastern side of Hispaniola. Despite the fact that it had technically been French territory since 1795, France had not previously seen fit to cash in on its rights, and the Spanish colonial military had made it clear it would not simply allow Toussaint to waltz in and claim it. Once he had succeeded, however, Toussaint made sure that the Governor, Joaquin García, under whom he had served in the early 1790s before defecting to Republican France, handed him the key to the city. Toussaint refused to pick up the key himself, insisting that it be physically given into his hands by García.

This kind of storytelling and political theatrics, evidenced on numerous other occasions, was indicative not only of Toussaint's awareness of the narrative arc of his political career and of his willingness to wait for satisfaction but also of the broader context in which he conceived each of his individual actions and how they would affect his image. This obsession with how he was perceived was intertwined with his deep appreciation for and crafting of the written word in lobbying efforts intended to advance his cause. Still functionally illiterate at the outbreak of the 1791 insurrection, Toussaint hired a tutor for his sons and sat in the background of their classes. While other rebel leaders had their secretaries compose texts and letters for them, from the very beginning, Toussaint did not wish for others to control his words. Embarrassed of his own penmanship, he would dictate letters to his secretaries—often multiple letters to multiple secretaries at the same time—but would then re-read everything before it was sent to ensure it conveyed his precise meaning. Many an admiring historian has remarked on Napoleon's administrative stamina; in D.G. Wright's classic *Napoleon and Europe*, he remarks that, "Capable of working an eighteen-hour day and astonishing subordinates by the range of his knowledge, [Napoleon] drove perspiring secretaries to distraction." Wright continues by estimating that Napoleon dictated "an average of fifteen letters per day."[43] Impressive though this is, it pales in comparison with Toussaint, who according to one contemporary French observer dictated an average of 200 letters a day.[44]

In 1795, Toussaint intensified his lobbying efforts, sending deputies to Paris to protect his image and interests on the international political stage. It was around this time that he also began sending regular letters to the French government—first to the Legislative Assembly, then to the Directory, and then to the Consulate—outlining his positions on key issues and setting out his recent achievements. He also began sending "fluff pieces" to the US and Paris for publication in newspapers.

## Napoleon's Thorn

In November 1799, Napoleon Bonaparte ousted the French Directory and formed the Consulate, establishing himself as First Consul.[45] The constitution he introduced in December of the same year marked a clear change in French domestic and colonial policy: it did not include a declaration of rights, and Article 91 stated that "special laws" would apply to the colonies—laws that would take into account specific local circumstances. Toussaint was aware that this turn of events signified that the political will now existed in France to reintroduce slavery and walk back on the racial egalitarianism the government had previously endorsed. He was also aware that Napoleon had appointed several former colonial officials to important offices in the naval ministry.[46]

The tension that had been mounting between Toussaint and the French administrators ever since Laveaux's departure from the colony now came to a head. Toussaint's back-and-forth with Governor Roume prior to his unauthorized invasion of Santo Domingo had in fact been about far more than Toussaint's desire to unify the island on principle, or to prevent slave abductions across the border. The French clearly preferred to keep the eastern part of the island free of Toussaint's authority, if for no other reason than to have a potential landing place for French troops. Hédouville had himself disembarked on the Spanish side of the island, and Toussaint had no doubt picked up on the significance of his choice of port, and what this could mean for the future. When Toussaint wrote to Napoleon to inform him of the capture of Santo Domingo, Napoleon, angered by Toussaint's refusal to respect Roume's authority, did not respond. He would later issue a decree nullifying the takeover of the Spanish colony.

In 1801, Toussaint appointed a small committee composed of several white and mixed-race planters to draft a constitution for the entire island territory. Crucially, the constitution sought to negate the dangers presented by recent counterrevolutionary trends and by Napoleon's apparent ambivalence to the practice of slavery, as evidenced by his failure to press for emancipation on a number of French colonial islands after planters rose up to reject it. The constitution drafted by the committee and subsequently edited over a two-month period by Toussaint, specified that slavery in any form was irrevocably abolished in Saint-Domingue. There were other freedoms it neglected, however, including freedom of religion.[47]

The constitution established a legislative assembly, chosen by local government officials appointed by Toussaint, that was to meet to approve or reject the laws proposed by the governor, who was to be Toussaint. It gave Toussaint complete authority to appoint civil and military officials, and, in a move that would be copied by Napoleon just two years later, made him ruler for life with the right to appoint his successor.

This constitution remains one of the stains on Toussaint's record and its significance and implications are regularly debated among Haitian history specialists. Toussaint perhaps believed in the necessity of his leadership and the stability it brought to the colony. He must have realized that he was the only actor whose reputation and standing gave him the authority to keep European powers at bay and that he was the only one among his generals with the ability to successfully navigate complex domestic and international negotiations and conflicts. As he himself once said, what set him apart from those around him was his ability "to see and to foresee."[48] This may have appeared to him to justify the authoritarianism implicit in his new constitution. It will always remain unclear whether, when appointing his successor, Toussaint would have changed the nature of the subsequent succession of power. After all, he frequently acted to reduce friction in the short term in order to better position himself to make decisions in the long term.

This was, it must be said, far from the only controversial decision Toussaint took. In the mid-1790s, for example, as the economy was reeling from the years of fighting, famine loomed. Just as bad, lacking the money to buy arms, the island was vulnerable to invasion. It is against this backdrop that Toussaint negotiated a trade agreement with the British—at the time France's enemy—and their American ally. But these agreements had a catch: in order to close the deal, Toussaint had to promise not to interfere in internal Jamaican affairs—one of Britain's most lucrative island possessions. Toussaint upheld his end of the bargain, and when he got word of a plan to stir revolt in the neighboring island, he informed the British who promptly executed the ringleader.

The most controversial aspect of Toussaint's legacy involves the labor reform he introduced in October 1800, which imposed military oversight over what had, since Hédouville's decree mandating minimum three-year contracts, effectively become a system of indentured servitude.[49] A number of writers have characterized the draconian military oversight of the *cultivateur* system, the negotiations with the British for the purchase of trafficked Africans, and the undermining of the Jamaican slave rebellion as betrayals of Toussaint's egalitarian principals and the struggle for Black liberty, and therefore as an indication that he was more concerned with amassing personal wealth than with the good of the colony. But it is also possible to view these moves as born of the necessity—or what Toussaint believed was the necessity—of warding off French intervention. For much of Toussaint's time as Commander-in-Chief of Saint-Domingue's army, he had effectively held real authority by maintaining a deference to other authorities that disguised the extent of his own political aims. But this was a delicate balancing act. It is possible that Toussaint believed that a strong enough economic output would lead the French to see the situation in Saint-Domingue as advantageous to their interests, and therefore best left alone. The build-up of enough money in the colony's coffers would also facilitate the purchase of large amounts of weaponry and military equipment, and this would lead the French to understand that any intervention would carry with it a heavy cost: while they might not revel in the fact that a Black former slave was in control of their most lucrative colony, it would be in their economic and military interests to leave Saint-Domingue well enough alone. As even historian Phillipe Girard, one of Toussaint's harshest critics in this respect, acknowledges, without income from plantations, "Saint-Domingue could not pay for imports of flour and gunpowder, and without flour and gunpowder it was exposed to famine, foreign invasion, and re-enslavement."[50]

In October 1801, the British and French signed a peace treaty that effectively ended the British naval blockade of the Atlantic and thereby opened up a channel for the French navy to reach Saint-Domingue. The British Governor of Jamaica, Sir George Nugent, broke off talks about further trade deals with Toussaint in late November and ordered all British subjects in Saint-Domingue to take up residence in Jamaica. Toussaint would have been in no doubt as to the reason for the sudden change and what it foreshadowed. He issued a proclamation to the people of Saint-Domingue stating that the French were likely to invade the colony with the aim of reintroducing slavery. He was right: six days earlier, Napoleon's troops had set sail under General Charles Leclerc, with instructions to oust Toussaint from power.

Toussaint had tried extremely hard to develop a relationship with Napoleon. In 1799, Josephine Bonaparte had asked for Toussaint's help in re-establishing production on her family's sugar plantations in Léogane, and Toussaint had duly complied. Napoleon, on a military campaign in Egypt at the time, heard about the intervention and was pleased. From 1800 onward, Toussaint began writing to Napoleon himself, but all his letters went unanswered.[51] At the beginning of 1801, encouraged by a number of Toussaint's allies in Paris, Napoleon decided to support him and finally wrote to him, thanking him for his many letters and appointing him "capitaine-général" of the French-speaking part of the island.

By 1801, however, Napoleon had changed his tune. The invasion of Santo Domingo without French authorization had displeased him, but this alone did not lead him to send a significant military force to Saint-Domingue to depose Toussaint. Rather, the influence of the colonial lobby played the key role in his decision: the French general Kerverseau had written in a memorandum to Napoleon that Saint-Domingue had been "taken over by Africans" and advocated "a political rehabilitation of the whites." Kerverseau was among those who would travel to Saint-Domingue soon afterward to attempt to wrest back control from Toussaint's army.

A number of other prominent figures who had Napoleon's ear believed that the abolition of slavery had been a mistake. The decision to invade was no doubt racially motivated and had far more to do with the return to fashion of racialized pro-slavery ideas than with any of Toussaint's actions. Despite Toussaint's every effort to ensure the economic strength of the colony by introducing a harsh and productive system of agricultural labor, at the cost of losing favor with many farm workers and inciting a rebellion by his nephew, and despite his good relations with the white *colons*, by whom he was considered extremely favorably, Napoleon still decided to unseat him. Of his decision he said, "I am for the whites, because I am white...how can we have given liberty to Africans, to men without any civilization, who had not the slightest idea as to what a colony, or for that matter France was?"[52]

## The Final Act

On 29 January 1802, Toussaint responded to the first sighting of a fleet of French warships off Cape Samana. He arrived on the scene and saw that 25 naval vessels were already anchored, ten of which were the most advanced of the time and could carry 1000 men each. In the distance, emerging one by one, were more ships. Toussaint understood that he was looking at the full seaborne might of the French Empire.

Though the sight was certainly unwelcome it was not surprising—he had long been expecting French intervention. Now Toussaint himself, the man who had spent years urging restraint and non-violence, who had repeatedly instructed his troops not to burn plantation buildings or crops in order to keep the island's economic infrastructure as intact as possible, told his second-in-command, Dessalines, to "tear up the roads with shot, and throw the carcasses of dead horses into the springs; destroy and burn everything, so that those who come to re-enslave us always have before their eyes the image of hell they deserve." On his instructions, Henri-Christophe would burn the city of Cap-Français to the ground and with it its considerable granaries.[53]

In characteristic fashion, Toussaint had long been preparing for the possibility of invasion. For much of 1801, he had put a good portion of his customs revenues from the United States toward a supply of weapons and ammunition, and there is evidence to suggest that he had also struck a deal with Jamaican authorities for the import of arms. These acquisitions had been stored in specially designed mahogany containers and transported to munitions depots in the mountains. Toussaint had the roads leading to these secret outposts widened so that artillery pieces could be transported on them. These hidden stores of weapons were crucial to the eventual defeat of the French forces. Once again, Saint-Domingue's troops fought valiantly, and once again, they were helped by their strategy of retreating into the mountains and waiting for disease to do its worst to the foreign soldiers.

General Leclerc began making overtures to Black senior officers in Saint-Domingue, offering them the retainment of their properties, positions and wealth if they pledged allegiance to Napoleon. He met with some success, and a number of Toussaint's generals defected. Toussaint had by now become uncompromising; he sought to rally laborers to battle by citing the violence, torture, and mistreatment their ancestors had suffered at the hands of the French. The French, he said, had returned now to bring back slavery. Toussaint was right to think the French promises to his generals were false—before even setting off from France, Leclerc had received instructions that, during the final phase of his mission, he was to commit a "purge of Saint-Domingue's revolutionary leadership."[54]

In early 1802, Toussaint launched his final military campaign. He slept only a few hours a night, moving frenetically across the mountains and causing the French to undertake long and arduous treks to track him down—none of which were successful. He drew on his reserves of weapons hidden in the Cahos mountains and prevented his enemies from getting any rest through strategic ambushes. One French officer observed that "the enemy was like a hydra with a thousand heads: it would be reborn after every blow we struck. An order from Toussaint Louverture would suffice to make his men reappear and cover the entire territory in front of us."[55]

By February 1802, Toussaint's troops had killed more than 4000 of Leclerc's men. Leclerc was desperate and in March requested that Napoleon recall him to France. By early March 1802, Toussaint had retaken Saint-Michel, Marmelade, Saint-Raphaël and Dondon, and by the end of March he had begun thinking about a truce. He began discussing the matter with the French general Jean Boudet.

Toussaint's motivations for this move remain unclear. It is possible that he sought to use the stalemate that had developed—the French had control of many of the coastal areas, while Toussaint held much of the interior—to allow for the spread of disease among French troops, much as he had done while fighting the British. But he also recognized that he did not have the troops to decisively repulse the French, and the French were having increasing success in convincing his lieutenants to switch their allegiance. It is possible Toussaint was concerned about these losses and felt he needed time to regroup. In May, Toussaint and Leclerc came to a cease-fire agreement. Toussaint was able to negotiate amnesty for all his officers and soldiers, as well as their formal inclusion in the French army. Toussaint demanded that Dessalines be among those pardoned. Leclerc agreed to the terms.

Despite Toussaint's unwavering loyalty to Dessalines, there is evidence that Dessalines did not return it in kind. Leclerc had been left humiliated by the terms of the peace agreement, which were seen by many as a victory for Toussaint. When a rebel leader, Sylla, refused to agree to the terms of the cease-fire, Dessalines informed Leclerc that Toussaint was behind Sylla's resistance. At this point, Napoleon reiterated to Leclerc that he wanted Toussaint arrested and brought to France.

During the cease-fire, the French general Jean-Baptiste Brunet stationed a number of his men on a plantation belonging to Toussaint, and disagreements arose between the French soldiers and the Saint-Domingue laborers. Toussaint's son Isaac reported that the French were going all the way up to the door of the plantation to harvest bananas and plantains. When Toussaint wrote to Brunet to complain of his troops' conduct, Brunet invited him to the Georges plantation to discuss the matter. Brunet had assured Toussaint he was his "sincere friend," and, uncharacteristically, the usually wary Toussaint showed up with just a single aide-de-camp, who remained outside. Toussaint was invited into the house; the men talked; Brunet excused himself for a moment and left the room. At this point, a number of soldiers entered and placed Toussaint under arrest. He did not resist but handed his sword over silently. Toussaint and his wife and children, who had also been detained, were escorted to the *La Créole* in Gonaïves harbor. Addressing the ship's captain, Toussaint said that in capturing him, the French had tried to fell "the tree of Black liberty," but that its roots "were many and deep," and it would rise again. From Gonaïves he was brought to Cap-Français, and from there he was transferred to the *Le Héros* and transported across the Atlantic.

On the morning of 13 August 1802, Toussaint was escorted off the ship at the port of Brest in Brittany. It was the last time he would ever see his wife and children. Rather than make a public example of him, Napoleon decided to disappear him quietly. He ordered that he be brought across the country in an enclosed carriage under military escort. Toussaint was not informed of his destination; he believed that he was being taken to Paris to finally sit face-to-face with Napoleon. But the carriage was not to stop in Paris; instead, it steadily climbed up the uneven roads of the mountains above Pontarlier, near the Swiss border. When the carriage doors were opened, Toussaint found himself in the central courtyard of the Fort de Joux, a medieval fortification in the French Jura. He was brought to a dark cell deep inside the fort. The only window had been shuttered, and the room was pitch dark even in the daytime.[56]

Despite the miserable conditions in his cold, dark cell, Toussaint rallied and befriended the prison director. The two frequently discussed Saint-Domingue politics, and Toussaint was allowed to employ a local secretary. He set about composing a final appeal to Napoleon, whom he tried to convince to offer him a formal trial. Napoleon instead sent his aide-de-camp, Marie-Francois Caffarelli, to the Fort de Joux to extract a confession from Toussaint that he had been planning another uprising, but he left dissatisfied, carrying only a copy of Toussaint's 16,000-word appeal. Napoleon never read it.

In October 1802, Toussaint made a final attempt to reach out to Napoleon, writing "allow me to request again your justice and kindness."[57] The First Consul responded by ordering Toussaint's writing materials confiscated, silencing him forever. Toussaint Louverture died on 17 April 1803 in his cold stone cell, in the darkness, in a foreign continent and climate.

Later on, when he had been removed from power himself and exiled to the island of Saint Helena, Napoleon expressed regret for his treatment of Toussaint. He wrote that the invasion of Saint-Domingue had been a mistake and put it down to the "shrieks of the colonial lobby" that had poisoned his opinion of Toussaint. In fact, he thought Toussaint "was not a man without merit. .. astute and clever." And while these reflections and regrets would probably have been a great solace to Toussaint, it was by then far too late for both men to reverse course.

## The Endgame without a Hero

Thanks to Toussaint's incredibly well-disciplined army, his shoring up of vast supplies of weapons and munitions, and his scorched-earth policy, Saint-Domingue conclusively threw off French rule shortly after he died, and what had long been a French imperial colony has ever since been independent Haiti. If we are to measure Toussaint's success, it should surely be according to this metric: before he became involved in revolutionary politics, Saint-Domingue was a racially segregated slave society. By the time of his capture, Toussaint's army of predominantly free Black men had defeated the Spanish and the British and was on the brink of defeating the French imperial army, while systemic slavery had been permanently abolished from the island.

Toussaint's former second-in-command, Jean-Jacques Dessalines, who had betrayed him shortly before the cease-fire, was brought back around to Toussaint's cause in October 1802, when news that Napoleon had reintroduced slavery in neighboring French colonies reached Saint-Domingue. In November 1803, Dessalines' army decisively prevailed over French forces in Vertieres. The French troops had been decimated by disease during the intervening rainy season, just as Toussaint had predicted. After the battle of Vertieres, they had had enough; those who were still alive sailed back to France, and Saint-Domingue was forever free of its former European masters.

On 1 January 1804, Dessalines, a former slave who had once belonged to Toussaint Louverture, no less, declared Saint-Domingue independent and renamed it Haiti, the indigenous Taíno name for the island. Yet, he departed swiftly from the egalitarian and non-violent principles that had been the core of Toussaint's political philosophy, and which had guided the political and military course of the previous decade. In his speech declaring the establishment of independent Haiti, Dessalines declaimed "Anathema to the French name, eternal hatred to France: that is our cry."[58] Only a few months later, he ordered the mass-killing of whites on the island, resulting in the deaths of an estimated 3000 to 5000 white people in just a few weeks. This action led to a diplomatic break with the former colony's trading partners: the British ended negotiations immediately, and Haiti was henceforth treated as a pariah state by the Western powers. Everything that Toussaint had so insisted on—non-violence whenever possible, amnesty, a functioning economy, and good trade relations—had been thrown to the winds.

The fact that military rule and poverty have characterized much of Haiti's political history since has occassionaly been laid at the feet of Toussaint and the first Haitian constitution, with its restrictions on civil liberties, endorsement of censorship, lack of an elected legislature, and provision for Toussaint's lifelong rule. This was, in a sense, Toussaint's ultimate failure. However, it was not, in fact, Toussaint's constitution, but rather the steps Dessalines took after Toussaint's death that led to exactly the kind of political isolation that Toussaint had feared and sought so fervently to avoid. Under these circumstances, the new country was isolated, its economic opportunities utterly stifled.

There can be no telling whether, once Saint-Domingue's situation had fundamentally changed, Toussaint would have changed his approach to government. As we have seen, he was a leader and politician whose decisions were very much based on what was right for the moment rather than what was right, period. It is impossible to know how things would have turned out if he had not been captured or what he himself foresaw as the colony's future at the time of his detainment.

There is a more sinister reason behind Haiti's contemporary challenges, one that has nothing to do with Toussaint's legacy. In 2022, after an exhaustive investigation, the *New York Times* revealed for the first time the staggering burden of what the authors call Haiti's "double debt." As the *Times* explains, a few years after Haiti secured its independence, the French government forced the Haitian government to pay compensation to the former slave owners. In the words of the authors, "Without the funds to pay, Haitians had to take out a loan from French banks. This would come to be known as the 'double debt,' and is part of the reason Haiti is one of the poorest countries in the world today." The statement is hardly an exaggeration. The investigation revealed that the reparations amounted to $560 million in 2022 value—and that the actual cost of this debt on potential economic growth was between $21 and $115 billion.[59] Here is a window into the twisted logic upon which European colonialism was based. In the very decades that France touted its revolutionary and democratic credentials, it self-righteously imposed a crippling fine on an island nation for no other reason than because it had freed itself of France's brutal oppression. It's hard to think of a more sinister plan to utterly sabotage the future of a people.

## The Legacy of a Forgotten Leader

In 2019, the authors of *Harvard Business Review's Leaders Handbook* wrote of the power inherent in visionary leadership: "A simple, bold, inspirational vision can feel almost magical: it brings people. .. together around a common goal and provides a focal point for developing strategies to achieve a better future." Writing from a business perspective, they urge that it is not only CEOs who can and should lead through grand visions.[60] That it is difficult enough today to spawn visionary leadership in the ranks of those outside of the executive suite makes it even more difficult to fathom that the vision that would eventually emancipate France's most important colony emerged from an individual on the bottom rung of society's ladder. Herein lies perhaps the most amazing, near magical, quality in Toussaint's leadership. For anyone in the eighteenth century to imagine a world in which a Black people could one day rule the very island on which they were enslaved is mindboggling.

In this regard, Toussaint's influence—the true legacy of his leadership—goes far beyond his small island home in the Caribbean. For while established writers have shunned him, Toussaint has served as a stirring example for future Black freedom fighters and those working to define a Black culture and historical narrative.[61] More than anything he did, the fact that he believed so indelibly in the abilities and equality of Black men and women reverberated in their struggle to come through the next decades and centuries.

Yet to say that Toussaint's leadership relied purely on vision is false. Toussaint had a long-term vision, but his feet were firmly rooted on the ground of his present reality, and what enabled him to achieve what he did—the permanent end of slavery in his territory and the establishment of the first Black republic in the world—was not only lofty ambition and a stirring ideology, but rather its combination with pragmatism, creativity, and meticulous administration. He could switch allegiance on a dime, as his allies' political usefulness waned and waxed. This dexterity provided him with firearms and rations (the Spanish in 1793), conferred power on him (the French general Etienne de Laveaux in 1795) and provided the colony with flour and weapons (Britain and the USA in 1798). It was these short-term logistical realities as much as any lofty principles that preoccupied Toussaint and defined his policies, which were often a matter of necessity rather than choice. Toussaint understood that he needed infrastructure, financial security, and logistical capabilities to support his military; that only a well-fed and disciplined army would enable him to attain power; and that only a well-fed population would allow him to retain it. Once in a position of power, he would be able to do what he liked, to implement the underlying vision he had had all along: that of a meritocratic multiracial society.

While balancing the realities of short-term needs with his long-term vision, Toussaint, too, was able to switch seamlessly between two hats: that of a military leader and a public administrator. While history is rife with glorious military leaders whose abilities, once they traded in their gun for a pen, failed to impress, Toussaint was of a different mold. He stands out for being as brilliantly effective as a guerilla leader as he was behind an administrator's desk—a true rarity. He also stands out as a masterful storyteller and as a negotiator. Above all, he understood, better than anyone else, the currents of his time, and he knew when to press his advantage and when to wait for circumstances to play into his hand. More often than not, they did exactly that.

# "If the women of the English are like her, the men must be like lions." Gertrude Bell

Even a century ago, Switzerland was a tourism hotspot. Each summer, Victorian tourists in their hundreds flocked to Interlaken, Grindelwald, Zermatt, and a host of other mountain towns, eager to breathe fresh air and take in the views of majestic, glaciated peaks. As one ascended the trails above these bustling hamlets, however, the crowds grew increasingly thinner. This was definitely true of the Engelhörner, a series of needle-like peaks above the Rosenlaui Valley, high above the Bernese town of Meiringen. Yet on 7 September 1901, these desolate and nearly vertical peaks were the scene of a most curious spectacle. If anyone had been observing the mountain range from the opposite side of the valley with a telescope, they might have picked out, on the almost vertical limestone face opposite them, a kind of circus act playing out between a col known as the Gemsensattel and a peak called the Klein Engelhorn. Standing on a ledge below a smooth section of overhanging rock, a local mountain guide named Ulrich Fuhrer clambered onto the shoulders of his brother Heinrich in a daring attempt to reach a hold that would allow him to master the overhanging section. But there was no hold to be found. The third member of the party, Ulrich and Heinrich's client, describes what happened next:

> I then clambered up onto Heinrich, Ulrich stood on me and fingered up the rock as high as he could. It wasn't high enough. I lifted myself still a little higher—always with Ulrich on me, mind!—and he began to raise himself by his hands. As his foot left my shoulder I put up a hand, straightened out my arm and made a ledge for him. He called out "I don't feel at all safe—if you move we are all killed." I said, "All right, I can stand here for a week", and up he went by my shoulder and my hand. It was just high enough.[1]

© The Author(s), under exclusive license to Springer Nature Switzerland AG 2023
M. Gutmann, *The Unseen Leader*, https://doi.org/10.1007/978-3-031-37829-4_5

Once Ulrich had reached a moderately safe position, the client, climbing off of Heinrich's shoulders and hauling on the rope, made it up the overhang as well. Heinrich, however, "could not manage it. The fact was, I think, that he lost his nerve." The client and Ulrich had no choice; they left Heinrich behind, secured to the rock "like a second Prometheus—fortunately there were no vultures about!" The two went on to the top of Klein Engelhorn—the first ever to reach its foreboding summit—and then return to Heinrich, at which point all three set off to make an afternoon's work of the first traverse of the most imposing mountain in the range, the Ürbachsengelhorn. Over the course of two weeks, the three climbers made a total of seven first ascents.

Within the community of British mountaineers, this two-week foray was newsworthy in its own right. These were stout accomplishments, the types that would surely be the talk of the town at Alpine Club meetings or other similar social gatherings back in London. What made it all the more spectacular, especially considering the norms of this time, is that Ulrich and Heinrich's client was a woman: Gertrude Lowthian Bell.

Bell was an accomplished mountaineer. In the years before her foray into the Rosenlaui Valley in the summer of 1901, she had already climbed such formidable Alpine peaks as the Mont Blanc, the Grepon, the Dru, and the Meije—once out of sight of civilization, she would take off her skirt and climb in her petticoats—and having made the first traverse from the Lauteraarhorn to the Schreckhorn, she would become even better known in mountaineering circles after surviving an epic 53-hour attempt on the northeast face of the highest mountain in the Oberland, the Finsteraarhorn. During that climb, she and her two guides became trapped in a snowstorm and forced to spend two nights in the open—first on the iced-over rock face and then on the glacier below. She escaped the ordeal with frostbitten fingers and toes but mentally no worse for wear.

In 1904 she embarked on what would be her last climb, the Matterhorn from the less frequented Italian side, and once again in the company of Ulrich and Heinrich. She described it as "beautiful climbing, never seriously difficult, but never easy, and most of the time on a great steep face which was splendid to go upon." The party descended on the more usual route down to Zermatt, which she described as "more like sliding down the bannisters than climbing."[2]

That she climbed with a guide was hardly out of the ordinary; in fact, it was not only an acceptable but an expected practice among the British well-to-do who stormed the summits of the Alps beginning in the second half of the nineteenth century. Even so, she stood out. Ulrich later told E.L. Strutt, the editor of the *Alpine Journal*, that "of all the amateurs, men or women, that he had travelled with, he had seen but very few to surpass her in technical skill and none to equal her in coolness, bravery and judgment."[3]

## An Extraordinary Life

Ulrich and Heinrich Fuhrer's client was Gertrude Lowthian Bell. Bell's mountaineering alone would have made for an extraordinary lifetime accomplishment, but she rang up many firsts besides her mountain ascents. She was the first woman to earn a first in modern history at Oxford; the first woman officer ever employed by British military intelligence; the first female political officer in the entire British Empire; the first woman to write a White Paper; the first Director of Antiquities in Iraq.[4] Two of her archaeological works, meanwhile, remain classics in the field; they were reprinted in 2008 and 2013.[5] Her translation from the Persian of the poetry of Hafiz is, according to the great authority on Persian letters, E.G. Browne, writing in 1995, "probably the finest and most poetical rendering of any Persian poet ever produced in the English language."[6] Her six desert treks between 1900 and 1913, on foot and camelback, made independently and on her own initiative and covering distances between 900 and 1600 miles over the course of several months, gave her a knowledge of the geography and tribal makeup of Arabia that was unmatched by any other westerner's. After Bell's death in 1926, Faisal ibn al-Hussein, the leader of the Arab Revolt against the Turks during World War I and later King Faisal I of Iraq revealed that "in one of the critical phases of our history, when some of our men were wavering, the great white woman herself led them in an attack on the Turks."[7] Earlier in the war, Faisal continued, the Turks had put a bounty on her head. "The price was such that might have tempted the cupidity of men, but such was the esteem in which our people held her that none could be found to denounce her to her enemies."[8] Summing up his assessment of her, Faisal asserted that "Gertrude Bell is a name that is written indelibly on Arab history—a name which is spoken with awe…One might say that she was the greatest woman of her time."[9] Few others remembered her so fondly; in fact, most remembered her not at all.

In the annals of British colonial history and in the well-established genre of action-oriented, charismatic leaders, few names hold as much cache as "Lawrence of Arabia." T.E. Lawrence, as we will learn in the pages to come, was in fact a dashing and fearless leader, who is credited with instigating and leading the "Arab Revolt" against the Ottoman Turks during the First World War, which in turn eased the pressure on other British fronts and, perhaps more significantly, reshaped the Middle East.

Bell, when her name appears at all, is sometimes referred to as "the female Lawrence of Arabia," and Faisal's description of her leading an attack against the Turks during the Arab Revolt might seem to justify this statement. Perhaps a more accurate description, however, would be to assign the opposite labels— Lawrence was, in many ways, a male version of Bell. By his own admission, Lawrence relied heavily on Bell in much of his work. He was the first to admit that he could not match her knowledge of the tribes and geography of desert region. He relied in no small fashion on her expertise and guidance in his quest to raise the Arab Revolt, the historical episode which lent Lawrence his fame and moniker.[10]

Lawrence himself wrote of Bell that, "She stood out as the one person who, thinking clearly, saw the true ultimate goal of our work with the Arabs and, daunted by nothing, worked unsparingly of herself toward it.[11]" The Bell-Lawrence dichotomy has been challenged more recently as well. Helen Berry, professor of British history at the University of Newcastle, also upends the Lawrence-Bell dichotomy, stating that "Churchill relied heavily on Gertrude, not Lawrence."[12] We may give the final word to the man in the best position to judge their influence, Faisal, who stated that "[Gertrude Bell] was...mainly— I will even say entirely responsible for establishing the Iraqi Nation."[13]

The two, however, it would appear, were not always amicable. A curious episode is recounted in the Conservative politician Leopold Amery's memoir, that,

> [in] organising Arab forces against the Turks [Bell's] field of operations had to some extent overlapped with that of Lawrence, and she was credited with a signal victory in the desert in which her protégés defeated Lawrence's and captured all their machine guns.[14]

Bell, it seems, is a character worth getting to know better.

## Managing up in a Complex World

The desolate situation in Iraq today may not appear to provide a very good credential for the person mainly or entirely responsible for establishing the Iraqi nation. At Bell's death in 1926, however, for all its problems and tensions, and even taking into account all the hesitancies the reader might bring to anything smacking of white westerners practicing nation-building in former imperial territories, the land now known as Iraq was arguably better governed than it had been in 500 years. King Faisal I, a tolerant and inclusive leader, sat on the throne of a constitutional monarchy, intent on building a pluralistic and independent modern state; formal independence and League of Nations membership was six years away. Bell's "ultimate goal"—"a free, prosperous and cultivated Iraq," as her obituary in the *Times of India* put it—appeared within reach.[15]

It is worth pausing here to note how remarkable Bell's accomplishment was. The complexities of the post-World War One Middle East are almost unmatched by those of any other time and place: here, a panoply of historical currents clashed in a confused and uncontrollable torrent. The odds were powerfully weighted against any given individual achieving enough influence to realize a set purpose. When we consider that the individual in question was a woman working within and between two highly patriarchal cultures—those of imperial Britain and of the Arabian desert—the odds become even less propitious. It is, in other words, hard to fathom that anyone should have managed to build a state in the postwar Middle East (the recent American attempts in Iraq and Afghanistan have been hard enough, despite funding, knowledge, and resources wholly unavailable a century earlier); that a woman played a key leadership role in the endeavor is little short of miraculous.

And yet, for all the accolades, what Bell actually *did* to promote her cause is far more nebulous than what Toussaint, Amundsen, and Churchill (as we will see in the next chapter) did for theirs. The only woman in her milieu, Bell's influence made few headlines, and her work was generally fronted by that of powerful men. Lawrence relied on Bell's intelligence about the tribes and geography of the Arabian desert in his quest to raise the Arab Revolt; General Stanley Maude, on his push north from Basra to Baghdad, relied on her to smooth the way by winning over the local tribes and their sheiks to the British side against the Turks (which she did, and quite successfully; one sheik informed his followers that "…we all know that Allah has made all women inferior to men. If the women of the Angiliz [English] are like her, the men must be like lions, in strength and valour. We had better make peace with them."[16]) and High Commissioner Sir Percy Cox, the British proconsul in Mesopotamia, was dependent on her knowledge of the situation on the ground, her relationships with sheiks and other notables, and her political acumen in establishing the British administration in Baghdad. Bell was a powerful voice pushing for Arab independence, both in Baghdad and at the Paris Peace Conference in 1919; she was a key figure at the Cairo Conference of 1921; she was instrumental in putting together the first Iraqi provisional government and constitution and in garnering support among important Iraqi personages for Faisal's rule; and she was, at least at first, a trusted adviser to Faisal as he took on the kingship.

All of these roles, however, might be seen as those of an advisor rather than a leader. Her written output—the weekly intelligence reports that she delivered to London, Cairo and Delhi over the course of many years, in which she outlined her take on the situation in the Middle East; her White Paper presenting the state of affairs in Iraq in 1920 and arguing against an immediate British withdrawal; her manual for new British officers assigned to Iraq; and the wealth of informal communications she delivered to men in high places, often outside of regular channels (incurring no little wrath from her superiors) in her push to have her vision realized—might be regarded as fitting into an advisory framework.

In looking below the surface, however, we immediately recognize that Bell was more than an advisory. Because Bell's work should not only be seen from the narrow perspective of its place in the British imperial hierarchy. While she was neither the one to sign official documents nor to take center stage at diplomatic events, she designed and drove policy behind the scenes. Bell was the main point of contact for innumerable local personages, who both realized her influence on her nominal superior, the High Commissioner Sir Percy Cox, and felt safe to unburden their concerns, needs, and desires to her. That Bell's name is still remembered with fondness by many in Baghdad suggests a powerful and highly appreciated leadership role *from the point of view of the Iraqis*. This sentiment was expressed in the epithets by which she was known: al-Khatun ("important lady," or "lady of the court"—in Persian, the word means "queen"), Umm al Muminin ("Mother of the Faithful," a term otherwise reserved for Ayishah, the wife of the Prophet Muhammad), and, especially notably, Kokusah—the female form of "Kokus," which was the common rendering of "Cox" by speakers of Arabic.[17] For the local population, that is, Bell was indeed a leader—the female version of the High Commissioner. Leaders, this suggests, may not always be those who hold the most exalted official titles but may instead be those to whom people actually turn in order to effect change.

That this is a different form of leadership from the one we are used to is highlighted by the fact that the story of the founding of the modern state of Iraq can plausibly be told without mentioning Bell at all—as it often is. Lawrence, Churchill, Cox, Maude, Cox's successor Arnold Wilson, and Faisal will almost inevitably appear in a historical account, but Bell seems to be optional. This may render my inclusion of Bell in this book somewhat surprising. It would be impossible to tell the story of polar exploration without Amundsen, the Second World War without Churchill, or the Haitian Revolution without Toussaint Louverture. Yet what we have seen in the preceding chapters is that the decisive elements in the success of the first two leaders were often not their heroic public actions but instead their reading of the powerful natural and historical currents at play in the situations in which they found themselves, and the behind-the-scenes preparations that harnessed these currents to propel them toward their goals. With Bell, the heroic public actions fall away altogether. We are thus left, in a sense, with our proposed form of leadership in its pure, unadulterated form. Bell led, as it were, from behind—behind the curtain, behind the scenes, behind powerful men. Today we call this *managing* (or leading) *up*—a concept popular enough that the *Harvard Business Review* recently ran an entire series on it.[18] The term didn't exist 100 years ago, but Gertrude Bell's work epitomizes it.

## The Power of a Comma

The Ottoman Empire, from its capital in Constantinople (today's Istanbul), was the great power in the Mediterranean basin for more than six centuries, ruling territories from the Balkans to the Persian Gulf and North Africa. By the time Gertrude Bell first visited it in 1889, it had lost a significant amount of territory. The Russo-Turkish War of 1877–78 had led to the independence of Romania, Serbia and Montenegro, and Britain had established a de facto protectorate in Egypt in 1882. The Young Turk Revolution of 1908 and the series of coups, countercoups, and botched coups that followed it led to the establishment, in 1913, of a three-man dictatorship that received considerable support from Germany. The Ottomans thus, fatefully, entered World War I on the side of the Central Powers.

British interests in the Ottoman area included the Suez Canal, which it oversaw from Egypt, the land and air routes to India via Mesopotamia and the Persian Gulf, the oilfields in Abadan, and the prospect of oil in the region around Mosul, in southern Kurdistan—a prospect that would become ever more intriguing as Winston Churchill pushed to transform the British Navy from a coal-based to an oil-based operation.[1]

As the Great War bogged down in the trenches of France, the British conceived of the idea of sending battleships to the narrow Dardanelles straits to pound the Turks in Constantinople, opening a new front that would force the Germans to divert troops to the east. When three of its battleships were sunk by mines, the British Navy retreated. Plan B was to land troops on the beaches of Gallipoli; when this operation was carried out, British forces—largely

---

[1] Churchill's decision is one of the most profound and yet underdiscussed of the twentieth century. Unfortunately, we cannot dwell on it here.

composed of Australians and New Zealanders—were massacred by Turkish machine guns as they waded out of the water onto the beaches. After eleven months of battle in the Dardanelles, the British withdrew, affording the Ottomans a singular victory.

The debacle of Gallipoli not only saw 115,000 British and dominion casualties and cost Winston Churchill his post as Secretary of the Navy, but also placed the British in a dangerous position: the governor of Egypt, Sir Henry MacMahon, now feared a Turkish counterattack on the Suez Canal. Given the precarious economic situation in Egypt, MacMahon especially feared that such an attack might spark a revolt against the British by Egypt's mostly Muslim Arab population—particularly as the Ottoman sultan, who was simultaneously the caliph (religious leader) of Muslims the world over, had called for jihad (holy war) against the empire's enemies.

MacMahon's Oriental Secretary, Ronald Storrs, came up with an ingenious—and in the end, calamitous—way to get MacMahon and the British out of trouble. Storrs knew that Sharif Hussein, the emir of Mecca (telephone number: Mecca 1), was unhappy with Ottoman rule and had in the past asked for British arms to help him overthrow the Turks. Hussein's position as the ruler of the most holy city in the Muslim world, and as a direct descendant of the Prophet Muhammad—so went MacMahon's thinking—might be enough to discredit the sultan's call for jihad against the British, and, in fact, to effect the opposite: an Arab revolt against the Turks. MacMahon thus, fatefully, took up correspondence with Hussein.

To MacMahon's horror, the Sharif demanded significant recompense for raising a revolt: that Britain support his claim to found and lead an independent pan-Arab state not only on the Arabian peninsula, but also including Syria, Iraq, and Palestine. When MacMahon tried to put him off, Sharif responded that he spoke not for himself, but for "our people who believe that those frontiers form the minimum necessary to the establishment of the new order for which we are striving."[19]

When intelligence reached MacMahon suggesting that the Arab nationalist movement was widespread, he found himself in a dreadful predicament. He wired London that "unless we can give them immediate assurance of [a] nature to satisfy them they will throw themselves into the hands of Germany."[20] In reply, he received instructions "to be as vague as possible … [but] if something more precise than this is required you can give it."[21]

MacMahon did exactly as instructed: he was somewhat more precise than as vague as possible. Aware that the British had no intention of ceding Syria, Iraq and Palestine but desperate to prevent the Arabs joining the Ottomans, he took refuge, of all things, in a comma—or, to be precise, in the absence of one. He wrote Hussein that "'we accept these limits of boundaries," and offered his assurances "in regard to those portions of the territory therein in which Great Britain is free to act without detriment to the interests of her ally France."[222]Since France had traditional interests in Syria and Palestine, MacMahon was in effect offering only Mesopotamia. Yet—and English teachers everywhere can be grateful for this example of the existential import of punctuation—had there been a comma between "therein" and "in," the meaning of the sentence would have been entirely different: he would then have been offering all three territories, and furthermore asserting that Great Britain was able to act in all of them without bothering about France. ("We accept these limits of boundaries and offer our assurances in regard to those portions of the territory **therein, in** which Great Britain is free to act without detriment to the interests of her ally France.")

MacMahon's letter was translated into Arabic by a secret agent named Ruhi, who was working for Storrs, and then sent to Hussein. Ruhi translated badly, or perhaps mischievously: he acted as if the comma were present. Thus, it was that Britain offered one deal, and Hussein and the Arabs accepted quite another. The consequences of this comma would be enormous; arguably, they still reverberate today. The Arab Revolt led by Hussein's son Faisal was the first of these consequences.

## Under Lawrence's Shadow

In 1962, director David Lean shot an epic blockbuster based, with a hefty dose of poetic license, on T.E. Lawrence's role in the Arab Revolt of 1916–1918. With its stirring orchestral score, its vast and awe-inspiring shots of the desert landscape, its hordes of camels and horses, the tortured intensity of Peter O'Toole as Lawrence, Anthony Quinn's cynical wisdom as Faisal, and the early-60 s western stereotypes it applied to almost all the other Arab characters, it was a great box-office hit. As for the Bechdel test—which asks whether a movie includes at least two women who talk to each other about something other than a man—…well, *Lawrence of Arabia* fails it about as thoroughly as any movie ever has: the only female roles are as harem members who appear

---

[2] This is the text of the English original. Most English sources provide a translation back into English of the Arabic letter actually sent to Hussein, which accounts for the discrepancies between them and, as we shall soon see, between them and the English original quoted here. MacMahon was quite proud of his maneuver, as can be seen by his quoting the key formulation, without the comma, in a later communication.

in the background of a couple of scenes. There are also, at times, a few scattered female corpses.

This did not have to be the case. At least one prominent female role was spectacularly on offer. Gertrude Bell worked at the same Arab Bureau in which we see Lawrence burning with frustration at the beginning of the film; she was his friend and colleague; she supplied him with the intelligence he needed to negotiate the tribal intricacies of the desert; and, if we are to believe Faisal and Amery, she led tribes into battle as Lawrence did, once even taking on his forces and outdoing him.[3]

Ironically, Lean's movie opens with Lawrence drawing maps, an activity toward which he expressed a rather cavalier attitude. Of a map he had drawn of roads and wells in the Sinai, he once wrote, "Some of it was accurate, and the rest I invented." He admitted to fearing that one day he might have to find his way in the desert with only his own cartography to go by.[23]

Gertrude Bell's mapmaking, on the other hand, was a more serious affair. Trained by the Royal Geographical Society, she often stood with theodolite and compass in hand during her desert journeys, making her readings. It was not only her intimate knowledge of the desert tribes, but also her skills as a cartographer that resulted in her being summoned to the nascent Arab Bureau of the Admiralty Intelligence Division in Cairo in 1915. At the time of the summons, she was in London running the Wounded and Missing Enquiry Department of the British Red Cross, but the archaeologist David Hogarth, now a lieutenant commander with the Intelligence Division, wrote her from Cairo to say she was needed there. As Bell confided to David's sister Janet, "I've heard from David, he says anyone can trace the wounded, but only I can map northern Arabia. I'm going next week."[24]

The maps Bell made of northern Arabia became known as the Bell maps and were essential for British operations during the Arab Revolt. They are referred to in another Hollywood movie, *The English Patient*. In it, several British soldiers are examining a map of the desert. One asks, "But can we get through those mountains?" Another replies, "The Bell maps show a way." This meets with a disgruntled, "Let's hope he was right."

---

[3] It remains obscure why they would have been fighting one another.

# The Original Line in the Sand

The consequences of the mistranslated comma in the MacMahon-Hussein correspondence—the comma that allowed Britain to offer only Mesopotamia in English, but Mesopotamia, Syria, and Palestine in Arabic, in return for Hussein's raising the Arab Revolt—were so enormous because, at the same time as MacMahon was wrestling with Hussein's demands, Britain was secretly negotiating the postwar borders of the very same region with its uneasy ally France. The British negotiator, Sir Mark Sykes, was a near neighbor of Gertrude Bell's family in Yorkshire, and there was little love lost between Gertrude and Mark. Bell quarreled with Sykes in 1905 when he referred to Arabs as "cowardly," "diseased" and "idle." She may also have noted a singular entry in the index to Sykes's book *The Caliph's Last Heritage*: "Arab character: *see also* Treachery." It didn't help that Bell once outfoxed Sykes when they were both intending to set off across the desert to the Jebel Druze—she let drop to a local ruler that Sykes's brother-in-law was the Prime Minister of Egypt, which precluded his getting a permit to travel—a humiliation Sykes much resented.[4] When they met again at the Arab Bureau in Cairo, she was offended by his references to Arabs as "the frocks." Sykes's less-than-generous opinion of Bell will be quoted below.

The result of Sykes's secret negotiations was the (also secret) Sykes-Picot agreement, which divided up the postwar spoils in the Middle East through an arbitrary "line in the sand." Without respect for communities, languages, or religions, Sykes, referring to the map in front of him, had proposed to "draw a line from the 'e' in 'Acre' to the last 'k' in 'Kirkut.'" The northern, French zone would include the Syrian and Lebanese coast and extend into modern Turkey, while the southern, British zone would include most of Mesopotamia, Transjordan, and part of Palestine. When this idea was approved by the British Prime Minister Henry Asquith, Sykes and his French counterpart François George-Picot negotiated the deal, which they shared with Russian leaders—their allies in the war—but otherwise kept secret from the world.

The Sykes-Picot agreement of May 1916 represented a massive betrayal of the promise relayed to the Arabs in the MacMahon-Hussein correspondence, but as Hussein had no knowledge of it, he remained willing to fight alongside the British. The agreement became known to the members of the Arab Bureau in Cairo, however, and this meant, as Christopher Hitchens puts it, that these

---

[4] Bell, in turn, considered Sykes a foolish traveler and resented him for overpaying for mules, camels and dragomen, driving up local prices.

men, including Lawrence, were "objectively committed to living a lie"—
promising a pan-Arab state that they knew would never be delivered.[25] In the
Arab world, this betrayal still reverberates today. Sykes-Picot has become a
catchword for ISIS, among others; Caliph Abu Bakr al-Baghdadi announced
in 2014, for example, that "This blessed advance will not stop until we hit the
last nail in the coffin of the Sykes-Picot conspiracy."[26]

Bell, who had by this time left Cairo, was not party to this knowledge, and
learned of Sykes-Picot only a year and a half after the fact, when the agreement was exposed by the new Bolshevik government in Moscow—a move
designed to embarrass the British and the French. Those in the know, including the Arab Bureau members with Lawrence prominent among them, nevertheless continued to support the spectacularly successful revolt raised by
Hussein and led in the field by his third son, Faisal. The Revolt played a key
role in the defeat of the Turks by the British. On 1 October 1918, having
surpassed all British expectations, Faisal's army stormed into Damascus ahead
of General Allenby's Egyptian Expeditionary Force. Faisal and the Arabs
would rule there, with British financial and military support, for the next two
years; on 7 March 1920, Faisal was declared king of an independent Syria.

This better-than-expected and at the same time worse-than-expected course
of events placed the two contradictory promises the British had made in
direct, live opposition to one another. After much diplomatic wrangling and
soul-searching, Britain determined that its interests were better served by not
antagonizing the French than by backing what they now knew to have been
the explicit promise delivered to the Arabs.[5] On 1 November 1919, they
began to withdraw their forces from Syria, knowing full well what would follow. French troops moved into Damascus, and Faisal fled to British-controlled
Palestine. He was allowed to remain there only briefly before being escorted
to the Egyptian border and left at a train station, sitting on his luggage.[27]

## A Saint or Saddam

"Let's hope he was right"—the comment of the disgruntled soldier on examining the Bell map in *The English Patient*—provides at least a partial illustra-
tion of why Gertrude Bell may be the most amazing woman you've never
heard of. "She is a remarkably clever woman...with the brains of a man,"

---

[5] "This passage [MacMahon's English version without the comma]...had been our sheet anchor...It is
extremely awkward to have this piece of solid ground cut out from under our feet," wrote one official on
learning that Ruhi's translation had assumed the comma.

wrote the Viceroy of India, Lord Hardinge.[28] Sir George MacMunn, the inspector general of communications in Mesopotamia, wrote that she was "a little wisp of a human being, said to be a woman."[29] Mark Sykes pulled out all the stops, calling Bell a "bitch," an "infernal liar," and the "terror of the desert," and wishing "10,000 of my worst bad words on the head of that damned fool"—before losing, if not 10,000, at least a considerable number of such words: "Confound the silly chattering windbag of conceited, gushing, flat-chested, man-woman, globe-trotting, rump-wagging, blethering ass!"[30] Of course, the fact that Sykes had so much to say about Bell—toxic though it was—speaks to the fact that he was keenly aware of the great influence she had. Needless to say, neither Sykes nor other British officers of the time spent much time thinking about other women in their midst.

Beyond the small cabal of officers working on Mesopotamia, Bell was as invisible as most other women. Like her maps, many of Bell's works were assumed to have been written by a man. Her collection of essays commissioned to orient British political officers new to Iraq, "The Arab of Mesopotamia," was published anonymously. Replying to a question from her family, Bell affirmed, "Why yes of course I wrote all the 'Arab of Mesopotamia.' I've loved the reviews which speak of the practical men who were the anonymous authors etc. It's fun being practical men isn't it…"[31] Bell's white paper, *Review of the Civil Administration of Mesopotamia*, was presented to both houses of Parliament in 1920, received a standing ovation, and caused a "fandango" in the press.[32] On seeing some of the newspaper clippings, she commented, "The general line taken by the press seems to be that it's most remarkable that a dog should be able to stand up on its hind legs at all—i.e., a female write a white paper. I hope they'll drop that source of wonder and pay attention to the report itself."[33]

But the reason Bell remains so unknown outside a small circle of specialists is more complex than mere British imperial misogyny. Even feminist scholarship has steered away from her and on two counts: first, she was herself undoubtedly part of the British imperial machine (even if she was highly critical of much of it), and second, she was an anti-suffragist in her youth—and no mean anti-suffragist, but a founding member of the northern branch of the Women's National Anti-Suffrage League.[34] That later on in life she was reported to be "amused by her own [earlier] attitude"[35] has not removed the stain on her feminist reputation, and she remains, as Helen Berry writes, "an unlikely candidate for rehabilitation among the feminist pantheon."[36]

There are yet more reasons for the relative obscurity of such a remarkable woman. Lawrence, like Shackleton and other members of the pantheon of heroic leaders, was keenly interested in promoting his own image. At one point, he worked with the American journalist Lowell Thomas on an immensely popular stage show titled *With Allenby in Palestine and Lawrence in Arabia*. Bell, on the other hand, was utterly uninterested in publicity of any kind. She avoided the press, condemning it as "the whole advertisement business," and threw all letters asking for interviews or photographs "straight into the wastepaper basket."[37] And while Bell's extensive preserved correspondence, mostly with her father and stepmother ("one of the great correspondences of the past century," according to James Buchan, a fierce critic of Bell) reveals much, it also keeps much mum—in particular her secret political maneuverings and the dangers she ran up against, which are arguably the most important elements for an evaluation of her work.[38] Thus, while we know a good deal of what Bell actually did in the Middle East, there is also a good deal—and we don't know how much—that we don't know; and as her influence was so often behind the scenes and unrecorded, there is little hope we ever will.

As a result of all these ambiguities, evaluation of Bell's achievements varies widely according to whom you ask. Bell's 2006 biographer, Georgina Howell, adopts an adulatory attitude; Werner Herzog, in the flop that was to be his Hollywood breakthrough, skips Iraq altogether after many scenes of Nicole Kidman on a camel; Christopher Hitchens approvingly places Bell among those "English people who thought other peoples, too, deserved their place in the sun."[39] Faisal, as we have seen, credits her more than anyone else with the creation of the state of Iraq. The British academic and politician Rory Stewart notes that "When I served as a British official in southern Iraq in 2003, I often heard Iraqis compare my female colleagues to 'Gertrude Bell.' It was generally casual flattery…"[40] And James Buchan, writing in 2003, states that while "the historical waters have closed over T.E. Lawrence," who, by the 1970s, was no longer remembered even "at the scenes of his exploits…'Miss Bell' is still a name in Baghdad."[41]

Yet, the same James Buchan also lambasts Bell's legacy: "…Bell and her superior as British high commissioner, Sir Percy Cox, laid down policies of state in Iraq that were taken up by Saddam's Arab Ba'ath socialist party. Those policies included to retain, if necessary by violence, the Kurdish mountains as a buffer against Turkey and Russia; to promote Sunni Muslims and other minorities over the Shi'a majority." Karl Meyer and Shareen Brysac concur, delivering the verdict that "Gertrude Bell helped drown Iraq in a bitter sea filled with what Virgil called the 'tears of things.'"[42] Saad B. Eskander notes that "some political analysts attribute the present ethnic and religious troubles in Iraq to Bell's unrealistic ideas, hopes and ambitions."[43] Myriam Yakoubi takes yet another tack, judging that Bell overestimated her power, and doubting whether she had "such a decisive influence on political events in Iraq, let alone in the whole Arab world."

This is cynicism at its finest and smacks of the same imperial arrogance that Bell abhorred. The alternative to an independent Iraq was domination by the British, French, or the Turks. To suggest that this would have been a better alternative for the Iraqi population then or that it would have provided a better foundation for their later success is a troubling perspective. At the time of Bell's death, as we will see, the Middle East had its first functioning and reasonably well-governed modern state. Its failure in the long run is due to a set of complex circumstances, all of which were outside of Bell's control. But this is getting ahead of ourselves.

Returning to interpretations of Bell's role, we see that the entire spectrum is covered; by some, Bell is seen as almost saintly; others compare her to Saddam Hussein; and still others deny that she had much influence at all. That such an exceptional woman should be seen in such divergent ways, that her contributions and her legacy should be so obscure to most people and so much in dispute by scholars suggests that something is amiss. I suspect that the ambiguity and confusion arise from three sources: first, a misreading of the reign of King Faisal I and the causes of the current chaos in Iraq; second, a lack of appreciation for the depth of Bell's relationship to the natural world, and in particular to the desert; and third, and most relevant for the theme of this book, the fact that, as already noted, Bell's leadership was largely invisible. For while Bell took on many formal leadership roles in her life—from Secretary of the League of Anti-Suffragists to the head of the Red Cross Missing and Wounded Enquiry Department, from the leader of her own desert expeditions to the Director of Antiquities in Iraq—her greatest accomplishment, the creation of an Arab kingdom in Iraq, was achieved from the lowly position of "Oriental Secretary to the Political Department of the Indian Expeditionary Force in Iraq," a position granted her in an attempt to give some kind of title to a role that escaped all categories. We might wish for more clarity in a subject of a leadership study; we might prefer to examine Bell leading a charge of desert tribesmen against the Turks—the kind of thing hinted at by Faisal and Amery. But this is the Action Fallacy rearing its head. As we have seen already several times in this book, real leadership takes place mostly in the quiet, in the recognition of greater natural and historical currents and in an alignment with them in such a way that they support one's efforts rather than destroy them. Yet, this type of leadership is rarely recognized. In short, the standard leadership story doesn't know what to do with Gertrude Bell.

# Building a Nation from Behind the Scenes

What, then, exactly did Bell do? Unfortunately, it is difficult to recount her work in the same meticulous detail as that of Amundsen or Churchill, or even Toussaint (who lived a century earlier). For, unlike them, we have far fewer sources at our disposal in reconstructing her influence. And we must contend ourselves with the fact that some of what she did will remain forever shrouded in mystery, as she neither advertised it nor wrote home about it. Moreover, she had no inhibitions about using irregular channels in her work that did not figure in any official reports. But, with that said, we do know quite a lot.

Born into a wealthy industrial family in Yorkshire, Bell was precocious and extremely adventurous from her childhood. Climbing around on roofs and trees, jumping off walls, galloping away on horses, she ran roughshod over a series of governesses. At her oral exams at Oxford, she saw fit to contradict one of the dons examining her on a point of geography while informing the other, the great historian S.R. Gardiner, that she disagreed with his assessment of Charles I.[44]

After Oxford, this well-connected young woman traveled the world; she spent nine months in Tehran, where she got her first taste of what was called at the time "the East," and made a name for herself as one of the best climbers in the Alps—escapades with which we are now intimately familiar. During a stay in Jerusalem in 1900, she discovered a love for the desert that from then on would eclipse her climbing career. Preternaturally gifted at languages, she became fluent in Arabic and undertook six epic journeys through the Syrian, Arabian, and Mesopotamian deserts. She visited and wrote about archaeological sites, mapped previously uncharted terrain, and became closely acquainted with the sheiks of innumerable desert tribes and with the politics that ruled the desert: "who had sold horses, who owned camels, who had been killed in a raid, how much the blood money would be or where the next battle."[45]

Bell's desert journeys—on foot, horse-, mule- and camelback—were dangerous, demanding, and unparalleled, the longest of them lasting six months and covering 1600 miles. Raids on travelers were common; warring tribes, suspicious of foreigners, rendered vast swathes of terrain perilous to cross; and the desert environment is, of course, inhospitable to say the least. It is a testament to Bell's force of personality and her ability to read geographic and social landscapes that she never came to any harm. She traveled in style, with her canvas bathtub that doubled as a drinking trough for the camels, her Wedgwood china, her silver hairbrushes and candlesticks, her fur coat and her two tents—one for writing and one for sleeping. Her entourages of camel drivers and local guides varied in size as her journeys progressed. She traveled with her signature wardrobe of carefully selected dresses, with a pistol or two in her petticoats and a crate of valuable gifts for the sheiks (rifles and collapsible Zeiss telescopes). When challenged by the Bedouin, this queenly presence demanded to meet with their leader; the high style of her outfitting convinced her interlocutors that they were dealing with royalty, and she then consistently won over the sheiks with her knowledge of Arabic poetry, Bedouin customs, tribal relations, and desert geography.

That Bell survived these treks is astonishing. We are tempted in their retelling to see her adventures as good sport and good fun. However, danger lurked behind many a corner, the same way it did in her mountaineering escapades. But like Amundsen, Bell stands out for avoiding or mitigating these dangers to the extent that they become barely visible in hindsight. Only once was she held captive against her will, in the dreaded fortress of Ha'il in the center of the Arabian peninsula; after eleven days, she not only talked her way out of imprisonment, but demanded that she be given a day to photograph the legendary city before continuing on her way.

The knowledge Bell amassed on these treks, from which she reported intelligence to various British officers in an unofficial manner, was so far superior to that of any other Westerner that, when the Admiralty Intelligence Division set up shop in Cairo in 1915, she was summoned to join it, and awarded the rank of Major. The fact that she was the only woman in the entire, vast British Empire to hold such a position gives an indication of the esteem in which she was held and the indispensability of her knowledge.

In Cairo, she fell in with T.E. Lawrence—whom she had previously met at an archaeological dig—David Hogarth, Sir Gilbert Clayton and others, who dubbed themselves the "Intrusives" and were all invested in the idea of an Arab Revolt against the Turks and, in return, British support for the founding of an Arab state in some way, shape, or form. Even before Lawrence's first liaison with Sharif Hussein in Mecca, Bell was sent to Delhi to allay the fears of the Viceroy, Lord Hardinge, who, afraid of a revolt by Muslims in India, was horrified by the plans that were being cooked up in Cairo. Impressed by Bell's profound grasp of Arab affairs, Hardinge then sent her to the Mesopotamian port of Basra, which Britain had occupied, along with the Abadan oilfields in southern Persia, at the beginning of the war. She was to join the staff of Chief Political Officer Sir Percy Cox and act as liaison officer between Delhi and Cairo. Cox immediately sent her to a trial by fire: lunch with four British generals who saw no place for a woman meddling in their midst; the upshot of the lunch, at which Bell astonished the military men with her expertise, was that she found herself in an expansive and comfortable office from which she was to prepare her reports. She was commended for these by the Foreign Office, which complained that "no important information had reached either Cairo or London before her arrival."[46]

In March 1917, after a difficult campaign that included what Jan Morris has called "the most abject capitulation in Britain's military history" following the 147-day siege of Kut, the British reached Baghdad, where they promised to act "not as conquerors or enemies but as liberators."[47] A British administration was set up, with the Arab officials who had run the country for the Ottomans replaced by British political officers. Cox became the Civil Commissioner of Mesopotamia and immediately called on Bell to join him. Cox was a specialist in Persian affairs and had little knowledge of the dynamics of Mesopotamian culture. Nor were the half dozen British administrators surrounding Cox Arabists; none knew much of Iraq. Bell became Cox's indispensable source of information, instruction, and advice.

The challenges were immense. First and foremost was averting famine, but public buildings, markets, irrigation systems, and the institutions of justice, education, policing, and health all needed to be rebuilt. The language of the law, administration, commerce, and schools was to be changed to Arabic from Turkish. None of this could be done without the backing of a population that consisted of a vast multitude of religions, races, tribes, and allegiances. Leaders of all these groups came first to Bell, who spoke their language and knew of their circumstances, interests, and politics. Bell would then refer them to Cox, with a briefing on who they were and what they wanted and could offer, and what might be advisable to offer in return. These leaders were driven, at first, by the scarcity of food; while many of them expected a return of the Turks before long, making friends with the British also served as an insurance policy in case, against all odds, the British were to remain. Cox wrote of Bell that, "she had all the personnel and politics of the local communities at her fingers' end."[48]

This is one of those places in the story where it may do to pause and reflect on the role Bell was playing—specifically, the role she was playing in the context of this most complex confluence of cultures, motivations, and personal ambitions, within a period of great uncertainty and ambiguity. We do not know what exactly Bell told Cox in her many briefings with him. Nor do we the details of the pleasantries and substantive exchanges of information in the discussions Bell held with the various local stakeholders. The detailed, personal records through which we can reconstruct the minutia of Amundsen, Churchill, and other's leadership is quite simply absent in the case of Bell. Yet that she was the de facto leader in all but name in this critical stage of a soon-to-be independent country is beyond a doubt. She was able to mobilize a tremendous amount of influence—her designs and intentions were carried out by those around her, British and Arab alike. And she was the person other would-be-leaders sought primarily to influence.

This, of course, was not limited to Cox or the local Iraqis. The myriad of specialist British administrators sent to confront the institutional and engineering challenges of putting the war-torn territory back on its feet may have been experts in their fields but generally knew nothing of their new surroundings. Their first stop in Baghdad would be an hours-long briefing with Bell, who alerted them to the specific needs, problems, and attitudes of the communities in which they would be working.

What we know, too, is that the results of her efforts—or, as it was termed at the time, the results of the first Cox administration were impressive. Public hygiene improved dramatically, a cholera epidemic was stayed, and a vaccination campaign halted an outbreak of the plague; agriculture—devastated by the Turks' scorched-earth retreat—was kick-started with seed, cash and repairs to irrigation systems, and famine was averted by a successful spring crop in 1918. In 1919, responsibility for irrigation and agriculture was handed over to locally staffed civil authorities.[49]

In September 1918 Cox was reassigned to Tehran and provisionally replaced by his deputy, Arnold Wilson. Wilson was a die-hard imperialist. He had described his vision in 1914 and did not waver from it: "I should like to see it announced that Mesopotamia was to be annexed to India as a colony for India and Indians"—its desert wastes peopled "with martial races from the Punjab." Under direct rule, he believed that Iraq would become "a shining jewel in the British crown."[50] He himself ruled arbitrarily, showing little respect for the native population or for the wishes of Faisal's supporters in Syria. Meeting Iraqi nationalists in Damascus in May 1919 to discuss their desire to set up their own administration in Baghdad, Wilson dismissed their hopes as "moonshine."[51]

Relations between Wilson and Bell deteriorated rapidly; while Bell had not yet settled into a firm position regarding the future of Iraq, her "Intrusive" past inclined her toward the nationalists. "I think we are on the edge of a pretty considerable Arab nationalist demonstration with which I am a good deal in sympathy," she would later write in a letter home[52]; she would also note that "we had promised self-governing institutions, and not only made no step toward them but were busily setting up something quite different."[53] At the same time, she was convinced that an abrupt British exit, as demanded by the extreme nationalists, would result in chaos and a Turkish invasion. She found Wilson's way of dealing with his Arab interlocutors disastrous and felt that it undermined the delicate balancing act she and Cox had attempted.

In October 1919, Bell was sent to the Paris Peace Conference as part of the British delegation. It was here that she first met Faisal and immediately took a liking to him. Then, on her way back from Paris to Baghdad, she visited nationalist leaders in Damascus and was astonished both by the strength of the Baghdadi faction and by the scope of its ambitions.[54] In her report *Syria in October 1919*, she argued that the British had no options other than supporting Arab self-government in Mesopotamia. While she noted flaws in the Syrian government under Faisal, she wrote that if it collapsed, it would be on account of "British indifference and French ambition"—an accurate prediction of precisely what would happen and why. While time is not permitting of our dwelling on this point, it is significant because in the annals of British administration, certainly in this most unpredictable of times, there are few predictions that nailed both the how and the why of an ongoing foreign policy initiative. Bell, it seems, made a habit of it. We may appreciate this now, but her boss at the time, Wilson, most certainly did not. He forwarded the report to London with a note of his own explicitly contradicting Bell's views: he described her assumption that an Arab-ruled state was possible and would be "practical and popular," as "erroneous."[55]

As hatred for Wilson grew ever more pronounced, and as the British government dithered on what to do with the territory it was now administering, relations between Wilson and Bell worsened further. Wilson resented Bell's dodging of the chain of command in sending statements of her own views to higher-ups such as Edwin Montagu and Arthur Hirtzel, Secretary and Deputy Under Secretary of State for India, respectively. When she shared with an Arab friend the draft of a constitution written by a nationalist, Wilson exploded; he wrote to Cox suggesting that Bell be fired.

Then, on 4 June 1920, a united Sunni and Shi'a uprising, in part incited by Faisal's agents from Syria, broke out all across Mesopotamia. Attempts to quash it were at first ineffective and only served to reveal British weaknesses, which encouraged the rebels and escalated the conflict. The revolt was eventually put down by British forces, but only at great expense in terms of both life (on the British side, mostly the lives of Indian soldiers) and money.

But life and money were in short supply: Britain had lost a generation of young men in the trenches of France and was broke after the war. Accordingly, while there was a powerful push by the government in India and its exponents like Wilson to rule Mesopotamia with an iron hand as an adjunct colony, there was also intense pressure from Parliament, in the press, and in public opinion in London to cut Britain's losses and get out. Had oil not been prospected in Mosul, this might well have been what happened.

A further consideration for Britain was that US President Woodrow Wilson was an outright opponent of colonialism and a proponent of the doctrine of "self-determination." President Wilson's stubbornness on this point led to the establishment of League of Nations "Mandates," in which the independence of former Ottoman territories was to be "provisionally recognized subject to the rendering of administrative advice and assistance by a Mandatory [in the Middle East, France or Britain] until such time as they are able to stand alone."

Nevertheless, oil *had* been prospected in Mosul, and the British government was not quite ready to cut and run. Arnold Wilson, panicked by the vehemence of the Sunni/Shi'a uprising, executed an abrupt about-face and on 31 July 1920, only four days after Faisal's expulsion from Damascus by the French, floated the idea to London of offering the Amirate of Mesopotamia to the very same Faisal.[56] Wilson was soon replaced by his predecessor, the immensely better-liked Percy Cox; his idea found resonance in the upper reaches of the British government, however—in large part due to Bell's and Lawrence's persistent advocacy. Thus it was that, on 5 August 1920, the newly reinstated Cox received instructions from the British Cabinet to install "Faisal as ruler in Baghdad, so long as there was 'spontaneous demand…from a sufficiently representative body of public opinion in Mesopotamia.'"[57]

Placing Faisal on the throne in Iraq would, of course, be a slap in the face to France, which had only that moment expelled him from Syria. The French were furious, fearing that their own mandate would be undermined. In order to allow Britain to evade full responsibility for its own plans, on 12 January 2021, Churchill, now Colonial Secretary, instructed Cox and Bell to carry out a plebiscite that would give the appearance of "spontaneous demand" for Faisal from the Arabs of Mesopotamia. "Western political methods," according to Churchill, were "not necessarily applicable." In other words, you may cheat, kick, and steal as long as Faisal wins the vote. Churchill also convened the Cairo Conference, which took place in March, having explained to the French "how difficult it would be for him…to return to the House of Commons and explain that all British advisers were in favour of the instalment of the Emir Faisal and that nevertheless he had to recommend evacuation…because of the French point of view." In Cairo, not surprisingly, "all British advisors"—Bell and Cox among them—did show themselves "in favour of Faisal." What was discussed was not the whether, but the details—while Churchill spent most of his time painting at the pyramids.

After the Cairo Conference it became Cox and Bell's assignment to make the Faisal kingship happen. What was for Churchill the "cheapest solution," for Lawrence retribution for his poorly treated ally, and for Wilson a grave misstep, was for Bell the opportunity to realize the idea of an independent

Arab state that she alone of the administration in Baghdad had nursed for years. Even at this point, however, she did not have full support. Cox was personally neutral on the question of who should rule a future Iraq, while the official sent to accompany Faisal on his first trip to Baghdad, John Philby (father of the notorious Kim), favored a republic rather than a monarchy. Philby informed Faisal of his and Cox's positions and was promptly fired for the indiscretion.[58] Faisal, meanwhile, who had never previously set foot in Iraq and spoke with a foreign accent, took lessons from Bell on the intricacies of Mesopotamian tribal politics. He received a distinctly lukewarm reception in the Shi'ite cities of Karbala and Najaf, and it was not at all certain that his kingship was in the cards.

Having been sidelined during the Wilson years, Bell joined Cox in doing what had to be done to win the support of enough influential Iraqis to create the Faisal kingship. With her web of contacts and relationships, she was the essential player. One of the first jobs that she took on—together with Philby—was to put together a provisional Arab government: a council of ministers, each sporting a British adviser. Though Bell was ill with bronchitis on Cox's return to Baghdad, she was afforded no rest: the summer house in her garden was besieged by notable personages with their worries and questions, and Cox, unwilling to proceed without her, moved a meeting to her drawing room to discuss the appointment of the ministers and advisers—a meeting Bell attended in her dressing gown.[59]

Another job was to organize the plebiscite. Bell had earlier described a 1918–19 plebiscite carried out by Wilson, ostensibly to test support for the British direct rule that he advocated, as follows:

> The rank and file of the tribesmen, the shepherds, marsh dwellers, rice, barley and date cultivators of the Euphrates and Tigris, whose experience of statecraft was confined to speculations as to the performances of their next door neighbours, could hardly be asked who should be the next ruler of the country, and by what constitution. They would in any case have done no more but re-echo by command the formula prescribed by their immediate chiefs, and it was just as profitable besides being more expeditious to refer those questions to their chiefs only.[60]

The 1921 plebiscite was carried out in a similar manner. Bell's anti-suffragist earlier self would have been proud—the argument was similar in both cases. It was hardly our modern conception of democracy, but then, Churchill's orders were orders—clear constraints within which Bell had to operate. And, of course, Bell was convinced that the best thing for Iraq was a Faisal kingship;

she noted that "I don't for a moment hesitate about the rightness of our policy."[6]

Meanwhile, when Bell heard that the only serious opposing candidate, the newly appointed Minister of the Interior Sayyid Talib, had complained at a dinner party about British bias toward Faisal and threatened to raise 30,000 rifles in the event of a rigged election, she alerted Cox. The next day Cox's wife invited Talib to a tea party, where Bell translated for him; after tea, Talib was arrested, stuffed into an armored car, and driven to Al-Faw, whence he was transported to Ceylon—safely out of the way. (Gertrude's stepmother Florence Bell would later write to a close friend, "For you only, I will remark that the less said of a very high-handed action taken with regard to Sayyid Talib for instance or indeed (I say *this* in a whisper) to some of the engineering of the plebiscite, the better!")[7]

The plebiscite, which took place in early August, unsurprisingly showed support for Faisal registering at 96%. The result was published on 15 August, and eight days later Faisal was inaugurated as King of Iraq. At his coronation he stood between Cox and the British General Sir Aylmer Haldane, with flags of British design waving around him and, there being no Iraqi national anthem as yet, a British military band playing "God Save the King." His throne, according to one account, had been hastily constructed of Asahi beer crates.[61]

Bell's involvement in the installation of Faisal ranged from the weighty and suspect to the uncontroversial and domestic. It was she who arranged for a specially decorated train to transport him from Basra to Baghdad, and for the carpets, wall hangings, and furniture to outfit his temporary residence. Once he had been crowned, she organized receptions and dealt with palace rituals.[62] During social events, she often translated for the King; she invited him out riding, went hunting with him, and took him to see the archaeological wonders of his new land. One scholar even speaks of Bell as "Faisal's Pygmalion."[63]

Bell was at first delighted with how it had all turned out. She was needed, her herculean efforts had been rewarded, and the solution she had been the strongest champion of in Baghdad had been the one realized.

King Faisal at first relied a good deal on Bell's knowledge about his new country. As time went on, however, while they remained good friends, their politics diverged. Anti-British sentiment became pronounced, and while on the one hand, Bell sympathized—she spoke of "the impediments born of the

---

[6] To be fair, our modern conception of democracy was not fully in effect in Britain, either, where until 1918 the electorate consisted only of property-owning males.

[7] The American novelist Jon dos Passos, who was in Iraq at the time, told of a local sheik who said that all important Iraqis were now "very much afraid to be invited to tea with Cokus." (*Kingmakers*, p 130)

insanity of Britain's Near Eastern policies,"[64] took on "more often than not the positions of the nationalists,"[65] and noted that the British would be better off if they did not try to "squeeze the Arabs into our mould,"[66] to quote just a few of many such sentiments in the written record—she also believed that some nationalist ambitions were simply unworkable. On a deeper level, she still carried in her heart the naïve hope that Britain and Iraq—the two poles of her life and devotion—would serve each other best as closely-knit allies. Faisal, however, had a different agenda; he had fought for independence and now aimed to seize it. Inevitably, he distanced himself from her advice, and, while they still picnicked together and went for swims in the Tigris, he was pursuing his own mission now. This both displeased and disappointed Bell. In time, with Cox gone and Faisal treading his own path, she came to realize that her life's mission had been accomplished. Her work as Iraq's Director of Antiquities, though she threw herself into it, was incapable of filling the void. Unneeded now, vaguely dissatisfied with the result of all her efforts, and unhappy in love, Bell fell increasingly into illness and depression. She died in her Baghdad home on the night of 11–12 July 1926, to all appearances after an intentional overdose of sleeping medication.

## "The work of an army of men"

Gertrude Bell's achievement was widely recognized at the time of her death. The *New York Herald* wrote that she had "accomplished a man's work, the work of an army of men," the *New York Times* referred to her as "the uncrowned queen of Mesopotamia" and "the Egeria of the Arab Emir Feisal," and the *Times of India* noted the

> astonishing position she had built up for herself in Iraq, a position which has made her responsible, more than any other single individual, for the shape and appearance of modern Iraq as it stands today.[67]

As we have seen, Faisal himself declared that Bell was "entirely responsible for establishing the Iraqi nation." Lawrence, meanwhile, wrote to Bell's parents that "her political work—one of the biggest things a woman has ever had to do—was as finished as mine…That Irak state is a fine monument"—even though he doubted it would survive for long.[68]

As the decades have passed, however, and imperialism and colonialism, whether Turkish or British, have increasingly been recognized for what they are and were—the brutal subjection of peoples on their own lands by foreign powers for self-interested purposes of economic and geopolitical gain—Bell's reputation, to the extent that she had one beyond the Arab lands, has declined. On the one hand, one can coherently tell the story of the founding of Iraq without her; on the other, many of those who do recognize her role tend to disparage it as part of the British imperial machine, and thus, at best, highly compromised. Added to this comes the later history of the state she helped found, which has been, to say the least, unenviable. The oft-repeated charge that the imperialists drew national borders without respect for the wishes, beliefs and cultures of the people who subsequently lived on one or the other side of those borders, and the belief that this represents a major cause of the lamentable state of Iraq today, seem to point directly at Bell as well, for she was engaged in drawing borders herself. On all these counts, then, Bell appears to have blood on her hands.

Yet, describing Bell as yet another self-interested agent of British imperialism whose calamitous nation-building has led to the lamentable state of affairs in the Middle East today is too simplistic—and on many counts, simply wrong. It is wrong for a variety of widely differing reasons.

First, it is a serious misreading of Bell's own views to say simply that she was a British imperialist—a person who believed in the superiority of British to other cultures and therefore of Britain's right or, indeed, calling to rule over them. On the cultural front, Bell was a lover of Persian and Arabic poetry, which she translated beautifully and which she would recite with her friends the sheiks of the desert after dinner in their black goatskin tents on her many journeys, astonishing them with her knowledge and fluency. As an archaeologist, she was captivated by early Middle Eastern civilizations and became convinced of Josef Strzygowski's view that Western art was primarily influenced by Near Eastern rather than Roman designs. In her vision of an Arab state, she foresaw a return to the former splendor of Arab civilizations after 500 years of Ottoman rule; and in general, her view of history was hardly Europhilic. As she wrote in 1905,

> We in Europe are accustomed to think that civilization is an advancing flood that has gone steadily forward since the beginning of time. I believe we are wrong. It is a tide that ebbs and flows, reaches a high water mark and turns back again. Do you think that from age to age it rises higher than before? I wonder—and I doubt.[69]

Her admiration for the freedom, bravery, and way of life of the Bedouins contrasted with her disdain for the cramped ways and customs of her own country. The imperial belief that the culture and character of the metropolis were superior to those of the colonies simply does not jive with any of these convictions.

On the contemporary political front, both with the Intrusives at the Cairo Arab Bureau and with Lawrence on an extended visit he paid to her in Basra, Bell fantasized of an independent Arabia. She was horrified by the Sykes-Picot agreement, which she saw as a massive betrayal of the promises Britain had made in return for the revolt. When push came to shove, she not only favored Faisal's independent Iraq, but also sympathized openly with the anti-British nationalists who wanted a speedier solution to the British problem. This was, as we have seen, one of the sources of her acrimonious relationship with Arnold Wilson. And indeed, she found common ground with many of the nationalists, who recognized that simply getting rid of the British immediately would not work. The "extreme nationalist" and future Prime Minister, Yasin al-Hashimi, for example, saw a ten-year British presence in Iraq as unavoidable. Bell was also critical of the 1922 treaty between Britain and Iraq, which she said "consists exclusively of injunctions to the Iraq, harshly worded as to what [Iraq] may not do; not a syllable as to what we will do except that we shall rapidly reduce our forces as occasion serves,"[70] and she sided with the nationalists in favoring a large conscripted army as a sign of sovereignty, rather than the small army backed up by the RAF that was advocated by her colleagues.[71]

There was, in fact, often little difference between Bell's position and that of influential nationalists. In a remarkable conversation, the future Iraqi prime minister Ja'far al-'Askari, himself a leading nationalist, complained to Bell of the irrationality of those who demanded instant independence, in Iraq as in Syria. Bell describes their exchange in a letter to her father:

[Ja'far:] I say to them, you want complete independence? So do I. Do we not each and all of us dream of a beautiful maiden, her age 14, her hair touching her waist? She does not exist! So complete independence under existing conditions is impossible." I [Bell] said complete independence was what we ultimately wished to give. "My lady," he answered—we were speaking Arabic—"complete independence is never given; it is always taken"—a profound saying. "But because I believe in your honesty of purpose," he continued, "I am ready to work with you for the salvation of my country—and when I go to my brothers to persuade them to help they turn aside and say 'You're English.'" I said, "It's your turn. For the last year when I spoke to my brothers they turned from me and said 'You're an Arab.'[72]

Many of Bell's letters and reports do propound the belief that not only was British support necessary, but that considerations of British interests were paramount; but then, her official reports were required to take that line, and her letters home were to thinkers not as radical as she. And other of her writings and sayings directly contradict this take on things.

I would suggest, following scholars intimately familiar with the period and Bell, such as Paul Collins, Curator for Ancient Near East, Ashmolean Museum of Art and Archaeology at the University of Oxford, and Charles Tripp, Professor of Middle East Politics, University of London, that Bell was both a British imperialist and an Iraqi nationalist—an evident contradiction in terms.[73] She was also a thinker who could and did change her mind as situations evolved on the ground—which makes citing any given Bell quote as proof of her "point of view" a rather pointless game. All of this makes casting her as a British imperialist, and then condemning her for it, a less than useful exercise.

This brings us to the second of the reasons I think Bell is unjustly maligned: she was, remarkably for a person exercising the influence she did, not a political careerist. Gertrude Bell was, instead, an adventurer. Her childhood escapades, her extreme mountain climbing in the Alps and her astonishing desert treks all make this very clear. She did not seek out a role in the British war effort, other than that of working in the Wounded and Missing Enquiry department of the British Red Cross (which she characteristically took over soon after her arrival). She was summoned to Cairo through no initiative of her own, sent on a mission to Delhi, ordered to Basra, and finally called to Baghdad. It was the next great adventure, and she took it on keenly and intelligently, making use of her considerable talents. Of course, she also believed in it and believed in the Iraqi people she was working with. Today, much of the in-literature on leadership tells us that a leader is one who is able to recognize the needs and wishes, as well as the strengths and weaknesses of those around him (or her). And, equally importantly, act with this knowledge in mind. If there was one British citizen on the ground in Mesopotamia at the time who did this, then it was Gertrud Bell. As an adventurer, however, she was motivated not primarily by the aspirations of an imperial civil servant, but by something very different: by her love of the desert, and the desert peoples, and the beauties and intensities of Middle Eastern civilizations. One sees this clearly in her letters home, in which her comments on political machinations are so often interspersed, as if she cannot stop herself, with the sights, sounds, and colors of her surroundings, with descriptions of architecture, apparel, flora, and landscapes, as if this is what was really important. This has been pejoratively dubbed a naïve romanticism—a charge also leveled at Lawrence.

This seems to me a strange verdict to pass on a woman whose Arabic was perfect (and ran circles around Lawrence's), whose knowledge of Arabic literature was profound, who had survived intrepid journeys through the desert and learned first-hand the politics of its tribes, and who had a profound knowledge of its archaeology and history. This is hardly romanticism in the sense of naivete; rather, it represents a poetic sensitivity to sensual impressions and to the facts on the ground. And while it is precisely this sensitivity that prevented Bell from falling into the dogmas and methodologies of the British imperial civil service, it also makes her difficult to place in her milieu, which was exactly that. If Bell also often spoke the language of empire—and one can drag up any number of quotes from her letters and reports to back up this assertion as well—it is hardly surprising, given that she grew up in the midst of Edwardian England and was writing reports for an imperial power. What is more relevant is how different her reports sound from the norm, how sparkling, witty, speckled, and iconoclastic they are, immediately recognizable as "other" than those of her colleagues.

The third and probably the most significant reason for dismissing Bell's achievements is the claim that her efforts led to failure. Look at Iraq today, we will tend to say—look at the Middle East: how much suffering, oppression, conflict. Clearly whatever was done, we suppose, was done wrongly. But Bell neither made today's Iraq nor did she design the Middle East. In fact, she was presciently horrified by the two main causes of the lamentable situation today, as we shall see. What Bell achieved, together with her fellows-in-arms (and they were all fellows), was to create a workable administration in Iraq and then place Faisal I at the head of a constitutional monarchy. The crucial question thus becomes, was Faisal's kingship a good thing? And the answer appears to be an emphatic "yes."

Faisal is a largely forgotten figure today, but a voluminous 2014 biography by Ali Allawi, published by Yale University Press, may help to remind us of him. Allawi, who has served as minister of defense, trade, and finance in post-Saddam Iraq, was a professor at Singapore National University and is himself a secular Shi'ite. While he does not refrain from criticizing Faisal on several counts, his overall verdict is immensely positive—so much so that he claims Faisal deserves the epithet "The Great." He characterizes Faisal's reign as one of moderation, realism, flexibility, and tolerance—rare and truly noteworthy qualities—and claims that Faisal "accomplished far more, on the battlefield and as king of Iraq, than any other Arab in the past several centuries."[74] "It would be hard to find an equivalent figure who combined the qualities of leadership and statesmanship with the virtues of moderation, wisdom and decency," Allawi writes. Tolerant and inclusive, he successfully built bridges to the most disparate communities in his kingdom, from Shi'as to Jews to Christians to Kurds, in his attempt to shape an open, pluralistic society. "Anyone who sows discord between Muslim, Christian, and Jew is not an Arab," Faisal admonished in 1918.[75] As King he reserved two days a week for audiences with ordinary Iraqis, permitted the Jesuits to establish Baghdad College, made contributions to schools of Sunnis, Shiites, Christians and Jews, and was a conservationist who planted trees throughout the country and founded the Iraqi Agricultural College and the Ministry of Agriculture. At the same time, he skillfully negotiated his country's increasing independence from British power and influence, confronting any number of apparently irresolvable dilemmas on the way. And this is the same man, we must remember, who led an "army" of Bedouins, aged 12 to 60, whose members "came and went," with no established chain of command, to a stunning victory over the forces of the Ottoman Empire—and on the way, paid his warriors a bounty for prisoners captured alive, in order to prevent the traditional throat-slitting of captives, which he deplored.[876]

What went so wrong, then? According to Allawi, it was not Iraq's constitution, not the country's gradual severance from Britain, not its borders and not the fact that a Sunni minority ruled over a Shi'a majority, nor the fact that the Kurds had no place in it, that destroyed the pluralistic project of Iraq. The real cause of the eternal battlefield that the Middle East turned into was the creation of the state of Israel on Arab-inhabited lands in 1948. This event gave rise to new kinds of leaders in the Arab world, among whom tolerance and inclusiveness were bad words. At this point, "Any recognition of the diversity of populations and the complexity of loyalties in the Arab Middle East [was] swept away by a stultifying and hollow [Arab] nationalism."[77]

Bell had argued against supporting Zionism and had firmly opposed the Balfour Declaration of 2 November 1917, which committed Britain to supporting the establishment of a "Jewish national home" in Palestine. She presciently predicted what it would lead to: "[T]o gratify Jewish sentiment you would have to override every conceivable political consideration, including the wishes of the vast majority of the population," she wrote in January 1918, and, on 4 February 1921,

---

[8] Allawi's admiration for Faisal is not shared by all. Rory Stewart describes Faisal's rule as "corrupt, inadequate, and violent," and the Baghdadi historian Elie Kedourie considered the Faisal solution a disaster, a result of "the fluent salesmanship of Lloyd George, the intermittent, orotund and futile declamations of Lord Curzon, the hysterical mendacity of Colonel Lawrence, the brittle cleverness and sentimental enthusiasm of Miss Bell, and the resigned acquiescence of Sir Percy Cox." (*Kingmakers*, p 189). I find Allawi's scholarship more convincing, and so have emphasized it here, but your views may well differ from mine.

The French in Syria, Zionism in Palestine, form a stupendous barrier to honest dealing with the Arabs, only in Mesopotamia can we pursue an honest policy…The impasse in Palestine differs considerably from that which has been reached in Syria; there is a quite obvious way out, namely the abandonment of the Zionist policy."[78]

Ironically, the Balfour Declaration was an utterly cynical act. Its purpose was to thwart French ambitions in Palestine while appearing "high-minded" enough to silence the anti-colonialist US President, Woodrow Wilson.[79] As the just-ousted British Prime Minister Henry Asquith said of his successor at the time of the Declaration,

Lloyd George…does not care a damn for the Jews or their past or their future, but thinks it would be an outrage to let the Christian Holy Places…pass in to the possession of "Agnostic Atheist France"![80]

Faisal himself, adopting a typically tolerant stance, had been willing to countenance Jewish immigration to Palestine, but was unambiguous in his opposition to a Jewish state, for the same reasons as Bell. Faisal only gave his conditional approval to the so-called Faisal-Weizmann Agreement on the advice of Lawrence, who deceived him on this count as he had on Sykes-Picot. Faisal could not read the English document and relied on Lawrence's oral translation, and on Lawrence's assurances that the Zionist leader would make no claim to a Jewish state.[81] Lawrence knew full well that the contrary was the case. Faisal was wily enough to append a codicil in Arabic, however, which effectively nullified the concessions he had been tricked into making.

To Alawi's reading of the true causes of the long-term troubles in the Middle East we can add yet another factor: the premature death of Faisal himself. In Faisal, Iraq and the Middle East as a whole had a capable and credible leader who, like Bell, was able to read the immensely complex circumstances and build solutions accordingly. The Balfour Declaration, the tumult of the Second World War and the creation of Israel in 1948 made a complex region all the more complex; if there was one person who could have negotiated this complexity and maintained Iraq on a productive course, it would have been Faisal. Faisal died young, however—at the age of 50—in murky circumstances while recuperating in Bern, Switzerland in September of 1933.

The Sykes-Picot agreement brings us to the fourth reason that Bell is often dismissed: the drawing of borders. Sykes-Picot can stand in for everything the imperial powers did wrong in the Middle East, and, as noted above, it still reverberates today (see the ISIS videos on YouTube). Not only did it represent an explicit betrayal of the Arabs by the west, and not only did it presume that the Middle East was a playground for imperial powers to divvy up as they chose, but it also made a border so arbitrary as to show a mind-boggling lack of concern, even for imperial powers, for the realities on the ground. "From the 'e' in Acre to the final 'k' in Kirkut" was a straight line for the sake of having a straight line.

That Sykes-Picot was never actually implemented made little difference—its principle of dividing up Arab territory into spheres of western influence without the slightest notion that the inhabitants might have something to say about the matter, and the fact that it did so in secret, breaking solemn promises, rendered all future western acts suspicious in the Arab world; its publication by the Bolsheviks just weeks after the Balfour Declaration reinforced this message. The arbitrary drawing of borders by Sykes-Picot is cited on all sides as an indication of Western arrogance and blindness. And it has, it seems, cast a shadow over *all* drawing of borders.

Gertrude Bell is often said to have drawn the borders of modern Iraq. This is, in fact, a gross exaggeration. The borders of the new Iraq remained pretty much those of the Ottoman vilayets of Basra, Baghdad, and Mosul. Bell did help Cox to draw up borders to the south, between Iraq and what is today Saudi Arabia. These became controversial not because they were poorly drawn, but because the Bedouins in the area didn't want any borders at all. In fact, no borders that would have satisfied them. Yet once the decision was made to establish Iraq as a modern state, borders had to be drawn somewhere, and Bell was probably not a bad choice to do it. The northern borders around Mosul, meanwhile, were drawn up after prolonged work by a League of Nations committee in 1926. It is true that Bell, like Faisal, argued for the inclusion of Mosul in Iraq, largely to balance out the Shi'a majority with an increased number of Sunnis; the real influence in determining the inclusion of Mosul, though, can be spelled in three letters—oil—and it is unlikely that anything Bell might have said pro or contra would have counteracted that influence.

Thus, the "line in the sand" drawn by Sykes and Picot and the borders that Bell did actually advise Cox on have little in common, either in their scale, their import or their effect. What joins them is that both were drawn by White westerners. Most would agree that White westerners had no place drawing any lines in the sand at all. But whether Gertrude Bell should have been drawing what borders she did draw at the time and in the circumstances in which she drew them, given that the imperial enterprise was a fact and that her desire was not to create a colony but an independent Arab nation has little to do with the much larger problem—and at the time, the given—of unwanted western presence in other parts of the world. Far from representing a betrayal and imperial arrogance, like the Sykes-Picot borders, Bell's were part of the attempt to establish, rather than undermine, an independent Arab state.

## Stuck in Between

Gertrude Bell's strength lay in her intimate knowledge of an area's geography and natural history (much like Amundsen) and the ways of life of its people (much like Toussaint). This knowledge allowed each of them to negotiate the perils of what in Amundsen's case were geographical and climatic and in Bell's case geopolitical givens. While Amundsen was the acknowledged leader of his expedition, Bell's "leadership" was entirely unseen, though some newspapers of her day referred to her as the uncrowned queen of Iraq. Bell's form of back-stage leadership by depth of knowledge, establishment of relationships and behind-the-scenes negotiations was imposed on her by her gender, but I would argue that it also fit her profile as an outdoorswoman, as a climber, and a desert explorer, as an admirer of wild and empty landscapes. Such a character is urged on by a desire for freedom—freedom from conventions, from restrictions, from established roles and, dare I say it, freedom from the state. Bell achieved all of these freedoms, and one of the contradictions in her life is that she, an outdoorswoman who literally outfoxed the rules of various governments in undertaking her desert journeys, should have been instrumental precisely in establishing a government.[9] Lawrence expressed a similar sentiment in a letter he wrote to Bell's parents on hearing of her death: "It seems such a very doubtful benefit—government—to give to a people who have long done without."[82]

If Bell was going to help establish a state, it could hardly have happened in the conventional manner of a senior civil servant, with all its trappings and regulations; she did it her way, a way that she invented on the spot. Her unorthodox methods and her lack of respect, at times, for authorities and regulations she was expected to kowtow to, drove certain people to dismiss her or to rage against her (Arnold Wilson, Mark Sykes, Edwin Montagu), but despite the fact that she was a woman working in an otherwise exclusively male world, and a woman who did not play by all the rules of that or any other world, she was so skilled at what she did and so acutely able to read the

---

[9] In 1914, for example, she was told both by the British and by the Turks not to venture past Ziza; she ignored the British Ambassador, told the Turkish soldiers she would only be visiting a couple of local archaeological sites, and "decided to run away." "I am an outlaw," she then wrote, as she escaped into the desert on her way to Ha'il. (Gertrude Bell diary entry, 16 January 1914. http://gertrudebell.ncl.ac.uk/diary_details.php?diary_id=1066)

relations and positions and aspirations of the people in the environment in which she moved, and the characteristics of the desert environment itself—having mapped its wells and wadis, dunes and mountains, crumbling churches and ancient cities—that she was (embarrassingly, one might even say) indispensable for the functioning of that male world.

At the beginning of this chapter, we met Bell in an awkward position between two men: standing on the shoulders of Heinrich Fuhrer, with Ulrich Fuhrer, in turn, standing on her shoulders, blindly searching for a grip. The best-known photograph of Bell shows her, on camelback, between two other men (both of them less accomplished camel-riders): Winston Churchill and Lawrence of Arabia—both also, in a sense, searching blindly for a grip.

Bell was also, twice, caught between two men in her emotional life. As a young woman in Tehran she fell deeply in love with the British legation secretary Henry Cadogan, with whom she galloped into the marvelous and secretive desert landscape and learned to love Persian poetry. But her father, the iron magnate Sir Hugh Bell, opposed their marriage; Cadogan, Sir Hugh's investigations had revealed, was a man of no means with sizable gambling debts. Squeezed between her love for Cadogan and her intense, lifelong reverence for her father, Bell chose the latter and informed Cadogan that they were impossible. It almost broke her.

Two decades later, in the run-up to the Great War, Bell fell deeply in love again, this time with a British Major turned military consul, Dick Doughty-Wylie. They spent little time together but developed a passionate and remarkably explicit epistolary relationship. The problem, this time, was that Doughty-Wylie was married. This did not stop him from meeting Bell secretly, both in her bedroom at her family's estate and for a four-day interlude in London, but it did prevent them from ever physically consummating their relationship (as far as we know). Bell was on the brink of throwing all to the wind and ceding to her desires, whatever the cost, but when it came down to it, she was unable to face what she knew would be society's—and, above all, her father's—reproaches for being a party to adultery. She begged her would-be lover to end his relationship with his wife, Judith, so that they could be together openly and honestly, and he was on the verge of doing so. When Judith threatened to kill herself if he left her, however, Doughty-Wylie was paralyzed. At the same time, Bell was threatening him with her own suicide:

Do you remember that my doctor made me take morphia with me on the last journey [through the desert]? I never used it, and now I have sent for it from home, and have it always by me…Two full tubes…enough to cut a thread even as strong as mine."[83]

In the end it was neither of the women who cut the thread; instead, it was Doughty-Wylie, torn between duty and desire, who came up with a novel way of doing himself in: he volunteered to return to the battlefield, then led one of the ill-fated assaults on Gallipoli—armed only with a cane. He thus attained both honor (a Victoria Cross for bravery) and a way out of his irresolvable problems. He left a broken Gertrude Bell, whose work in Iraq became a temporary palliative, but who succumbed to her pain when that work petered out.

In both of her love affairs, despite her brash nature and her imperturbable resolve, Bell was never able to take the final step and do what she knew would lead to a break with her father. This pattern held true also in the ultimate conflict she found herself in—this time between two kings. Arguably responsible more than any other actor for the establishment of the administration and then the monarchy of Iraq, her loyalties were torn between King George and King Faisal. Despite her embrace of Iraqi nationalism on many counts, despite her clear-sighted condemnation of the failures and hypocrisy of British imperial policies in the Middle East, and despite her initial (and well justified) admiration for and support of Faisal, she became disillusioned with him when he failed to take the harsh measures she judged necessary to quell the extreme nationalist movement in Iraq. Her judgment here was wrong—Faisal was a more skilled reader of this situation and acted out of more straightforward motivations. Bell's divided loyalties, both between Iraq and Great Britain, and between her father and her (almost) lovers, in the end proved too much for her and did her in. In the meantime, however, her leadership from behind cleared the way for the reign of a great king and for his bold attempt at creating a moderate, tolerant, and inclusive nation under the most difficult of circumstances.

# The Myth of the Phoenix and the British Bulldog. Winston Churchill

## Taking the Life of a Child

Sailors aboard the French fleet stationed in the North African harbor of Mers-el-Kébir woke up on 3 July 1940 to find a large British Naval formation just offshore. Its sudden appearance came as a surprise. The previous month, British and French troops had fought side by side against Hitler's invasion of France. Now, barely a week since the fighting on the continent had ceased, British ships were aiming their guns at the French.

The British fleet, known as Task Force H, had been dispatched by Winston Churchill, Britain's Prime Minister during the Second World War. Churchill is a regular contender on lists of history's greatest leaders. The iconic image of the top-hatted Prime Minister brandishing a Tommy Gun, a smirk on his face and a cigar in his mouth, evokes much the same spirit of dogged resistance today that it did to observers when the photograph was taken in 1940. He is an especially interesting subject for this book since the prevalent reading of his greatness as a wartime leader simply does not correspond to the historical facts. The Action Fallacy has reared its head and delivered a Churchill whose success is based on his rhetorical skill and his penchant for bold and daring exploits. Nothing could be further from the truth.

The incident at Mers-el-Kébir, which he later compared to "taking the life of one's own child," is a case in point.[1] Often cited as an example of his predilection for rash, unrestrained action, it was instead, as we shall see, a carefully calculated move that served several long- and short-term strategic purposes, part of a well-crafted plan based on an acutely accurate reading of the immensely complex circumstances with which he was faced. To make this

M. Gutmann, *The Unseen Leader*, https://doi.org/10.1007/978-3-031-37829-4_6

point, we have to leave the waters of the Mediterranean on that fateful day behind and examine the larger context of that eventful summer.

There can hardly have been a less enviable time to be Prime Minister of the United Kingdom than the summer of 1940. A year before, in September 1939, Hitler had invaded Poland, triggering the start of the Second World War in Europe. Though the ease with which his troops subdued Poland surprised many observers, it still seemed to most that he had limited room to maneuver. French and British troops had taken up defensive positions behind the concrete fortifications of the Maginot Line and along the border with Belgium and Luxembourg, ready to counter Hitler's army. They waited in place throughout the fall and winter, but no invasion came. The British Press dubbed it the *Sitzkrieg* (sitting war) rather than the *Blitzkrieg* (lightning war). Then, in April 1940, Hitler confounded expectations by sending his troops north to seize Denmark and Norway, whence British troops were forced to make a hasty and embarrassing retreat.

It was only on the very day Churchill took office, 10 May 1940, that Hitler sent his tank armies west. And west they went: over the course of the next few weeks, the combined armies of Britain, France, Belgium, and Holland collapsed under the attack by Hitler's smaller but far more agile forces. The British Expeditionary Force, Britain's preeminent land-fighting army, only narrowly escaped complete destruction by German tanks. Saved at the last moment by a naval evacuation, the decimated force abandoned the bulk of its weaponry and vehicles on French beaches outside the town of Dunkirk. France itself surrendered on 22 June. In Britain, rumors of an imminent German invasion made the rounds. The months ahead would see the loss of over 40,000 British civilian lives in the so-called *Blitz*, as waves of German bombing raids wreaked havoc on the island's cities.[2] It seemed that Britain stood alone. This was the turbulent summer in which Churchill sent 18 ships, including an aircraft carrier and two battleships, to Mers-el-Kébir.

Mers-el-Kébir, "Great Harbor" in Arabic, is a natural port at the foot of Mount Santon in the Gulf of Oman, in present-day Algeria. It had been vital for the projection of French power into North Africa and across the Mediterranean since the 1830s. With a mountain range stretching horn-like into the water and a sea wall paralleling the coastline, the base provided snug and secure anchorage. When the British arrived, they found four battleships and five destroyers moored in two neat rows. While the bulk of the British fleet remained in deeper waters, at optimal range for using their main guns, a lone destroyer, the *Foxhound*, sailed toward the harbor entrance to deliver an ultimatum to the French admiral: join the British Navy, intern the ships in an American or British port, or scuttle the fleet. If the French refused, the British would destroy them. But the French admiral, Marcel-Bruno Gensoul, proved a stubborn and evasive negotiator, and by early afternoon the resolve of the British task force Commander, Sir James Somerville, began to weaken. The temptation to find a peaceful way out was huge, as the moral and political costs of an unprovoked attack on France were bound to be significant. Somerville signaled to Churchill in London that he was "of the view that the use of force should be avoided at all costs."[3]

In his original orders to Somerville, Churchill had openly admitted that he was asking him to undertake the "most disagreeable task that a British Admiral has ever been faced with." Nonetheless, Churchill remained firm. He doubled down with an unambiguous reply: "Firm intention of HMG [her majesty's government] that if French will not accept any of your alternatives they are to be destroyed." Churchill knew that the French were playing for time, hoping that darkness or a French relief force would arrive before the British attacked. He spent the afternoon pacing nervously back and forth in the Cabinet Room in Whitehall in London. At 6:26 p.m., he fired off another message to the fleet: "French ships must comply with our terms or sink themselves or be sunk by you before dark." Unbeknownst to Churchill, this final message was moot. By the time he sent it, the carnage had already begun.[4]

When negotiations had finally broken down shortly before 6:00 p.m., Somerville had ordered his ships to open fire. Explosives rained down on helpless French sailors as they desperately tried to maneuver their ships into deeper water. Four massive 15-inch shells struck the *Dunkerque,* setting off fires and explosions below deck and disabling its steering and electronics. The ship ran aground. At 6:04 p.m., a shell struck the munitions hold of the French destroyer *Bretagne*, setting it ablaze. It sank rapidly, together with 977 of its crew. A few ships managed to escape from the harbor, but they were immediately set upon by British seaplanes. By the end of the engagement a few hours later, seven of the ten French ships had been sunk or disabled, and 1250 French sailors were dead.

At first glance, the attack at Mers-el-Kébir invites familiar conclusions about what made Churchill the wartime leader he was: impatient, offensively minded and above all thirsting for action. In looking back on Churchill's role in World War I, Kemal Ataturk remarked, "History is ruthless to those who lack ruthlessness."[5] At Mers-el-Kébir, Churchill did not lack for any. In fact, to many contemporary observers, the attack was not only bold but foolhardy. Somerville called it "the biggest political blunder of modern times…[one that] will rouse the whole world against us."[6]

Somerville's concern was understandable. At the beginning of July 1940, the disposition of the new French government was still far from certain. That

Germany was France's new overlord may have been clear, but the nature of the relationship was not. Would France be a thorn in Germany's side and use its colonial resources, outside of Germany's grasp, to keep the spirit of French resistance alive and help its British friends?[7] Or would it be an eager accomplice in Hitler's dark designs for the continent? No one knew, but sinking the French fleet seemed a sure-fire way to tip the balance of French opinion toward aligning itself with the country's new German masters, rather than with France's former ally, Britain.

Churchill understood this strategic dimension. He was also aware of the moral costs of an unprovoked attack on a French fleet. Why, then, did he order it to go ahead? The answer has little to do with a penchant for action, and everything to do with Churchill's understanding of the strategic dimensions of the long war ahead. The sinking of the French fleet was a brilliant chess move on the complex strategic board of that summer—the consequences of which few but Churchill understood at the time.

## The Churchill Myth

Churchill must be celebrated with care. He was an unabashed colonialist, racist in his thinking and more-than-once brutal in his policies toward the inhabitants of Britain's far-flung territories. We should in no way place Churchill on a figurative pedestal when there is legitimate talk about removing him from several literal ones. At the same time, the Second World War remains the most profound event of the twentieth century and represents one of the most complex leadership challenges imaginable. As the chief architect of the Allies' success in defeating Italy and Germany, Churchill remains a legitimate, if not obligatory, target of inquiry for a book examining leadership.

Despite his fame, or perhaps because of it, Churchill is a difficult figure to study. As a subject of academic inquiry, few events in human history can match the word count produced by the Second World War, and within this literature, Churchill figures prominently: over 10,000 books bear his name in their title (not to mention the many tens of thousands more that discuss his life and work).[8] But it is not only the voluminous nature of work on the Second World War and by extension Churchill that makes it a challenge to try to understand him. Unlike events remote in time or irrelevant to the contemporary observer, the Second World War continues to evoke emotional responses from observers today. How politicians of the former combatant nations choose to apologize or take credit for various dimensions of the war still creates shock waves at home and abroad. This makes sense; the war touched the lives of billions of people and upended nearly every aspect of life as they knew it. Much of what has been written about the war and Churchill, especially when it is centered on the war's most iconic moments, is steeped in lore—in deep narrative ruts in which myth and reality can be hard to tell apart. Because we may only just have enough distance between us and the event—and the role of one man in it—to examine it soberly, it requires extra care.

This is nowhere more true than of the events of the summer of 1940, which left Britain, in Churchill's words, "standing alone in the breach." The classic story of the war has it that, at this dramatic nadir of their fortunes, the British establishment and population were on the verge of caving to Nazi pressure, that the country stood alone in the face of an imminent Nazi threat, and that it was only Churchill's stubborn grit and eloquent words that staved off disaster. Elements of this myth can be gleaned in numerous places. The American Public Broadcasting Service (PBS), for example, has a twelve-event timeline of the war up until 1941 on its website. Starting at entry 8, they are "Churchill becomes Prime Minister," "The Miracle of Dunkirk," "Paris falls to the Nazis," and, tersely, "Britain fights for its life."[9] A recent article in *Forbes*, one of dozens that extract leadership truths from Churchill's example, sums the situation up as follows: "The Germans had absolute control of all of Europe. It seemed impossible that Britain could survive."[10] One author writes, "[Churchill] led a nation fighting for its life [...] At his best in adversity, he showed a never-say-die attitude that was infectious."[11]

The Churchill myth, then, has two components. The first is that Britain's survival was at stake—that, had it not been for the intervention of one bold leader, the country would have fallen to Nazi Germany. The second piece of the myth is that Churchill won the war by inspiring his fellow Britons through his fiercely eloquent words and ceaseless agitation for action.

This view is steeped in misinterpretations, both of the contours of the war and of Churchill's role in bringing it to a successful conclusion. When one digs below all the mythology, it becomes abundantly clear that Churchill's success was not in fact determined by his oft-cited mastery of language or his offensive spirit. Equally clear is that there are scant facts to support the narrative of a nearly beaten island standing alone and then rising again like a phoenix. Historians are nearly united in the judgment that Britain was never in any danger of being invaded. The decision to fight on was thus neither heroic nor bold, neither outlandish nor foolhardy. Churchill knew perfectly well that if Hitler ever decided to launch a cross-channel invasion the Germans would face almost impossible odds. This much is indelibly clear from the last decades of historical research. Nonetheless, since the phoenix interpretation has been so persistent in popular culture, it is worth taking a closer look at all the evidence that speaks against it.

There was no doubt that Hitler's victory in Western Europe had been crushing and Churchill and others certainly had the utmost respect for the fighting abilities of the German armed forces. In the short campaign for France and the Low Countries, 90,000 Allied soldiers had been killed, 200,000 wounded and mind-boggling 1.9 million captured.[12] Yet, Hitler's tanks could obviously not sweep across the waters of the Channel the way they had across the flatlands of northern France. With the Royal Air Force on a par with the *Luftwaffe* and the British Navy far superior in quality and quantity to the German *Kriegsmarine*, German troop and vehicle carriers—likely a collection of barges and other hastily acquired civilian craft—would have proved easy targets for British gunners. The internal assessments of German military planners in the summer of 1940 were themselves nearly unanimous in predicting doom should a cross-Channel invasion go ahead—a telling evaluation, coming as it did from a group of officers fresh off a series of stunning victories and not generally known for shirking from daunting exploits.[13] Although Hitler ordered preparations made for a possible landing, his senior officers could tell that his attitude was uncharacteristically half-hearted. The German Commander-in-Chief, Gerd von Rundstedt, didn't even bother attending trial beach landings.[14]

This point is hammered home when one thinks about how hard it was for the Allies to establish a firm foothold on the continent during their invasion of Normandy four years later, despite the fact that by that point, they had complete naval and air superiority—on D-Day the Allied air forces flew 14,000 sorties compared to the *Luftwaffe's 275*—and were able to call on a quantity and quality of dedicated material wholly unavailable to Germany in 1940: 11,000 support aircraft, 7000 purpose-built military landing craft and transport ships, an armada of 1213 naval warships in support, and a host of other custom-built technologies, such as floating docks, cross-Channel pipelines, a tide-predicting machine, and a variety of specialized landing and fighting vehicles.[15] In the summer of 1940, the only card the Germans could have played to even begin to level the odds involved in an invasion of Great Britain would have been to seize the ships of the French Navy. This card, however, had been taken from them when Churchill neutralized the French fleet in early July, in the operation involving the destruction of the ships in Mers-el-Kébir. Therein lies the first piece of strategic wisdom behind his controversial move. At the end of this chapter, we will be in a position to appreciate the second.

Churchill and the British military leadership knew that the threat of an invasion was chimeric. Looking back on the situation after the war, Churchill wrote soberly,

> Those of us who were responsible at the summit in London understood the physical structure of our Island strength and were sure of the spirit of the nation. The confidence with which we faced the immediate future was not founded, as was commonly supposed abroad, upon audacious bluff or rhetorical appeal, but upon a sober consciousness and calculation of practical facts.[16]

In addition to facing no outright threat of invasion from Germany, Britain was never in fact alone. British historian David Edgerton recently took on this myth in his exhaustive book *Britain's War Machine*. Edgerton shows that Britain was in fact a "world island," with London at the center of an expansive empire that was able to call on resources, scientific know-how, and manpower from all over the world.[17] Alongside the exhaustive resources of the Empire, thousands of Polish, Czech, French, and other continental soldiers who had fled the advancing German army were now encamped on the island, all of whom were eager to get back into the fight.

Where then did the myth of Britain's standing alone, and its imminent collapse in the face of a Nazi onslaught come from? It was in fact Churchill, as much as anyone else, who was the architect of this myth. But why? For one, Churchill was, as we will see below in detail, preparing his citizens for a long fight. This required what modern leadership scholars call a "burning platform" attitude—the sense that one's back is against the wall and that the only option is to take the plunge.[18] The "crisis" of the summer of 1940 was to a large extent a creation of Churchill's fancy, rather than a real one. In a series of speeches during the summer and fall of 1940, Churchill wove a particular narrative about where Britain was and what it needed to do—what modern management scholars would call "storytelling." With his evocation of the possibility of Britain's "long island story" coming to an end with "each one of us [lying] choking in his own blood upon the ground," and his claim that Britain was "to stand alone in the breach," he intentionally cultivated what he knew to be a myth.[19] Not everyone fell for it. A popular cartoon from the summer of 1940 shows two British soldiers looking out from a beach onto the water beyond. One of them says, "So our poor old Empire is alone in the world." The other responds, "Aye, we are—the whole five hundred million of us."[1]

---

[1] As David Edgerton and others have pointed out, when Churchill spoke of "alone" and "we" he was always referring to the British Empire, not the English nation—a point that was largely obscured after the war.

Churchill's masterful leadership stroke was not to rouse a reluctant nation to fight for its survival. Its survival was all but guaranteed, whether or not the British public was motivated to fight. To be sure, by the end of 1940 the world was in a new equilibrium. Hitler was the undoubted master of the continent; his new empire stretched from the Norwegian Arctic to the Mediterranean. Yet at the same time, Britain was perfectly secure. There was no threat of an invasion of the island itself, nor to much of its extensive global empire. (The threat that did exist was to its possessions in Asia, where the Japanese were poised to threaten Hong Kong, Singapore, and other valuable British territories—though this was not yet evident in the summer of 1940.) Hitler was well aware of this fact, and repeatedly tried to sue for peace with Churchill—once in May and once again in July. Other politicians might have taken the bait, and Churchill was under some pressure from his cabinet to consider making a deal. He remained firm.

Yet in sticking to his guns—and this is the vital point—he was not leading a nation on the brink of destruction. Churchill made the decision to mobilize his nation to *fight and destroy* Nazism not in order to survive, but because he recognized in Nazism an evil of a wholly new order. As early as 1933, when Hitler had just assumed power, Churchill had been one of the few voices condemning the Nazi regime. When his colleagues began appeasing Hitler in the lead-up to the war, he unequivocally opposed it. When Hitler invaded Poland, Churchill told the House of Commons that Britain would not be fighting for Poland alone but rather,

> to save the whole world from the pestilence of Nazi tyranny and in defense of all that is most sacred to man. This is no war of domination or imperial aggrandizement or material gain: no war to shut any country out of its sunlight or means of progress."[20]

In the summer of 1940, Churchill doubled down on his conviction that Britain should fight to defeat Nazi Germany. It would cost Britain dearly. It would cost others even more.

# A New Kind of War

The Second World War is by most metrics the most catastrophic event in human history. If one includes the Japanese invasion of China—which I believe one should—the war lasted for nine years, from 1937 to 1945. It saw violent engagements on every inhabited continent, from the remote Aleutian volcanoes off Alaska to the island of Mauritius in the desolate reaches of the Indian Ocean. Armies battled in the deserts of North Africa and on the beaches of Normandy. The war was massive in both scope and scale. Guerilla bands harassed occupying armies from Indochina to Yugoslavia. Bombs rained down on civilians in London, Dresden, and Tokyo, as well as numerous forgotten towns like Wieluń in Poland, almost completely flattened by German Stuka dive bombers in 1939. And then there were what historian Timothy Snyder calls the "bloodlands"—the vast expanses of Eastern Europe (Snyder's focus) and the Chinese mainland where massive armies clashed repeatedly and inflicted hell on civilian populations. The war was global and brutal to an extent no previous conflict had ever been.

Well over 60 million people lost their lives during World War II. And beyond the sheer numbers come the deliberate and deliberately inhumane ways in which many of these individuals met their fate. The Nazi-orchestrated Holocaust stands out for the pernicious focus of its perpetrators and for its dedicated infrastructure of death. But remorseless cruelty to fellow humans took many forms and occurred under many flags. Long before Auschwitz became the center of Hitler's Final Solution, German soldiers and paramilitary forces machine-gunned Jewish men, women, and children into makeshift mass graves. On many occasions they were helped by eager locals—Ukrainians, Russians, Romanians, Lithuanians, and others.

I came across one of the uncountable such stories years ago when I was researching in the archives of the Swedish Military Intelligence Service and State Security. The Swedish authorities interviewed all Swedes returning from voluntary service in the German armed forces (yes, there were such men). During one of these interviews, a young Swede recalled how in the early months of the invasion of the Soviet Union, his elite "Wiking" Division had forced a group of Jews to dig a trench. The troops then took turns swinging rifle butts at the Jews' heads. Finally, "the rest were told to fight to the death with their shovels in the grave, with the promise that the survivors would be let out. They were also shot."[21] Perhaps as shocking as the story itself is the fact that the Swedish authorities simply noted this tale of barbarism by one of its citizens on a standard interview form, shoved it into a filing cabinet, and sent the young man on his way.

But Europe was far from the only stage on which atrocities occurred. In their campaign to subdue China, Japanese units murdered droves of helpless civilians and engaged in the highly ritualized mutilation of prisoners of war. This violence reached an early crescendo in 1937 with the so-called Rape of Nanjing. Japanese soldiers slaughtered some 30,000–40,000 civilians in this ancient Chinese city. Many of the victims were young women who were gang-raped and then speared with bayonets in their genitals.[22]

This was a war, then, in which instigated murder and misery—part of war since time immemorial—took on previously unknown dimensions. The brutality has often been explained as a relapse into medieval barbarism. In fact, however, the opposite is the case: the war took its dreadful toll on people precisely because of its modernity. It was the result of a toxic mix of ideological extremism, binding patriotism, industrial production, bureaucratic know-how, and technological advance.

The change had been long in the making, and the Second World War itself represented but the culmination of certain trends that had developed over the previous half century. It is difficult to single out one date at which these trends had their genesis, but a possible choice would be 1898. In that year, an Anglo-Egyptian army was sent up the Nile to quell a Sudanese uprising around the village of Omdurman. The battle that ensued marked the end of an age in military tactics, and the beginning of another. At one stage in the battle, General Horatio Kitchener ordered his cavalry to dislodge a group of Sudanese warriors taking shelter around a cluster of huts. Kitchener's horsemen, led by a young lieutenant, set off to accomplish the task. Unbeknownst to them and obscured from view, a large trench filled with Sudanese warriors lay between the horsemen and their target. The charging cavalry, men and horses all, plunged into the mass of enemy soldiers. As the lieutenant leading the charge later recalled, the result was vicious hand-to-hand combat with "horses spouting blood, men bleeding from terrible wounds, fish-hook spears stuck right through them."[23] Twenty-two cavalrymen lost their lives along with an unknown number of Sudanese. The lieutenant, who emptied his 10-shot pistol before retreating to safety, was Winston Churchill.

The cavalry charge, a staple of military tradition since the days of the Mongols, would never be employed by British forces again. Nor was its replacement far away. On the exact same battlefield on which Churchill's cavalry was fighting for its life, other British soldiers were training a new weapon—a stubby cylinder mounted on a tripod—on the main party of Sudanese. The Maxim gun, capable of firing over 500 rounds per minute, ensured that the battle was a one-sided affair. 11,000 Sudanese were killed in the fighting, most of them mowed down by the Maxims and long-distance fire by British infantry. The British suffered fewer than 50 deaths.[24] The significant development here lies not only in the technological capability of the Maxim gun, but also in the willingness of officers and gunners to mow down what at that moment were essentially helpless human beings.

By the turn of the century, the British Empire had become the largest the world had ever seen. The small island nation directly controlled a quarter of the world's population and a fifth of its inhabited landmass, and exerted influence over much of the rest. Military intervention to subdue those who resisted British rule was, if not a regular occurrence, hardly an exception. The Battle at Omdurman may have been, from the perspective of the British, little more than another colonial adventure (from the perspective of the Sudanese, of course, it was a massacre), but it was also a model for things to come. When war broke out in Europe a decade and a half later, the consequences of modern weaponry like the Maxim gun became clear for all to see. In 1915, while Shackleton and his crew were battling for their lives in the South Atlantic, scenes played out in the trenches of Europe that had no parallel in history. On one sunny June day in 1916—let me repeat, on *one* day—the British Army lost 57,000 men.[25] This was twice as many casualties as had occurred during the entire 14-year War of Spanish Succession.

Such unfathomable numbers obscure the agonizing individuality of the deaths that occurred in the trenches, day in and day out. After the war, a French soldier recalled the death of one of his colleagues when an Austrian shell exploded:

> His face was burned; one splinter entered his skull behind the ear; another slit open his stomach, broke his spine, and in the bloody mess one saw his spinal cord gliding about. His right leg was completely crushed above the knee. The most hideous part of it was that he continued to live for four or five minutes.[26]

A British officer recalled sitting in a shell hole with a group of captured Germans.

> From other shell holes from the darkness on all sides came the groans and wails of wounded men; faint, long, sobbing moans of agony, and despairing shrieks. It was too horribly obvious that dozens of men with serious wounds must have crawled for safety into new shell holes, and now the water was rising about them and, powerless to move, they were slowly drowning.[27]

What had changed to make this new kind of war possible? Technology is certainly one of the answers. During World War I, for the first time, highly lethal *defensive* weapons were facing each other. Machine guns and rifled artillery guns with high explosive shells could lay down an impenetrable curtain of fire on any opponent who ventured too close. These weapons were not yet mobile, however, so while they were available to the defending side, they could not be used effectively by attackers. The result was the famous stalemate of trench warfare.

Weapons alone, however, cannot explain the full scale of the calamity. What made the trench warfare of the First World War possible, if not inevitable, were other attributes of modern industrial societies. In the past, armies had had to live off the land; this was true even during the Napoleonic wars. This fact limited both an army's size and the duration of any battle. There is no way Napoleon or any other pre-modern general could have concentrated more than a million men in a narrow zone of battle for years on end, as happened in World War I. Their soldiers would quite simply have starved to death. The modern economies of Europe, by contrast, with their industrialized production of food and materials and the railroads to deliver them, were able to provide their troops a steady stream of canned goods, clothing, weapons, ammunition, building supplies, and whatever else was needed to prosecute a war practically in perpetuity. The disrupting of enemy supply chains, such as the attempted blockade of Britain by German submarines, thus became a critical dimension of war.

Two things changed between the First and Second World Wars that made the Second even bloodier. First, the artillery guns and machine guns that had made the trenches so deadly became mobilized in the form of tanks and fighter planes. These weapons were thus available to the offensive as well as the defensive sides.

Second, ideological restrictions on targeting civilians were entirely removed by the fascist ideologies of Hitler, Mussolini, and Hirohito's Japan. Being German, according to National Socialists, was a racial characteristic that defined an individual by blood, not by legal or political status. For the fascists, history consisted of a struggle between races, one in which all means were justified in protecting one's own race against the supposed harmful designs of the others.[28] Meanwhile, violence and warfare were seen not only as a means to an end, but as an elixir that kept a race sharp and vital. Mussolini famously wrote that "War is to man what maternity is to women."[29]

Of the five major protagonists of the Second World War—Churchill, Roosevelt, Stalin, Hitler and Mussolini—two spoke admiringly of this elixir. These two were Hitler and Mussolini. But only one of the five leaders was truly fluent in the mechanics of modern warfare, and this was Winston Churchill. Churchill had experienced war in every dimension and from every angle—as an officer, as a journalist and author and as a politician. At the time of his cavalry charge in the Sudan, he was already on his third overseas campaign, having previously served in Cuba and India. When the First World War broke out, Churchill was First Lord of the Admiralty, in charge of the mighty British Navy—a post he held in the early months of the Second World War as well. After a foiled British landing in Turkey in 1915–1916—largely attributed to Churchill's miscalculation—he resigned and signed up to serve on the Western Front as a Lieutenant Colonel. From 1917 to 1919 he again worked in government, as Minister of Munitions and, after the war, as Secretary of State for War and Air.

It is in this context—that of deeply understanding the real determinants of modern warfare—that we must read certain of Churchill's remarks during the turbulent summer of 1940. On 20 August, Churchill addressed the House of Commons in a speech remembered as "The Few" for its acknowledgment of the Royal Air Force pilots who were engaging German fighters on a nightly basis. "Never in the field of human conflict was so much owed by so many to so few," he said, in a brilliantly simple phrase that perfectly captured human heroism. Yet in the same speech, in lines less frequently quoted, Churchill showed a canny awareness of what this war would bring, and how it could ultimately be won. This was a conflict, he said, "of strategy, of organisation, of technical apparatus, of science, mechanics, and morale."[30] None of the other leaders was as prepared to fight such a war as Churchill.

## Keep Buggering On

The British Isles were not threatened in the summer of 1940. There was no dramatic low point from which Britain rose like a phoenix. But by committing the country and its far-flung empire to a protracted struggle against Hitler and Mussolini (and eventually Hirohito), Churchill launched it from a position of moderate strength and security into a slogging match that would result in a long series of early defeats. In fact, at the time he made his decision not to accept Hitler's offers of peace, Churchill's experts were predicting over a million British civilian deaths as a result of German bombing raids.[31] The death toll ended up being nowhere close to a million, but the fact that this was the prediction says a lot about the type of commitment Churchill was making. And while the early, often spectacular defeats followed hard on one another in the first years of the war, Churchill patiently played a long game, building up the organizational structures, producing the overwhelming quantity and quality of machinery necessary to take on his tactically superior enemies, and pulling a staunchly reluctant US into the war.

In July 1937, the Japanese Imperial Army invaded China from Japan's colonial territory Manchuria. Within a month they had captured both Beijing and Shanghai. The countryside was harder for the Japanese to win and hold, as nimble Chinese forces, such as those led by Mao Zedong, employed guerrilla tactics. A long and excruciatingly bloody land war ensued; of the approximately 28 million civilian deaths during the war, 7.5 million occurred on Chinese soil.[32] Tension with the US over access to oil, as well as a growing sense among the Japanese military leadership that war was inevitable and that a sooner-rather-than-later surprise attack was the best strategic move, led to the infamous bombing of Pearl Harbor in December 1941. Simultaneously, Japanese forces attacked the US-controlled Philippines, Guam, and Wake Island, but also territories of the British Empire in Malaya, Hong Kong and Singapore.

This escalation of the war in the East was two years in the making when Hitler launched his invasion of Poland in September of 1939. Hitler had already led the continent to the brink of war through his aggressive expansion eastward into Austria and Czechoslovakia. After the Allies' defeat in France, Churchill focused his offensive on the Mediterranean. Initially, his instinct for action served him well. In November of 1940 he sent a task force to the Italian naval base at Taranto; it sank three Italian battleships and severely bruised Italian confidence. In December, in the deserts of North Africa, General Archibald Wavell's Western Desert Force launched a raid against the Italian army that turned into a 2-month, 400-mile advance. One British officer described it in an uncoded signal as "fox hunting"—to Churchill's delight and Mussolini's fury.[33] But here Churchill's penchant for offensive action, for wanting to do all things at once, got the better of him. He took crucial forces away from Wavell and sent them to Greece, just as Wavell's force was bearing down on the hapless Italians (a point over which military historians mercilessly fault him).[34] From that point on, British luck began to run out. Mussolini's army suffered from incompetent leadership and poor morale. It had been easy pickings for the career officer Wavell, who was used to brushing aside under-armed foes. This is exactly when Hitler sent Rommel to assist his struggling Italian ally. With this, Wavell was for the first time in his career, picking on someone his own size. He was not up to the task.

British troops stationed in Greece to bolster King George II's armed forces were expelled in an utter rout by German forces in April 1941. Most of these troops escaped to Crete. Crete was a strategically vital outpost—a long and rocky island in the eastern reaches of the Mediterranean with a natural harbor at Suda Bay and three operational airfields. It served as a vital link in Britain's Mediterranean chain—which stretched from Gibraltar at one end of the sea, via Malta in the middle, to Alexandria in Egypt at the other end—and was a natural launching pad for bombing raids on the Ploesi oil fields in Romania, the main supplier for Hitler's tank armies. It was therefore vital for the British to maintain control of Crete, and Churchill knew this.

At the end of May 1941, 35,000 British and Commonwealth troops were based in Crete under the command of the New Zealand Lieutenant General Sir Bernard Freyburg. Churchill had great faith in Freyburg. While many British officers had spent their pre-war years in pomp and inaction at one of Britain's many colonial outposts, lacked an offensive spirit, and were a constant thorn in Churchill's side, Freyburg was an exception. A bold and brazen commander who flouted discipline for its own sake in favor of respect and hard work, he once quipped that, "You cannot treat a man like a butler and expect him to fight like a lion."[35]

When the Germans launched an airborne invasion of Crete on 21 May, Churchill and Freyburg were confident that they would easily fend them off. For one thing, thanks to the British ability to read coded German messages, they knew the invasion was coming. Moreover, inserting troops into a field of operations by parachute and glider landings was risky. In four days, 17,500 German troops landed on and around the three main airfields. The landings went badly. Many paratroopers missed their mark and landed on rough, arid terrain through which they wandered, alone and thirsty, in search of their units. Others were shot on their slow descent to earth, some of them by Cretan civilians. Several gliders crashed. Slowly, however, the tide turned against the British; the German paratroopers regrouped and began tenaciously harassing them. Finally, between 28 May and 1 June 1941 the much larger British force was evacuated from Crete in yet another humiliating defeat.

Defeats like those in North Africa, Greece, and Crete were a constant for the following year and a half. Committed to fighting Germany and Italy, Britain left its possessions in Asia poorly defended. Hong Kong fell to Japanese forces after a feeble defense on 25 December 1941. It had been doomed from the start; with a large civilian population to feed, the island had always been vulnerable to being cut off. Singapore, however, was another matter. Home to the largest British naval force in Asia, this colony on the tip of the Malaysian peninsula boasted an ideal defensive position, with impenetrable marshes on the land side and a massive coastal fortress on the other. And yet, less than a month after the surrender of Hong Kong, British and Imperial forces in Singapore surrendered to a Japanese force half their size. In April, meanwhile, British troops were outfought in Burma and forced into a humiliating 600-mile retreat.

Even more upsetting to Churchill was the sinking of the *Prince of Wales* in December 1941. The pride of the British Navy, this brand-new battleship, escorted by the battle cruiser *Repulse* and a small armada of supporting ships, was sailing north from Singapore to intercept a Japanese amphibious landing on the narrow isthmus connecting Thailand to Malaysia. Shortly after ten in the morning, the British warships were ambushed by Japanese torpedo planes. The first hit caused the *Prince of Wales* to list to the side and took out its steering. A British survivor later recalled thinking, "It doesn't seem possible that those slight-looking planes could do that to her."[36] Three more hits sent it to a watery grave. 840 British sailors went down with the *Prince of Wales* and its accompanying ships.

Churchill was in bed when he received the call from First Sea Lord Sir Dudley Pound who managed first only to utter "a sort of cough and gulp," before informing the Prime Minister of the ship's fate. "In all the war, I never received a more direct shock," Churchill later wrote.[37] A few months earlier, off the coast of Canada, he and President Roosevelt had agreed to the historic Atlantic Charter on the deck of the *Prince of Wales*. But the reasons for Churchill's shock ran yet deeper. It is often said that in planning for a new war, all military leaders are chained by their experience in the previous war. Losers therefore find themselves in a more natural position to innovate. On land, the German armies drew the right lessons from the bloody stalemates of the World War I trenches; they developed the highly mobile and adaptive form of operations later known as *Blitzkrieg*. In naval warfare, meanwhile, the British, unlike the Japanese, continued to privilege the battleship in their planning and operations. This turned out to be poor doctrine—and no British politician had contributed to it more than Churchill, who had two tenures as the Navy's head behind him. With tiny airplanes able to exert massive punches, on land and on sea, battleships, powerful though they were, were naked without aircraft to defend them.

For our purposes, the details of these numerous debacles are less important than the overall narrative they produce. There was in fact no slow and steady rise of British fighting power after the defeat in France in the summer of 1940 and the "Miracle at Dunkirk." The phoenix moment was years off. Dunkirk was repeated in Greece, on Crete, and in the deserts of North Africa. Some sailors in the Royal Navy grew so tired of evacuating their infantry from yet another beach that they redubbed the British Expeditionary Force (BEF), "Back Every Fortnight."[38] In Asia, the record was worse. There could be no "miracles" because there was no British flotilla to come to the rescue of beleaguered British troops in Hong Kong and Singapore.

For the first half of the war, well into 1942 and 1943, Britain simply had to "keep buggering on," as Churchill liked to say when confronted with bad news from the front—a frequent enough occurrence that he began referring to this mantra by the acronym "KBO." Of course, buggering on was not going to win the war.

## Organizing to Fight a Superior Enemy

One of the incontrovertible facts about the Second World War in Europe is that German soldiers consistently outperformed their Allied opponents. In nearly all scenarios where an equal number of troops armed with comparable weapons squared off, the Axis emerged victorious. While more recent motion pictures have been honest about this fact, earlier films tended to whitewash this unpleasant truth. In an op-ed piece in the 1980s, the prolific military historian Max Hastings castigates the myth of the on-par Allied solider:

> The inescapable truth is that Hitler's Wehrmacht was the outstanding fighting force of World War II, one of the greatest in history. For many years after 1945, this seemed painful to concede publicly, partly for nationalistic reasons, partly also because the Nazi legions were fighting for one of the most obnoxious regimes of all time.

Hastings goes on to cite a US military analysis performed in the postwar period that determined that,

> [o]n a man for man basis, German ground soldiers consistently inflicted casualties at about a 50 percent higher rate than they incurred them from the opposing British and American troops under all circumstances. This was true when they were attacking and when they were defending, when they had a local numerical superiority and when, as was usually the case, they were outnumbered.[39]

Despite the bravado of military correspondents and the portrayal of the conflict in postwar films, many Allied soldiers reached the same conclusion. A British general in 1942 admitted, "We are still amateurs. The Germans are professionals."[40] This can easily be seen when one looks at the dry statistics of battle orders and casualties.

Take, for example, the Battle of Kursk in the summer of 1943, one of the turning points in the conflict on the Eastern Front. During the first phase of the battle, the German army launched a pincer attack on entrenched Red Army lines. 780,000 German soldiers deploying 2900 tanks faced off against roughly 1.9 million Soviet soldiers with over 5000 tanks.[41] German casualties were 54,000; Soviet casualties 177,000. Some 300 German tanks were destroyed, versus 2000 Soviet tanks. After another four weeks of fighting, the Red Army managed to push back the Germans, with each side once again suffering similar losses. The German leadership, from Hitler on down, considered the battle an utter failure. The Soviet leadership was exuberant. The Germans had failed to reach their objective, certainly. Nonetheless, we get a clear sense of the lopsided nature of the capabilities of the two fighting forces when an army inflicts nearly four times as many casualties *while on the offensive* against a well-entrenched enemy and deems this an utter failure.

Bearing this in mind, it is clear that Britain would not have been able to defeat Germany on its own. What it needed was, quite simply, to overwhelm Germany with much more material, many more men, and a far superior organization to deliver men and materials to the front. The only way to win against the far superior German army, Churchill saw, was with far larger numbers—numbers of tanks and airplanes, numbers of soldiers, and numbers of shots fired—and the way to larger numbers was international coordination. This required creating new mechanisms for promoting and effecting the manufacture and delivery of hardware; it further required finding partners to undertake a major part of the fighting, and therefore also creating a means for coordinating an unprecedented international war effort. All of these tasks were characterized by an extremely high degree of complexity, and Churchill excelled in all of them. Despite his unfaltering jingoism, Churchill was both the architect and the heart and soul of an unlikely and unprecedented international military collaboration. To create and manage this unwieldy but ultimately effective military machine, Churchill brought his full pallet of leadership competencies to bear, foremost among them his ability to launch and sustain an international advocacy campaign and his knack for behind-the-scenes organization.

Churchill's major "action" began with reorganization at home. By the time he became Prime Minister in May of 1940, he had served in Parliament for close to 40 years. In his decades of experience in government, he had held ministerial responsibilities over briefs such as the Admiralty, Armaments, and Labor, and been exposed to most domains of governance—finance, industry, foreign affairs, and military matters. During the First World War, he had experienced first-hand the difficulty of coordinating multiple ministries in wartime, when focus and aligned agendas were a must. One of his priorities as Prime Minister was therefore to establish a ruthlessly effective administration that could leverage the most out of the country's war effort. He appointed a Minister of Defense—General Hastings Ismay—to occupy the critical juncture between himself and the Chiefs of Staff of the Army, Navy, and Air Force. The five men met regularly, often daily.

Churchill set a new tone of consistency and clarity in internal communications. He emphasized to Ismay and his Cabinet Secretary Sir Edward Bridges and the Chief of the Imperial Staff, Sir John Dill, early on in the war, that "all directives emanating from me are to be made in writing, or should be immediately afterwards confirmed in writing."[42] What seems like a pedantic request was born from Churchill's experience in the First World War, where oral directives, sent from on high, became muddled, confused, and redirected as they made their way down and through those tasked with their implementation. Later we will compare this protocol to Hitler's penchant for issuing vague but vociferous—and often contradictory—orders to his various deputies, many of whom leveraged this "will of the Führer" to accumulate power for their ministry at the expense of others.

To ensure that items that required immediate action not be passed over, Churchill's secretaries stuck preprinted colored stickers with the words "Action This Day" onto the relevant dossiers. Martin Gilbert, the British historian and author of *Churchill: A Life*, the six-volume *Winston S. Churchill*, as well as numerous other detailed works on the war, writes that "[t]he combination of intense thought and consultation, followed by a clear instruction for action, enabled the war machinery to advance."[43]

Part and parcel of these clear initiatives was Churchill's information management. For Churchill to make informed decisions in the face of overwhelming complexity, he not only needed access to relevant information but also an efficient structure for digesting it. For this purpose, he rearranged the traditional "locked box" method of delivering messages to a prime minister. He insisted that every day his staff place inbound correspondence and reports in a consistent and coded order which he himself had designed, and which placed necessary information regarding fighting, production, diplomacy, and other areas at his command. Churchill began his days working through the box in bed and shooting off a series of answers, follow-up thoughts or queries in response. One official, quoted by Gilbert, called the boxes, "peculiarly Winston's own, and it was in a sense the nerve centre of his war effort."[44]

Churchill also built up an independent assessment mechanism, entrusting his old colleague Professor Frederick Lindemann with the position of head of the statistical branch. Churchill demanded of him "one pagers" summarizing particular aspects of wartime production. The two men were friends and frequently spent the weekends together. This did not spare Lindemann harassment from Churchill: "You are not presenting me as I should like every few days, or every week with a short clear statement of the falling off or improvement in munitions production. I am not able to form a clear view unless you do this."[45]

Churchill's appetite for information and his ability to soak it up, to consider the significance of a new item and then make appropriate decisions, was uncanny. In addition to his constant meetings, his voluminous correspondence, and the ceaseless reports he had to sift through, he read up to ten newspapers before going to bed in the evening or getting up in the morning. And beyond his own ability to manage a ceaseless flow of information, Churchill knew how to engage the levers of various ministries to put and keep the country on track, or design new processes for making and implementing decisions. When Franklin Delano Roosevelt sent his trusted aide Harry Hopkins to visit Britain and report back on its warfighting, the latter was stunned by Churchill's, "absolute mastery of Britain's governance."[46]

## Building the Grand Coalition

In his groundbreaking *Britain's War Machine*, David Edgerton dispatches with the myth that Britain was mortally wounded after Dunkirk and a junior player in bringing the war to a successful conclusion. While bested by the US in sheer output and far behind the Soviet Union in number of casualties, Britain steadily built up an effective mechanism for fighting a modern war. Edgerton writes in summary that,

> Britain [was] a first-class power, confident, with good reason, in its capacity to wage a devastating war of machines. It had the resources to spare, was wealthy enough to make mistakes, and could fight as it chose to rather than had to.[47]

Even so, it certainly did not fight alone. Nor had that ever been Churchill's intention.

On 14 July 1940, less than two weeks after the attack on Mers-el-Kébir, Churchill gave one of his signature speeches to the British people.

> And now it has come to us to stand alone in the breach, and face the worst that the tyrant's might and enmity can do. Bearing ourselves humbly before God, but conscious that we serve an unfolding purpose, we are ready to defend our native land against the invasion by which it is threatened. We are fighting by ourselves alone; but we are not fighting for ourselves alone.[48]

The last two sentences were utterly disingenuous. As we have seen, Britain was not threatened by an invasion. And as we will see shortly, Churchill had absolutely no intention of fighting the war alone. Despite his rhetoric, he was already working overtime to build an international fighting force. Over the vociferous objections of his generals, he had set to work integrating the thousands of soldiers from Poland, Holland, France, and other countries who had taken refuge in England. Two days before his broadcast to the British people, Churchill sent an exasperated message to the three service departments, dismissing their reservations and insisting that they put their full effort into organizing the exiled service personnel into national units. "It is most necessary to give to the war which Great Britain is waging single-handed the broad international character which will add greatly to our strength and prestige," he told his chiefs of staff. He possessed a clear understanding of the strategic benefits, both militarily and politically, that came with organizing foreign soldiers. By incorporating them into his forces, he aimed to enhance the persuasive power of his appeal for assistance from the United States. This approach aimed to showcase that Britain's fight was not solely for its own preservation but also for the defense of "rights and freedom" and the preservation of "Christian civilization." Additionally, Churchill dedicated considerable efforts toward recruiting support from Britain's former colonial territories, particularly New Zealand, Australia, South Africa, and Canada. As evidenced during the critical battle of El Alamein in autumn 1942, where Rommel found himself outmatched by his British adversary Bernard Montgomery, only 55% of the forces fighting under the "British" banner were actually British. The remaining 45% comprised soldiers from India, Australia, New Zealand, South Africa, Free French, and Greek nationals.[49]

But Churchill aimed for a coalition that would extend well beyond refugees and the soldiers of former and present colonies. In building it, he was immensely aided by a decisive move by Hitler. In the early morning hours of 22 June 1941, the anniversary of Napoleon's doomed Russian invasion of 1812, Hitler sent 150 German divisions—600,000 vehicles, 3600 tanks, 7000 artillery pieces, 2700 planes, and 600,000 horses—into the Soviet Union. This, the largest army ever assembled, achieved impressive early gains, with the tanks armies encircling swaths of hapless Soviet defenders. The sheer number of Red Army prisoners captured in the first few months of the conflict stands as a testament to the scale of these encirclements. In the Kiev pocket alone, the Wehrmacht captured an astounding 665,000 prisoners. By the autumn of 1941, the total count of Soviet prisoners was rapidly approaching three million. By the subsequent summer, Germany had conquered a substantial portion of Soviet territory, encompassing 45% of the pre-invasion

Soviet population, 33% of its industrial capacity, and 47% of its agricultural production.[50]

The invasion was a turning point in the war, and Churchill seized on it. He made the decision to support the Soviet Union, despite his misgivings. On 21 June, he broadcast a speech in which he said, "No one has been a more consistent opponent of Communism than I have for the last twenty-five years. I will unsay no word that I have spoken about it." These were understatements. Churchill had been a staunch critic of Communism and the Soviet Union for decades and was largely responsible for a failed British intervention to crush the Bolshevik revolution in its early days. At one point he had even complimented Benito Mussolini on his no-holds-barred approach to weeding out Communism in Italy. That Churchill would side with Stalin was an unimaginable about-face.

Yet, Churchill recognized that, without any of his own doing, the tide of the war had changed. Rather than swim against it or try to skirt around it, Churchill doubled down and joined it. After his quip about "unsaying" none of his previous critiques of the Soviet Union, he went on to say,

> But all this fades away before the spectacle which is now unfolding…any man or state who fights on against Nazidom will have our aid…that is our policy and that is our declaration. It follows therefore that we shall give whatever help we can to Russia and the Russian people.[51]

Churchill did exactly this; over the course of the next several years, he sent equipment his own troops could ill afford to lose to his new Soviet ally, while working hard to build a personal relationship with Stalin.

In the same speech, Churchill daringly invoked the United States, a country also not predisposed to an alliance with a Communist country. "The Russian danger," he said, "is therefore our danger, and the danger of the United States." That this may not strike us as surprising today is only because we know how the war turned out. At the time, the idea that Britain, the US and the Soviet Union would fight together represented a long shot. In the summer of 1940, few in Washington saw the war as any of their business. Even when Japan attacked the US at Pearl Harbor in 1941, this might have drawn the US into no more than a war against Japan. That the US would contribute so mightily to defeating Hitler's armies, that it would end up following a policy of "Europe first," as Roosevelt denoted it, could not in any way have been taken for granted. That it happened was not solely due to Churchill. But if we were to single out one decisive factor in making it happen, it was Churchill's incessant behind-the-scenes coalition-building.

The Grand Coalition, as it came to be called, was Churchill's brainchild, and his paramount creation. While the inclusion of the Soviet Union was helped on by circumstance, the idea of bringing the US into the war had taken seed in Churchill's mind during the very first days of the war. Just eight days into his premiership, on 18 May, he confided in his son his plan for winning the war: "I shall drag the United States in."[52] Seen in this context, his disingenuous rhetoric in the summer of 1940 served both to lay the foundation for a long war *and* to create a story that would eventually bond the US and Britain in the most comprehensive military alliance the world has even seen.

The alliance between the US and Great Britain was unlikely for a number of cogent reasons. The Churchill biographer and World War Two historian Max Hasting, in his masterpiece, *Finest Years: Churchill as Warlord,* exhaustively details the obstacles to such a partnership. Antipathy was rife on both sides of the Atlantic. When Britons thought of Americans, the words that regularly came to mind were "arrogance," "ignorance," and, above all, "apathy." Many worried that the US would join the war only at the last minute, if at all, yet claim credit for victory. In preparing his country for a partnership with the US, Churchill had to overcome objections from his generals and ministers on down to regular folks on the streets. Yet, as one of Churchill's confidants recalled, Churchill "quite understood the exasperation with which so many English people feel with the American attitude of criticism combined with ineffective assistance; but we must be patient and we must conceal our irritation."[53]

Forming the Grand Coalition required what management scholars today would call an advocacy campaign. Churchill spent an enormous amount of time building and managing his relationship with the US. Over months and years, he influenced US policymakers, above all Roosevelt, with a carefully crafted barrage of messages across all available lines of communication. Over the course of the war, he wrote over 1300 telegrams to Roosevelt—in total they exchanged some 2000 written messages. They spoke frequently over the phone—Churchill from inside a dedicated phone cabinet in the depths of the underground Cabinet War Rooms, disguised behind a door that proclaimed the room to be the Prime Minister's bathroom, so as to keep disturbances to a minimum.[54] Churchill was also one of the great travelers of the war, often putting himself at serious risk and discomfort to travel to Washington, Moscow, Tehran and wherever else he felt he needed to exert his personal influence (logging 107,000 miles of air travel during the war).[55]

At the same time, he bent over backward to accommodate and impress the various emissaries Roosevelt sent to London. This is rather remarkable.

Churchill was known by all, and despised by many, for being a loud-mouthed, overbearing, and brash conversationalist. Yet in dealing with American guests, he showed a remarkable and consistent restraint. Hastings concludes, "He subordinated pride to need, endured slights without visible resentment, and greeted every American visitor as if his presence did Britain honour."[56] As a man used to speaking his mind, one of Churchill's most remarkable feats in the war was the repressing of his most natural instincts for the sake of a long game that at first only he understood.

## The Materiel of War for a War of Materiel

While Churchill was determined to bring the US into the conflict, his first concern in 1940 was war materiel—airplanes, tanks, trucks, ships, and all the other hardware necessary to fight a modern war. Along with ramping up its own production, at home and in its vast empire, Britain bought what it could from the US. By the fall of 1940, however, Britain was beginning to reach the limit of what it could afford, just as German U-Boats were starting to squeeze the island. A letter Churchill sent almost exactly a year before the Japanese attack on Pearl Harbor and half a year before the German invasion of the Soviet Union outlined Britain's need for assistance from the United States beyond what it could pay for. Churchill spent two weeks working on this letter, laboring over it day and night.

The letter is a masterpiece on many levels. Its brilliant rhetoric and eloquent style bear all the hallmarks of Churchill's authorship. He explained, in no uncertain terms, that Britain could no longer afford to pay for the weapons it was purchasing from the US. In addition to suggesting an alternative arrangement—what would become the Lend-Lease Program—he framed the struggle Britain was fighting as one undertaken on behalf of the US and the whole western world, and stressed, in no uncertain terms, that Britain was willing to bear the consequences of this struggle.

> You may be assured that we shall prove ourselves ready to suffer and sacrifice to the utmost for the Cause, and that we glory in being its champion. The rest we leave with confidence to you and to your people, being sure that ways and means will be found which future generations on both sides of the Atlantic will approve and admire.

Being careful not to accuse the US of complacency in the face of a global threat, he underlined that Britain's war was being fought on behalf of the West, and that the assistance he was requesting was more than warranted.

> If, as I believe, you are convinced, Mr. President, that the defeat of the Nazi and Fascist tyranny is a matter of high consequences to the people of the United States and to the Western Hemisphere, you will regard this letter not as an appeal for aid, but as a statement of the minimum action necessary to the achievement of our common purpose.[57]

The letter paid off: a few weeks later, Roosevelt agreed to the Lend-Lease Program (an idea that had already been circulating among a small group of his advisers), through which the US distributed some $50 billion in war materiel to over 30 countries during the rest of the war, including $30 billion to Great Britain and $11 billion to the Soviet Union. The US also became a belligerent in all but name, taking over the protection of Greenland and Iceland and escorting British merchant vessels halfway across the Atlantic. In selling this move to a weary American public, Roosevelt mobilized his own rhetorical muscle, speaking of the need to be "the arsenal of democracy" and comparing the scenario to lending a hose to a neighbor whose house is on fire.

Lend-Lease ought not to be read simply as good-willed American largesse. Churchill had to open up the Treasury books to American scrutiny to prove that his country was essentially bankrupt—a truly remarkable act for a sovereign nation. The sales of arms to France and Britain also injected the US economy with much needed cash and launched it on its recovery from the Depression.

That the Allies were able to out-manufacture the Axis was a crucial factor in deciding the war. Countless books have been written about every aspect of this "industrial war." A few numbers will suffice to represent the magnitude of the accomplishment: in the crux years of 1942 to 1944, the Allies outproduced the Axis at a ratio of 3.5 to 1 in rifles, 4.7 to 1 in machine guns, 5.2 to 1 in tanks, 10.6 to 1 in major naval vessels, and a whopping 15.6 to 1 in machine pistols.[58] Superiority in the quantity of war-fighting tools was one of the most significant way in which the Allies compensated for the deficit in their war-fighting ability. Lend-Lease was a small but important component in this effort, particularly in the east—in total, American materiel amounted to around 7% of Soviet wartime production.[59] Yet, critically, it put fighting materiel into the hands of those who were willing and able to use it. And it laid yet another stone in the foundation in the intimate relationship Churchill was envisioning with the United States.

## Forging an Alliance

Throughout all of these early years, from the summer of 1940 to late 1942, Churchill had to balance the impression that Britain was in imminent danger—and therefore desperately required American help—with the impression that it would win the war, and that therefore American help would not be wasted. Above all, he had to be able to show that Britain was in the fight, doing what it could to wrestle with the Nazi menace while the Americans were still making up their mind. This, in part, explains Churchill's willingness to commit British troops to forlorn campaigns across the Mediterranean.

And slowly but surely, the coalition took shape. First it happened in the air and at sea. Then, in November of 1942, British and US troops landed on the North African coast. Rommel now had to fight a two-front war. US troops first encountered the Germans in the Atlas Mountains along the border of Algeria and Tunisia. At Faid Pass, the American first Armored Division, naively believing the Germans in front of them were retreating, drove headlong into a German ambush of hidden antitank guns. "It was murder," recalled one survivor.[60] The subsequent larger battle at Kasserine Pass was a typically lopsided affair. The Allied attackers, mostly Americans with some Free French Units, suffered 10,000 casualties, compared to 980 for the Germans. While a 10 to 1 ratio would be a resounding success in any other war, however, the Germans could ill afford such losses, while the Allies, with their superior numbers, could.

Such casualty figures pale in comparison with the daily carnage that played out on the Eastern Front. While American, British, and other Allied forces learned to work together and embarked on comparatively small-scale adventures, the Soviet Union was suffering and inflicting violence of yet another order.

After his troops were stopped on the outskirts of Leningrad and Moscow in the winter of 1941—as much by the particularly cold weather as anything else—Hitler continued the offensive in the summer of 1942. Over the objections of his generals, he sent the bulk of his army south into the Caucasus. He believed that if he could gain access to Soviet oil fields, the war would be won. In the city of Stalingrad, scenes of some of the most bitter close quarters combat of the war, the Red Army finally stopped the Germans and, after Hitler's refusal against all military reason to retreat to a holdable line, his 6th Army surrendered in the winter of 1943. Hitler's once invincible army had suffered over 800,000 casualties (the Soviet Union over one million). From then on, the war slowly and painfully ground its way back westward with massive battles unfamiliar to most Western readers—Kursk, Bagration, Korsun…and the list goes on.

From a military standpoint, casualties typically refer to soldiers who are irretrievably lost—whether though death, a serious injury, or by being captured. During the chaos of war, however, cataloging such figures reliably is a fraught business. Double counting, destroyed paperwork, deliberate fudging, and other happenstance conspire to make numbers unreliable. Nonetheless, what can be said with certainty is that the Soviet Union paid a heavier toll in lost lives than any other combatant in the war. And the bulk of the German army was destroyed in the east (many estimates suggest that up to 80% of German casualties were inflicted on the Eastern Front). In what is today accepted as one of the most accurate studies, Rüdiger Overmans puts German military deaths at 2,742,909 on the Eastern Front, compared to 339,957 on the Western Front (this includes, of course, both the Battle of France in 1940 *and* the Allied invasion of Normandy).[61]

Assessments are less precise for Soviet losses, but the figure seems to rest somewhere between 8 and 13 million military deaths (out of 26 million total war deaths).[62] Throughout the war, the Soviet leadership was able and, crucially, willing to sacrifice its soldiers in a callous, near to careless fashion. Undeniably, the Red Army's performance had improved by the second half of the war. Despite this, it was the Soviet reserves of manpower and Stalin's willingness to draw on it, come what may, that made the Red Army successful. The Red Army was the most resilient organization of the war. Historian Roger Rees, who dedicated a book-length study to this issue, writes soberly,

> I conclude that the Red Army was effective because it was able to keep fighting, despite weak large- and small-unit leadership, inadequate training, slipshod planning, unreliable logistics, confusing command structures, meddlesome political interference, a disrupted economy, and above all massive casualties.[63]

Rees's conclusion bears out Churchill's reading of the war from the beginning: in order to defeat a superior fighting force, the Allies would have to rely on numbers, and hence on a grand coalition. Interestingly, popular accounts of the war in the west tend to see it largely as an American and British endeavor, neglecting both the disproportionate contribution of the Red Army *and* Churchill's essential role as a coalition builder. These two facets are intimately linked. Still, defeating the Germans required more than an unfathomable number of Soviet casualties. It also required an invasion of the continent from the west. And here, too, Churchill played the crucial role, not only in having involved the Americans, but, surprisingly—given his supposed penchant for immediate action—in having *delayed* what would become known as D-Day for over two years.

## Back to France, with a Delay

On 6 June 1944, German soldiers stationed along France's Normandy coast awoke to an astonishing sight. "I had never seen such an assembly of ships, and I'm sure nobody will ever see such a thing again, perhaps not in human history. The sea was absolutely solid with metal," wrote one defender.[64] Since midnight, field telephones in military headquarters across much of north-western France had been ringing to report airborne landings, bombing raids, and sabotage activity of various kinds. At around 6:30 a.m., soldiers of the 4th US Infantry Division disembarked from their landing crafts onto Utah Beach, followed in the next few hours by troops at the four other target beaches, code-named Omaha, Juno, Gold, and Sword. D-Day—termed Operation Overlord by Allied planners and "the longest day" by a German staff officer—was underway. By the end of the day some 150,000 troops had crossed the channel.

D-Day was a triumph of organization and a triumph of international coop-eration. Never before and, it could be argued, never since have independent nations worked so intimately to design and implement an endeavor of such scale and complexity. Operation Overlord involved the careful coordination of some 7000 ships and 11,000 aircraft, the first-time implementation of a host of new technologies—from amphibious tanks to portable harbors—the processing of mountains of data from meteorological to signal intelligence, and the directing of soldiers and sailors representing some 13 countries. By the end of the month over 850,000 men, 148,000 vehicles and 570,000 tons of supplies had crossed the Channel. This is a monumental achievement.

Though the bulk of the organizational effort and the subsequent fighting rested on American, British, and Canadian shoulders, Australian, Belgian, Czech, Dutch, French, Greek, New Zealand, Norwegian, Rhodesian and Polish soldiers, sailors and airmen played a role as well. The only Allied ship to be sunk by German torpedoes during the invasion was the Norwegian Svenner, resulting in the loss of 32 Norwegian sailors. The efforts of the French resistance—numbering over 300,000 by the time of the invasion—in sabo-taging railway infrastructure was vital in preventing a quick inflow of German reinforcements into Normandy. Even the Soviet Union contributed to the endeavor's success by timing the launch of its massive Operation Bagration on the Eastern Front to coincide with the Allied invasion, at least in part to prevent the Germans from transferring troops to the West.

The amazing coordination evidenced during Operation Overlord would not have been possible without the most remarkable institution of the war: the Combined Chiefs of Staff Committee. Though rarely discussed, the Committee marked a radical innovation in the history of warfare. To be sure, alliances had long served a vital role in war-making. It was the dense network of alliances on the continent during the First World War that contributed to the war's remarkable scale, beginning with Germany's desire to help its ally Austria. Yet, military policy—how each army engaged the enemy—had always remained the business of individual countries. The full independence of a head of state to direct his top generals—the Joint Chiefs of Staff in the US and the Chief of Staff in the UK, for example—was considered the sacrosanct right of a sovereign nation. The institution of the Combined Chiefs of Staff upended this practice; for the first time, the military efforts of two great sovereign nations were coordinated at the highest level, their command structures melded together into one. This innovation owed much to Churchill.

The Committee, which was based in Washington, served to transform the strategic decisions made by Churchill and Roosevelt into concrete military actions. It was chaired by Admiral William D. Leahy and met on a weekly basis, though at times the CCoS reported back to London hourly. Field Marshal Alan Brooke, Chief of the Imperial General Staff, had been skeptical of the institution at first; he later called it, "the most efficient organization that had ever been evolved for co-ordinating and correlating the war strategy and effort of the Allies."[65] Without the Committee, it is inconceivable that Operation Overlord could have been implemented with such success.

D-Day opened a second front against Hitler. Together with the massive Soviet effort in the east, it led to the defeat of his regime. It has been written about exhaustively and has served as fodder for innumerable films. One aspect that is usually left out of these accounts, however, is the timing of the invasion.

That D-Day took place in June 1944, rather than a year or even two earlier, was down to Churchill. He alone among the Allied leaders correctly read that the time was not ripe in 1942 or 1943. To delay the invasion, he mustered all his abilities and charm to undermine a wave of public and political pressure for an earlier date. Ironically, given today's prevailing leadership paradigm, this key determinant of his and the Allies' success demonstrates the exact opposite of a propensity for action. Churchill in fact showed immense restraint and a deep commitment to postponing action in the face of massive pressure to act.

Dwight D. Eisenhower, one of the most lauded generals of the war, appealed vociferously in February 1942 for launching an invasion of continental Europe during the following summer. With the scars of Pearl Harbor still raw, he and his fellow generals saw the British strategy as lethargic and overly careful—to the dismay of many Britons, who had been engaged with Hitler's troops in one theater or another since the start of the war. Roosevelt agreed with Eisenhower. In April 1942, he dispatched his trusted aide, Harry Hopkins, and his Chief of Staff, George C. Marshall, on a mission of persuasion to London. There the two men advocated for a 1943 invasion of the continent by a mixed US and British force consisting of 38 divisions, or, alternatively, for a drastically smaller September 1942 invasion.

During their stay in London, Hopkins and Marshall were treated with the utmost courtesy. They delivered a personal letter from Roosevelt that noted that "Even if full success is not attained [by the proposed invasion], big objectives will be." Roosevelt further noted that "the Russians are today killing more Germans and destroying more equipment than you and I put together."[66] Churchill called Roosevelt's letter a "masterful" document—but instead of supporting the implementation of its suggestions, he set about doing everything in his power to block it. Quietly and deliberately, yet without openly contradicting the president, Churchill steered planning and resources away from an early D-Day.

At home, too, Churchill faced pressure to open the second front. In March 1942, some 40,000 people took to the streets in Trafalgar Square to push Churchill into action. One officer described an "envy of the Russians, who are being allowed to fight all out." The American public was also less than impressed with the Prime Minister. A survey of Americans later that summer showed that 57% believed the Allies should launch a Second Front "within two to three months."[67]

Most of all, Stalin agitated ceaselessly for his allies to launch an invasion of the continent. He made little of their argument that the bombing campaign was an effective method of weakening Hitler's fighting abilities (a point still debated by historians). "Someone who is unwilling to take risks could never win a war," he derisively remarked to Churchill.[68] In fact, to this day many Russian works cite the fact that the invasion only took place in 1944 as a deliberate betrayal by the West, a gambit to grind the Soviet Union and Nazi Germany down while waiting for the opportune moment to finish off Germany. There is no evidence to support this view. Despite their objections to Communism and the Stalinist regime, both Churchill and Roosevelt genuinely supported the Red Army where they could. A premature invasion of France—a D-Day in 1942 or 1943—would have had the opposite effect. It would undoubtedly have failed. Weakened both politically and militarily after an aborted invasion attempt in 1942 or 1943, it is unlikely that the Allies could have launched another invasion the following year.

In August 1942, in a small trial run for an actual invasion, Churchill did send 6000 Allied troops, predominantly Canadian, to attempt an amphibious landing that was meant to temporarily seize the German-controlled port at Dieppe. This trial invasion took the German defenders completely by surprise and hit them in a spot that had few fortifications. Nevertheless, it was a fiasco. Of the 4963 Canadians who took part, over 3350 were killed, wounded, or captured.[69] Churchill took immense blame for the failed operation. Seen differently, however, it was at once a confirmation of his view that a larger invasion would have been a catastrophe, and a laboratory in which a number of lessons were learned for the D-Day invasion to come two summers later.

The fact is that in 1943, far fewer resources could have been sent across the channel to take on the Germans than a year later. Moreover, even the Normandy landing in 1944 was never a sure thing. Hitler's generals, including Rommel, advocated mobilizing their tank reserves to counter the invasion in its first few days. Hitler, however, overruled them, as he was convinced that another invasion was coming elsewhere. Had he listened to his generals, the outcome of the Allied operation might have been very different.

Meanwhile, as the Allies made their way inland, it was not only their material superiority that enabled them to advance. So too the British and Americans had begun to improve their ability to use men and machines together—combined arms as it is called in military jargon.[70] And precisely this capability had been learned in earlier "trial runs" in North Africa, in Italy in 1943, and in the disastrous raid at Dieppe.

In the end, then, Churchill got his way. Though leaders from the President of the United States and Josef Stalin all the way down to lower-ranking generals were itching to get on with the invasion, and while popular pressure mounted at home and abroad, Churchill knew that conditions were not ripe in 1942 and 1943. It is a powerful testament to his wiliness and diplomacy that, though he never openly advocated it, the strategic course that the Allies ultimately embarked on was of his design.

It is not an exaggeration to state that holding off on the invasion in the West was one of the pivotal decisions made during the war. And it was Churchill's.

# The War of Words and Hitler's Failed Leadership

That Churchill was a master wordsmith is, of course, beyond doubt. His writing and speeches have a crisp, poetic bite. At heart, he was a writer—over the course of his life, he made more money from writing than from any other source. In 1953, he won the Nobel Prize in Literature. From a young age, he was aware of his gift in formulating language. Well before he had been recognized for his rhetorical skills, the 23-year-old Churchill wrote that "Of all the talents bestowed upon men, none is so precious as the gift of oratory. He who enjoys it wields a power more durable than that of a great king."[71]

That he inspired the British people, and many others far afield, is undisputed. One British woman, speaking for many, wrote after the war that "gradually we came under the spell of that wonderful voice and inspiration." Yet, the impact Churchill's words had on the men he worked most closely with, the men tasked with prosecuting the war, was mixed at best. For one, when push comes to shove, inspirational oratory comes up against its limits. A year and half into the war, when Japanese troops were closing in on Hong Kong, the water supply was cut off and the city was under bombardment, the defenders' resolve lagged. Churchill dispatched a short but nobly worded cable to the colony's governor, Sir Mark Young, and the city's commander, Christopher Maltby, enjoining that "There must be no thought of surrender. Every part of the island must be resisted with the utmost stubbornness."[72] In such a case, however, words could have no material effect. Four days later, the two men surrendered to the Japanese commander in the candlelit lobby of the Peninsula Hotel.

If words could actually decide wars, it would likely have been Hitler and Mussolini, rather than Churchill, who emerged victorious at the end of the day. Even as the tide turned against Germany, Hitler's language held a magnetic sway over most of his soldiers. When the German 6th Army was surrounded at Stalingrad and disaster was unfolding, the men's letters—sent out on the same planes that brought them trickles of supplies—showed a stubborn resistance toward blaming Hitler for a military disaster that was so obviously and completely his making.

Hitler provides a perfect example of just how wrong the overall narrative so often applied to Churchill is. Hitler was an electrifying orator who won over the hearts and minds of his troops and his people. He believed that what was needed for victory was not careful planning and a reading of the currents of the times, but sheer willpower. And he had a propensity for action that was so extreme that he made blunder after blunder, against the advice of his generals.

Though every historian who examines the details of the war immediately recognizes Hitler for what he was, an incompetent and unprepared wartime leader, the myth in the popular imagination that he was a military genius remains persistent. He was not. While Churchill frequently annoyed and harangued his generals and other staff, he had an ingrained respect for the expertise of others. Hitler verbally abused his generals and consistently undermined their best attempts to keep the German war effort going. Willpower, for Hitler, was the one key to success. If everyone from the simple soldier to his top generals simply believed in victory, victory could be achieved.

When Rommel requested permission to retreat after being decisively beaten at El Alamein in early November 1942, Hitler responded, "in the position in which you find yourself, there can be no other thought than to stand fast, not to take even one step back and to throw every available soldier and weapon into the battle...this is not the first time in history that resolute determination will prevail."[73] Such orders were part and parcel of Hitler's leadership style; he insisted, completely disconnected from reality, that his soldiers should simply dig deeper and fight on.

Most of Hitler's generals saw through him, despite the fact that they remained committed to his leadership and the Nazi cause. On 23 July 1942, Franz Halder wrote in his diary that,

> this chronic tendency to underrate enemy capabilities is gradually assuming grotesque proportions and is developing into a positive danger...This so-called leadership is characterized by a pathological reaction to the impressions of the moment and a total lack of any understanding of the command machinery and its possibilities.[74]

Josef Goebbels, Minister of Propaganda and one of Hitler's most committed sycophants, is reported to have confided in a colleague during the war that "We have not only a leadership crisis but strictly speaking a 'Leader Crisis.'"[75]

As I have already noted, German troops consistently outperformed comparably sized and equipped units from any other country. But this was not, as Hitler would have it, due to the power of their will or their belief in their inevitable victory. Instead, it was the result of the superb training and organization enjoyed by German soldiers. While military historians almost unanimously condemn the British officer class between the wars as overly aristocratic, out of touch and ineffective, the German army boasted—in the first few years of the war—a nearly inexhaustible pool of extremely competent officers, from the lowest ranks up to the generals.

But the German army was poorly served by its *Führer*. While Churchill cultivated structures that allowed networks of experts and production facilities to produce an ever larger and better assortment of war-fighting technologies, Hitler did the opposite. A case in point is the German ME-262 jet fighter program. Toward the second half of the war, German aircraft designers were edging close to building the first operational fighter jet, a monumental achievement. Midway through its development, Hitler decided on a whim that he would prefer a jet *bomber* over a fighter. In a meeting with a collection of sycophants and engineers at his mountain retreat in May 1943, Hitler, according to his biographer Ian Kershaw, "exploded in fury, ordering the ME-262—despite all technical objections leveled by the experts present—to be built exclusively as a bomber."[76] Hitler's head of the *Luftwaffe*, Herman Goering, was well aware of the impossibility of following this order, but was unwilling to face his leader's wrath. He passed the buck down the line to his hapless engineers. Production was delayed for months while engineers scrambled to redesign the plane. Finally, it was put back on track as a fighter jet. And this is hardly the only case in which Hitler's "leadership" consisted of persistent meddling in business he knew nothing about, and a resort to shouting whenever he felt his subordinates lacked drive and willpower.

Like many German weapons systems, technologically advanced though they were, the jet ended up being too little too late to make a difference on the battlefield. Especially in the second half of the war, the Allies' ability to produce quality equipment at scale far surpassed the Germans'. Maintaining and increasing output while innovating was a balance Germany struggled to master.[77] While this was not only Hitler's fault, he certainly did not help. Adam Tooze, an expert on the German war economy, calls the German Mark XXI U-boat the "world's first true submarine," but goes on to say that "the problem, as with all Germany's wonder weapons, was the time required to develop the excellent [...] design into a fully functional weapon that was suitable for bulk production."[78] While countless German weapons systems became models for postwar development—the Panther Tank, the V2 Rocket, the Mark XXI submarine, the ME-262, and many others—they made only a modest contribution to the war for which they were initially developed. Tooze summarizes the German approach, spearheaded by Hitler, writing that "desperate need for a technical fix resulted both in exaggerated hopes being placed in individual weapons systems and in accelerated high-risk development programmes."[79]

While Hitler was an effective mass influencer—crucial in his ascension to power—he was a hopelessly ineffective administrator. The number of books that detail the bewildering bureaucratic mess that was Berlin during the war or the *Führer's* "un-systematic, dilettante style of governing" is too numerous to cite.[80] Winning the war required something Hitler didn't have: the fundamental understanding of the currents of this new type of war and the patience and vision to build structures and institutions that could leverage them. These were exactly the leadership qualities that Churchill brought to bear on his task, and they were far more important than any amount of rhetoric or hasty action.

## Winning the War

Churchill's mastery of the English language does not explain how his country managed to fend off and eventually defeat the most proficient army of the twentieth century. Nor were persuasive pep talks to his inner circle a decisive element. The standard narrative sees Churchill's leadership as impatient, offensively oriented, bristling for action, and of imperturbable resolve. Of course, he was all of these things—so much so that Stalin referred to him as the "British bulldog."[81] These traits characterized him throughout his life. In 1899, when he was a 25-year-old journalist reporting on the Boer War in South Africa, a train he was traveling on was ambushed. Churchill sprang into action, organizing the frightened British troops into a defensive line. Some managed to escape. Churchill did not. He was taken to a prisoner of war camp in Pretoria. One night he scaled the perimeter fence and set off across hostile territory, with no map or survival equipment save some chocolate and an old biscuit. Despite a large Boer search party on his trail, Churchill—with the help of some sympathetic miners—accomplished the 300-mile trip back to the British lines stowed away on a train (he was unable to acknowledge his helpers in his subsequent reporting, for fear that they would suffer Boer retribution, though he eventually gifted them inscribed watches).[82]

Churchill was a man who lived for action, and he expected the same of his subordinates. When his first two desert commanders— Archibald Wavell and Claude Auchinleck—failed to launch offensives as quickly as he wished, he ceaselessly agitated and prodded them. He wrote of Wavell that if his offensive ambitions remained small, "he will have failed to rise to the height of circumstances…I never worry about 'action' only inaction."[83]

Churchill's ceaseless yearning for action was, in a war against a ruthless and capable enemy such as Nazi Germany, certainly a valuable attribute. It did not, however, win the war. What made Churchill successful was not impatience, action, and resolve. It was rather that he could temper these impulses when larger forces demanded it: when dealing with his American guests, or

when deciding when to launch the cross-Channel invasion. Just as significantly, below his bluster, he managed to set up the kind of excellently coordinated administration required to effectively conduct a modern war, and to
design and implement a strategy that would bring the US into that war. It is
in this light that we must read his excellent and inspiring speeches of 1940.
They were the construction of a (fictional) narrative that would garner him
the necessary support at home and, even more crucially, win over support
from abroad, and particularly from the United States of America. Britain
required sacrifice (from within) and help (from without). Yet at the same
time—so the narrative Churchill spun—Britain's eventual victory was assured.

So what exactly was it that Churchill was so good at? In recent years, one
line of inquiry has proven quite robust in predicting leadership effectiveness
across various leadership scenarios: Emotional Intelligence.[84] The term refers
to a range of abilities that allow one to recognize, label, and respond to emo-
tions in oneself and in others. Leaders with high levels of Emotional
Intelligence, research suggests, are better able to gauge and leverage the motivations, fears, and other relevant emotional responses of their followers and,
at the same time, they are aware of how they themselves feel.[85] Quantifying
Emotional Intelligence and measuring it in individuals is obviously challenging. In looking at Churchill, however, the challenge of measuring is not very
grave; it is clear that he possessed *none of it*.

Admiral John Godfrey, British director of naval intelligence during the
Second World War, wrote that Churchill inflicted on those around him "persuasion, real or simulated anger, mockery, vituperation, tantrums, ridicule,
derision, abuse and tears."[86] Nor was this a new trait. Already during the First
World War, during which Churchill served in a variety of cabinet positions,
his colleague Herbert Asquith described him as "by far the most disliked man
in the cabinet by his colleagues," and continued, "He is intolerable! Noisy,
long-winded and full of perorations."[87] Churchill, for all his skills at writing
and speaking for the masses or pulling himself together when dealing with
Americans, was not particularly aware of how his behavior affected those in
his immediate environment. Nor did he seem to care enough to find out. (On
the other hand, Toussaint, Bell, and Amundsen, display all the hallmarks of
leaders with a high Emotional Intelligence).

This does not mean that Emotional Intelligence is a dead end. Instead,
Churchill's story would suggest that Emotional Intelligence is merely formulated too narrowly, as it applies specifically to challenges that were primarily
social in nature—where the challenge involved rallying a reluctant team or
convincing a recalcitrant client. But what about the leadership challenges in

which the challenge is bigger than any small group of humans with which you can reason—such as the Second World War?

We should take a quick detour here to have a look at one of the tricks of the historian's trade. When looking back at past events, historians frequently separate *manifest* from *latent* history. These terms may sound a bit cryptic, but the idea is quite simple. In the words of one of the twentieth century's best-known historians, Bernard Bailyn, *manifest* history is the "story of events that contemporaries were clearly aware of, that were matters of conscious concern, were consciously struggled over, were, so to speak, headline events in their own time." *Latent* history, in contrast—as you have likely already guessed—is the opposite, the currents and trends that propelled history forward but remained invisible to the men and women of the time, "however much they might have been forced unwittingly to grapple with their consequences."[88]

What if some humans were better able to recognize these latent trends than others? What if this basic ability, or intelligence, is what set truly effective leaders apart from others. Perhaps it is not just a matter of being able to read the human environment in which a leader operates—as the many proponents of Emotional Intelligence suggest—but reading the larger environment. An environmental intelligence, of sorts.

This type of intelligence, Churchill was flush in. His secret to success was his ability to recognize, in the earliest days of the war, the underlying forces at play: that Nazi Germany had to be defeated, that Britain could do so only with the help of powerful allies and through superior organization and quantity of materiel. He set his mind to achieving this outcome in the summer of 1940 and held true to the war's end, by crafting a consistent narrative and carefully building the administrative structures that aligned with these immovable truths of the war. (Incidentally, Bell, Toussaint, and Amundsen all excelled in this ability as well, the latter of whom wrote, "I may say that this is the greatest factor: the way in which the expedition is equipped, the way in which every difficulty is foreseen, and precautions taken for meeting or avoiding it.")

The rationale behind Churchill's most notorious act of 1940, the attack on the French ships at Mers-el-Kébir, can now be more fully understood. Sinking the French fleet was not a rash act of revenge against an ally who had abandoned Britain. It was a strategically brilliant move. The decision aligned short-term needs—to diminish the enemy's potential naval power—and the long game: *to clearly signal British determination and intentions to the United States.* Churchill knew that Roosevelt would have little interest in investing in Britain if he thought that its commitment might waver—and at the time, talk of its wavering was in the air. The US ambassador in London, Joseph Kennedy, believed that Britain's agitation against Hitler would eventually run out of steam. Mers-el-Kébir put paid to Kennedy's argument, convincing Roosevelt that Britain was in it for the long haul. By clearly burning all bridges with Vichy France, it rendered any future accommodation with the fascists unthinkable. Thus did the outlandish sinking of a French fleet bring the decisive alliance with the US—the main goal toward which Churchill was working determinedly behind the scenes—that much closer to reality.

# Part III

## Rethinking Leadership

# The Story We Tell

## Perkins and the Power of the Frame

In late January of 1912, Amundsen and his crew departed from the Bay of Whales for Hobart—from where they would spread word of their remarkable success at the South Pole. A few weeks later, Scott died in his quest to reach the Pole. The year was eventful in other corners of the world, too. In July, Winston Churchill, appointed First Lord of the Admiralty the previous year, set up the British Royal Commission on Fuel and Engines to ensure that the British Navy maintained access to an adequate supply of oil—a development that would shape the Middle East in his time and beyond. On 8 August, the Haitian National Palace exploded spectacularly, killing the president and much of his military entourage and launching the country into a new round of political chaos. Gertrude Bell, meanwhile, spent much of the year planning her most ambitious journey through the Middle East, a journey that would take her over 1500 miles from Damascus down the Arabian Peninsula, across to Baghdad, and back to Damascus.

It was also an eventful year for a man named George Perkins. Perkins was the campaign manager for Theodore Roosevelt, the rambunctious former US president known for his brazen patriotism and his love of all things Western. After his 1901–1909 stint in the White House, Roosevelt had quickly grown disappointed in how his protégé and successor William Taft was performing, and he decided to run again in 1912. It was Perkins's job to see to it that he won. (He didn't win—Woodrow Wilson did—but that's irrelevant to our purposes here).

© The Author(s), under exclusive license to Springer Nature Switzerland AG 2023
M. Gutmann, *The Unseen Leader*, https://doi.org/10.1007/978-3-031-37829-4_7

Perkins awoke one morning during what was a hectic campaign season to find that he had a major headache to deal with. An overeager campaign staffer had ordered three million copies of a pamphlet including one of Roosevelt's stirring speeches and, more importantly, a photo of Roosevelt on the cover. Copyright to the photo belonged to the Moffett Studio of Chicago. Yet, no one had thought to secure permission to reprint the photo. The studio owner was financially strapped and would be sure to make the campaign pay dearly for its mistake. What was Perkins to do?

It is easy to imagine the frenzied and panicked discussions that must have taken place among the campaign staffers that day. While we have no record of what was said, we can imagine that various options and mitigation strategies were discussed. Perhaps someone recommended sending an apologetic message with the offer to pay a goodwill sum. Perhaps someone else advocated for cutting losses and ditching the pamphlet idea altogether. An air of "we're done for" must have permeated the room.

Panic, however, was premature, for Perkins was a savvy guy. He didn't buy the various doomed narratives in circulation. Instead, he wired Moffett the following message, "We are planning to distribute millions of pamphlets with Roosevelt's picture on the cover. It will be great publicity for the studio whose photograph we choose. How much will you pay us to use yours? Respond immediately." Soon enough, the studio wrote back: they were willing to pay $250 for Perkins's exciting offer. Perkins agreed, no doubt with a smile on his face. He had just avoided disaster and made some money to boot.

This probably embellished story about Perkins, like those about Shackleton and Rommel, is a staple in contemporary business schools.[1] And the lesson typically drawn from his tale does not relate directly to leadership. Instead, the lesson in Perkins's story is his ability to *reframe* an unhelpful narrative.

A frame is a rigid structure that surrounds something, like a picture or a window. If we are standing inside a house and want to look out, our gaze is forced to the window. The frame around the window gives the outside world a familiar shape. It also concentrates our focus on whatever is in its center. It presents, in other words, a very limited picture of the world out there. A frame can take on a broader meaning as well. We often speak of someone's frame of mind when describing consistent themes in their thinking or behavior. So, too, dominant stories—rote narrative patterns in how we talk about recurring themes in life, such as leadership—are a frame of sorts.

What Perkins did was to look at the same facts as everyone else but assemble them into an entirely different story. Where everyone else on his staff saw a story of a costly mistake and the need to mitigate damage, Perkins saw an opportunity. He invented no new facts, nor did he say anything untrue. He simply worked from a different set of assumptions than everyone else and told himself, and eventually the poor photographer in Chicago, a different story. He gave the facts on the table a different frame. In contemporary business innovation literature, this is called a reframe.[2] And leadership itself is in dire need of it.

## Abandoning the Action Fallacy

The story we tell about history's great leaders (and by extension leaders today) is faulty. It is faulty because we have adopted a set of assumptions and recurring themes that seem intuitively correct—and are addictively entertaining—but fail to correlate with how historical research tells us events actually unfolded. The culprit in this gross misreading of history is the Action Fallacy—the belief that the best leaders were those who generated the most noise and sensational activity in the most dramatic circumstances. The Action Fallacy acts as a frame, putting distinct (and unhelpful) boundaries on how we talk about leadership.

Inherent in the Action Fallacy is the belief that history is at the mercy of a few brave and bold men and women and that it is, above all, their individual doings that steer events to specific outcomes. Inherent, too, is the mistaken belief that a crisis is the ultimate leadership challenge and the utmost testament to a leader's mettle. Because of these beliefs, the Action Fallacy traps us into telling a very limited set of stories about leaders and leadership. When events don't fit nicely into its frame, we ignore leaders entirely—like Amundsen, Toussaint, and Bell—or misinterpret their stories until they do fit—as in the case of Churchill. And the more we believe that leadership functions in this very specific way, the more likely we are to single out exactly the types of characters or characteristics that conform to it in our reading of the past and the present. And this makes it more likely that the types of people who fit this frame become promoted to positions of leadership. The Action Fallacy, in other words, fuels a self-perpetuating cycle, reinforced by our love of heroic stories and propped up by droves of guru-esque writers and commentators.

This is not to say that the more heroic qualities are bad to have. Indeed, we find plenty of cases in which our four protagonists acted briskly. Churchill ceaselessly hounded his generals to be more aggressive. Bell, if we are to believe Faisal, once even took to arms against Lawrence. When the warships Napoleon had sent to capture the recalcitrant slave-turned-revolutionary-leader appeared on the horizon, Toussaint immediately ordered Cap-Français burned to the ground. Even Amundsen, the epitome of a calm and deliberate leader, could embody a Shackletonesque spirit when occasion required it. During a fateful day navigating the Northwest Passage, when a fire broke out in the engine room, Amundsen did not remain calm but, he recalled, "we all flew into a frantic haste."[3]

Whatever the merit of this behavior in these specific circumstances— Churchill probably went after his generals too hard, while Amundsen's forceful reaction to the fire likely saved the ship and crew—we should not let these flashy examples distract us. Shiny and exciting though they are, in the grand scheme of things they are not behind these leaders' ultimate success. In these brief moments of stress, they did what they had to do: they responded. But these moments hardly define who they were as leaders.

To reframe leadership, we have to start by abandoning the Action Fallacy, once and for all. But it doesn't end there.

## Reframing Leadership

Karl Marx was proved wrong in many of his predictions. Capitalism did not implode under its own weight, as he confidently proclaimed it would. There was no communist revolution in either Germany or the US, the two countries he had his sights on, but instead in Russia—a country completely off his radar. In at least one area, however, Marx was spot on. He famously wrote that, "Men make their own history, but they do not make it just as they please; they do not make it under circumstances chosen by themselves, but under circumstances directly found, given, and transmitted from the past."[4] Leaders, like all people, are constrained by and subject to their circumstances.

To reframe leadership, we must first and foremost, appreciate that there is no steering wheel of history that a single individual can seize. Instead, historical events emerge from a complex web of technological, economic, and cultural drivers, as well as the decisions and actions of numerous individuals, near and far. The most effective leaders are those who recognize this fact and act in alignment with, rather than in ignorance of or against, these currents of history.

Roald Amundsen recognized that regardless of how well stocked your stores were, how much dynamite you packed, or how powerful your steam engines were, you could never bulldoze your way through the polar ice. A nimble and flexible approach was the only promising one. And rather than combating his crew's inevitable flagging of motivation with discipline, ceaseless chores, and lofty pep talks, Amundsen led with humility and honesty—and so made the brutal arctic winters not only survivable but enjoyable for his men. Toussaint recognized early on that an unrivaled network among the island's diverse social groupings was the key to launching and effecting a revolution. And when the European empires fought back to hang on to this most lucrative island, Toussaint leveraged strategic patience—hanging back and letting the island's hostile environment do the work for him, always keeping his eye on his long-term goal but willing to switch sides as the tides of battle and opinion dictated. Gertrude Bell recognized that rather than jostling for a seat at the table, she could exercise true power by subtly influencing the multitude of self-serving and pompous men she found herself among. While swashbuckling attitudes and desert raids captured the public (and eventually Hollywood's) imagination, Bell embodied the banal wisdom that the pen is indeed mightier than the sword. Churchill, whose island's survival was never truly threatened in the summer of 1940, took upon himself and his nation the task of defeating the vilest regime the world had ever seen. To do so, he knew that two things mattered most. He would need to devise the most sophisticated war-fighting machinery imaginable: a slick and well-oiled administration the likes of which Hitler could only dream. And, above all else, he had to cajole a reluctant United States to join the fight and yet, at the same time, restrain it from launching an invasion of Europe prematurely.

Their ability to do so was based on what I termed Environmental Intelligence in an earlier chapter. This exceptionally well-developed awareness of the unique currents of their particular time and place was not something any of them had come by easily. Each of them dedicated their life to developing a fluency in their domain. Churchill was not only a passionate career politician, if there ever was one, but a serial minister and an experienced officer. By the time he took over the war effort, there was no man or woman anywhere on the planet who had a more comprehensive understanding of the mechanism of government and the workings of a modern military. Amundsen, too, was determined from an early age to learn everything he could about being an explorer, just as Gertrude Bell was (and to some extent remains) the most knowledgeable Westerner regarding the cultures and workings of the Middle East. She gained this knowledge both through academic study—reading and reflecting in her writing on every conceivable aspect of the region—and through brave expeditions into uncharted deserts. Toussaint, though an illiterate slave at birth, built a network second to none and a fluency in the informal politics of slave owners and revolutionaries alike. In fact, in all of them we can recognize a stubborn obsession, described in Amundsen by his biographer as him "remain[ing] true to his childhood ideal and to the child within. Only thus could he pursue his ideas so single-mindedly, so stubbornly, so fanatically as he did."[5]

Perhaps some leaders are born. But there is no way to overstate how hard the leaders profiled in this book had to work to achieve the level of competency on which their later successes so fundamentally depended. This, then, might serve as an enduring insight: good leaders boast a mastery of their environment, a mastery gained by dedicated study, self-reflection, and a tenacious gathering of experience.

Second, to reframe leadership we must also learn not to judge all actions equally when evaluating the impact a particular leader has had. Instead, we need to distinguish between leaders whose actions exacerbated the challenge they faced and those whose actions reduced them. The Action Fallacy clearly privileges the former—a crisis, no matter its origin, is what makes a leadership story entertaining. But, as the cases in this book make clear, truly effective leaders, more often than not, forestall overly dramatic circumstances, either in their planning or in their handling of circumstances as they unfold.

Much of the trouble Shackleton's team suffered was self-inflicted; it could have been avoided with a more sober appraisal of how the expedition's resources and capacities lined up against the context of the extreme Antarctic environment. In contrast, Roald Amundsen's journeys make for boring reading not because he was lucky enough to meet with little drama, but because his reading of the environment, his long and careful preparation, and his innovative strategies all reduced the friction his team encountered to a bare minimum. Shackleton's mistake was similar to the mistakes of the various generals and governors who sought to ensnarl Toussaint or of the warlords who faced the same challenge as Churchill—foremost among them Hitler, who made it habit of clogging the wheels of the German military machine (something for which we can be grateful, of course).

The persistent habit of good leaders to reduce, circumvent, or mitigate the friction that inevitably lurks in any complex endeavor is exactly what makes their leadership so hard to spot. It makes them unseen. And, in contrast, the inability of some of their peers to do so is what makes their stories so entertaining.

We may return here to our opening example of leadership being akin to a swimmer crossing a river. While the swimmer who splashes around wildly with his hands on the surface of the water will certainly garner the most attention from those on shore, it is the swimmer who understands the nature of the river and can read the various currents who will make it across with the least effort. And the few actions this leader takes—say, gently moving her arms and legs to align her body with a favorable flow, like Churchill's carefully crafted letters to Roosevelt or Toussaint's subtle scheming to remove an unhelpful rival—occur below the surface of the water and will be largely imperceptible to the onlooker on shore. (Contemporary scholars have come to the same conclusion as well—"The evidence is clear that boring management matters," writes Harvard Business School professor Raffaella Sadun in a summary of her decades-long research into organizational effectiveness and the role of leadership.[6]) These actions, executed with careful deliberation and surgical precision—often over a long period and born from their deep understanding of their time—were much more decisive in facilitating their success than any spur-of-the-moment action or violent course corrections in response to last-minute hiccups.

## Beyond the Past

Approaching leadership, as this book has, as a question to which we should apply the historian's perspectives and tools is not in keeping with common practice in the field's top books and journals. Many academics engaged in contemporary leadership studies approach their work with the same quantitative rigor that physicists and biologists do. Studies are carefully crafted with defined parameters, measurable variables, control groups, and findings expressed with the same precision as a report on the prevalence of a genetic trait in a population of baboons. (One leadership study concluded with confident exactitude, in response to that ever-present question of whether leaders are born or made, that 24% of leadership traits are inherent from birth).[7]

This book was born in an entirely different place, and it purports neither to offer numerical precision nor easy-to-apply five-step recipes for leadership success. Instead, it had a more basic goal: to question an unwritten assumption that dominates how we talk about history's leaders. The result has been an entirely different leadership story from the one we are used to—a story that has remained unseen for too long.

Yet, it is a story that takes courage to embrace. A lot speaks against emulating unseen leaders. While this book has shown us that effective leadership has little to nothing to do with vociferous activity, it is a fact that exactly such activity generates rewards and recognition, whether it is in response to an actual crisis or for no particular reason. The sad truth is that it pays—at least in terms of recognition and reward—to be the Shackleton rather than the Amundsen of the office. One of the most prominent leadership scholars of the past three decades, Keith Grint, soberly acknowledges this point in his classic book *Leadership*, writing, "since we reward people who are good in crises (and ignore people who are such good managers that there are very few crises), [leaders] soon learn to seek out (or reframe situations as) crises."[8] Appearing to be an effective leader, rather than actually being one behind the scenes, is in most circumstances the path to promotion, bonuses, and fame.

To the protagonists in our book, this fact hardly mattered. They were motivated by something more than being recognized as good leaders. Amundsen wanted to cross the Passages and reach the Poles—the fact that his leadership efforts were subsequently ignored by the British annoyed but hardly distressed him. Bell was happy to work in the shadows, enjoying the intricate chess game of the postwar Middle East the same way she enjoyed mountain climbing or studying ruins in the desert—for her own satisfaction. Toussaint wanted to free his people from enslavement and colonization and engineered the first part of the revolution behind the scenes; that other men took credit seemed to hardly bother him—indeed it was a deliberate part of his strategy. Churchill, of course, was recognized even during his time for the leader he was, though the intricacies of his leadership remained hidden to most.

Of course, the story of the unseen leader is not solely theirs. The historical record is filled with extraordinary individuals, many of whom have gone unnoticed by the *action*-primed observer, but whose work for the betterment of their countries or companies was immense. Already in the 1980s, for example, the remarkable American historian Howard Zinn, in his best-selling *A People's History of the United States,* expounded on the profound impact that strike leaders in Seattle, little-known Civil Rights advocates, and many other unseen peoples had on shaping the healthiest parts of the American socioeconomic ecosystem. We can look farther afield as well: remarkable individuals—such as the Berber explorer Ibn Batutta, whose fourteenth century travels put Marco Polo's to shame and facilitated vital exchanges across disparate cultures, or the pioneering Black female entrepreneur C.J. Walker, who built a successful business empire against all odds in the Progressive Era US—are absent from the standard annals of leadership greats.

For this reason, the implications of this book extend far beyond Amundsen, Toussaint, Bell, and Churchill, indeed far beyond history itself. Each of us has a choice about which story we tell about leadership—whether we are telling that story about ourselves or others. And this choice matters. We don't have to look far today to find examples of (usually white) male leaders who feel simultaneously called upon and entitled to bulldoze their way forward, when more often than not they are fighting a crisis of their own making. The damage they cause in their ill-fated attempts at blazing their way through boardrooms or policy discussions is profound, as is evident in recent examples of political leadership—from Trump to Putin to Bolsonaro—as well as among the various narcissistic CEOs in the halls of Silicon Valley firms.

The choice of the leadership story we tell is a choice about the type of world we want to live in. Choosing to embrace the story of the unseen leader is both to commemorate the truly influential—not merely privileged or loud-mouthed—characters of history *and* to do our utmost to prepare for a challenging future by recognizing and rewarding the individuals in our midst today best placed to make a positive impact. It is about embracing ideas and insight from corners of the world or our teams that we may have long overlooked. (Recent research has highlighted the extent to which indigenous mindsets might provide a key to some of today's gravest challenges.[9]) It is about appreciating the quiet and subtle through the distractive noise of the brash and bold and the magnetic pull of a large ego. And it is about acknowledging that there are many things about the world that we cannot control. The key lies not in all-out bluster but in leveraging those currents we can, and in so doing, charting a wise, if unspectacular, course through the torrents. With a growing climate crisis, political tension spilling over into violence across the globe, social fabrics fraying, and corporate workers burning out, the urgency of this cannot be exaggerated.

Not all of us are in a position to change the world. But we don't have to be. Toussaint, Bell, and Churchill each left an indelible footprint on the course of history. Amundsen, on the other hand, did not. His expeditions had no real economic, social, or political impact. His leadership, in the intimate confines of the *Gjöa*, extended to fewer men than the average start-up has on staff today. Yet, in the limited space within which he operated, he was able to achieve remarkable things against the odds. And so can you. The next time you embark on a new venture, the next time you are standing on the edge of a river with a team behind you eagerly awaiting your first move—the first crisis already brewing and everyone's adrenaline running high—take a moment to think: how can I swim with, instead of against, the current?

# Chapter Notes

## Introduction: History and Leadership

[1]L. Loew and K. O'Leonnard, *Leadership Development Factbook 2012: Benchmarks and Trends in US Leadership Development.* Bersin by Deloitte (July 2012).

[2]M. Prokopeak, Follow the Leader(ship) Spending (2018), accessed 12 May 2020, https://www.chieflearningofficer.com/2018/03/21/follow-the-leadership-spending/; and industry analysts predict growth of another $26 billion by 2024, https://www.businesswire.com/news/home/20200311005401/en/Global-Corporate-Leadership-Training-Market-2020-2024-Increased-Spending-on-Corporate-Leadership-Training-to-Boost-Market-Growth-Technavio.

[3]S. A. Haslam, et al., *The New Psychology of Leadership: Identity, Influence, and Power* (Hove, East Sussex England: Psychology Press, 2010), 10.

[4]For more examples, see R. E. Wright, Teaching History in Business Schools: An Insider's View. *Academy of Management Learning & Education* (2010) 9/4, 697–700. The past is used to understand other complex contemporary issues as well. See, for example, McKinsey Global Institute, Forward thinking on what deep history might tell us about today's turbulent times with Alan Taylor. (15 February 2023).

[5]S. Cummings & T. Bridgman, The Relevant Past: Why the History of Management Should Be Critical for Our Future. *Academy of Management Learning & Education* (2011) 10/1, 77–93.

# The Polar Explorer, the Desert Fox, and the Action Fallacy

¹Parts of this section appeared in M. Gutmann, Consulting the Past: Integrating Historians into History-Based Leadership Studies. *Journal of Leadership Studies* (2018); E. Shackleton, *South: Shackleton's Endurance expedition* (New York: Skyhorse Pub, 2013).

²M. Gilbert, *The Second World War: A Complete History* (Rev. ed.) (New York: H. Holt, 1991), 266; R. Citino, Drive to Nowhere. *Quarterly Journal of Military History*, 24/4 (Summer, 2012).

³J. Keegan, *The Second World War.* (New York: Viking, 1990), 330–336; A. Beevor, *The Second World War* (New York: Little, Brown and Co., 2012).

⁴N. G. MacLaren, et al., Testing the Babble Hypothesis: Speaking Time Predicts Leader Emergence in Small Groups. *The Leadership Quarterly* 31/5 (2020).

⁵T. DeLong, The Busyness Trap. *Harvard Business Review* (May 2011), accessed 20 June 2022 at https://hbr.org/2011/05/the-busyness-trap

⁶E. Meyer, Being the Boss in Boss in Brussels, Boston, and Beijing. *Harvard Business Review* (July–August, 2017), accessed 2 May 2023 at https://hbr.org/2017/07/being-the-boss-in-brussels-boston-and-beijing.

⁷A quick google search reveals dozens of blogs that lead with this quote, including, https://www.castlebayconsulting.com/leadership-is-action-not-a-position/ and https://www.teamly.com/blog/leadership-is-action-not-position/.

⁸J. Henley, Merkel Protege AKK Given Defence Job Seen as Poisoned Chalice. *The Guardian* (17 July 2019).

⁹C. Davies, Bill Clinton Talks Loudly, Fails to Act. *The Guardian* (18 July 2019).

¹⁰Foreword to Martin Luther King, *Strength to Love* (Boston: Beacon, 1981), xii.

¹¹Accessed 22 April 2023 at https://www.wow4u.com/action/.

¹²M. Higgins, LinkedIn Post (December 15, 2022).

¹³L. Botelho et al., What Sets Successful CEOs Apart: The Four Essential Behaviours That Help Them Win the Tob Job and Thrive Once They Get It. *Harvard Business Review* 95/3 (2017).

¹⁴H. Bruch, *Bias for Action: How Effective Managers Harness Their Willpower, Achieve Results, and Stop Wasting Time* (Cambridge: HBR Press, 2004).

¹⁵See, for example, S. T. Allison & G. C. Setterberg, Suffering and Sacrifice: Individual and Collective Benefits, and Implications for Leadership. In S. T. Allison, C. T. Kocher, & G. R. Goethals (Eds), *Frontiers in Spiritual*

*Leadership: Discovering the Better Angels of Our Nature* (New York: Palgrave Macmillan, 2016).

[16]G. Ueberschär *Hitlers militärische Elite* (Darmstadt: Primus Verlag, 1998); W. C. Martel, *Victory in War: Foundations of Modern Strategy* (Rev. and expanded ed.) (Cambridge, England; New York: Cambridge University Press, 2011).

[17]R. Amundsen, *The North West Passage: Being the Record of a Voyage of Exploration of the Ship "Gjoa" 1903–1907*, vol. 1 (New York: E.P. Dutton and Company, 1908), 17. This quote referred specifically to the first part of the expedition, though similar sentiments were used to describe the expedition as a whole.

[18]H. Dick, et al., Introduction. In *Narrative in Sociocultural Studies of Language* (Oxford: Oxford University Press, 2017).

[19]H. Moarth, The Irresistible Power of Storytelling as a Strategic Business Tool. *Harvard Business Review*, (March 11, 2014).

[20]Most often this has been studied within the context of branding. See, for example, D. T. Kao, Is Cinderella Resurging? The Impact of Consumers' Underdog Disposition on Brand Preferences: Underdog Brand Biography and Brand Status as Moderators. *Journal of Consumer Behaviour*, 14/5 (2015), 307–316.

[21]Though not the first to describe the Hero's Journey, the most well-known work on the subject is Joseph Campbell, *The Hero with a Thousand Faces* (New York: Pantheon, 1949). I am far from the first to link leadership to the Hero's Journey, though most who do have used it as a model for effective leadership rather than a critique thereof. See, for example, https://kim-holeung.com/hero/ and http://theleadershipforge.com/2016/04/leadership-is-a-heros-journey/.

[22]Most recently, I found it quoted in a Washington Post article, P. Brennan, Shackleton's Successful Failure. *Washington Post*, March 24 (2022), accessed 20 April 2023 at https://www.washingtonpost.com/archive/lifestyle/tv/2002/03/24/shackletons-successful-failure/4c72b4b9-da9f-4bc4-93cc-ed4626d79509/.

[23]C. Schultz, Shackleton Probably Never Took Out an Add Seeing Men for Hazardous Journey. *Smithsonian Magazine* (September 10, 2013).

[24]The exact interaction between structures and individual agency has a rich discourse. See, for example, K. Dowding, *Power, Luck and Freedom: Collected Essays* (Manchester: Manchester University Press, 2016); A. Green & K. Troup, *The Houses of History: A critical Reader in History and Theory* (Second edition. ed.) (Manchester: Manchester University Press, 2016), 6,

204; G. Mukunda, *Indispensable. When Leaders Really Matter* (Cambridge: Harvard Business School Press, 2012).

# Holiday Trips in the Polar Wastelands. Roald Amundsen

[1] This chapter is based on a shorter text I authored on Roald Amundsen for the book M. Gutmann (ed.), *Historians on Leadership and Strategy* (Cham: Springer Nature, 2020). Additionally, two biographies of Roald Amundsen were particularly useful to me: Stephen Bown's *The Last Viking. The Life of Roald Amundsen* and Tor Bomann-Larsen's *Roald Amundsen - En biografi* (also available in English, from which I draw quotes in this chapter). Reading them in parallel is an enlightening exercise. While they are both meticulously researched, Bomann-Larsen is able to use more obscure Norwegian-language sources than the Canadian Bown and reviewed Amundsen's extensive financial records. Bown, on the other hand, meticulously scoured American newspapers and found hundreds of interviews and articles on Amundsen, many of them previously unused in Amundsen biographies. On the matter of Amundsen's character, Bomann-Larsen takes a more critical view. My interpretation aligns more closely with Bown's.

While I read Amundsen's original Norwegian manuscripts, I have used quotes from the English translations, most notably *The North West Passage: Being the Record of a Voyage of Exploration of the Ship "Gjøa", 1903–1907*, vol. 1 (New York: E.P. Dutton and Company, 1908) and *The South Pole: An Account of the Norwegian Antarctic Expedition in the "Fram", 1910–1912*, vol. 1 & 2 (Pantianos Classics, 2023), original publication in 1912.

[2] Useful here is *Sir John Franklin's Journals and Correspondence: The First Arctic Land Expedition, 1819–1822*, The Publications of the Champlain Society, vol. 59 (Toronto: Champlain Society, 1995).

[3] A. Wilkinson, *The Ice Balloon: S.A. Andrée and the Heroic Age of Arctic Exploration* (New York: Knopf, 2001).

[4] J. Niven, *The Ice Master: The Doomed 1913 Voyage of the Karluk* (New York: Hachett Books, 2001); W. Mills, *Exploring Polar Frontiers: A Historical Encyclopedia* (Santa Barbara: ABC-CLIO, 2003).

[5] F. Fernandez-Armesto, *The World. A History* (New York: Pearson, 2006).

[6] R. Amundsen, *The North West Passage: Being the Record of a Voyage of Exploration of the Ship "Gjøa" 1903–1907*, vol. 1 (New York: E.P. Dutton and Company, 1908), 9.

[7] D. Kennedy, *Reinterpreting Exploration: The West in the World* (Oxford: Oxford University Press, 2014).

[8] There are many books on the British attempts, including Franklin's. Particularly noteworthy is F. Fleming, *Barrow's Boys. A Stirring Story of Daring, Fortitude, and Outright Lunacy* (New York: Grove Press, 2001), e-book.

[9] R. Amundsen, *The North West Passage: Being the Record of a Voyage of Exploration of the Ship "Gjoa" 1903–1907*, vol. 1 (New York: E.P. Dutton and Company, 1908), 4.

[10] R. Amundsen, *My Life as an Explorer* (New York: Doubleday, 1927), 2.

[11] R. Amundsen, *The North West Passage: Being the Record of a Voyage of Exploration of the Ship "Gjoa" 1903–1907*, vol. 1 (New York: E.P. Dutton and Company, 1908), 4.

[12] The only detour he took was a brief stint as a medical student—at his mother's insistence. When she died in 1893, he left his studies behind and returned to his obsession.

[13] R. Amundsen, *My Life as an Explorer* (New York: Doubleday, 1927), 4.

[14] Polar Worlds Collection. National Maritime Museum and Archives, London.

[15] R. Amundsen, *My Life as an Explorer* (New York: Doubleday, 1927), 18.

[16] T. Bomann-Larsen, *Roald Amundsen* (London: The History Press, 2006), 47.

[17] R. Amundsen, *The North West Passage: Being the Record of a Voyage of Exploration of the Ship "Gjoa" 1903–1907*, vol. 1 (New York: E.P. Dutton and Company, 1908), 6.

[18] T. Bomann-Larsen, *Roald Amundsen* (London: The History Press, 2006), 58.

[19] F. Nansen, Introduction. R. Amundsen, *The South Pole: An Account of the Norwegian Antarctic Expedition in the "Fram", 1910–1912*, vol. 1 & 2 (Pantianos Classics, 2023), x.

[20] R. Amundsen, *My Life as an Explorer* (New York: Doubleday, 1927), 77.

[21] Bomann-Larsen, whose biography relies on a more in-depth examination of Amundsen's finances than any previous work, claims that Amundsen later exaggerated the extent to which the expedition was financially strapped, see T. Bomann-Larsen, *Roald Amundsen* (London: The History Press, 2006), 60–61.

[22] R. Amundsen, *The North West Passage: Being the Record of a Voyage of Exploration of the Ship "Gjoa" 1903–1907*, vol. 1 (New York: E.P. Dutton and Company, 1908), 14.

[23] R. Amundsen, *The North West Passage: Being the Record of a Voyage of Exploration of the Ship "Gjoa" 1903–1907*, vol. 1 (New York: E.P. Dutton and Company, 1908), 47.

[24] R. Amundsen, *My Life as an Explorer* (New York: Doubleday, 1927), 2.

25R. Amundsen, *The North West Passage: Being the Record of a Voyage of Exploration of the Ship "Gjoa" 1903–1907*, vol. 1 (New York: E.P. Dutton and Company, 1908), 64.

26R. Amundsen, *The North West Passage: Being the Record of a Voyage of Exploration of the Ship "Gjoa" 1903–1907*, vol. 1 (New York: E.P. Dutton and Company, 1908), 75.

27R. Amundsen, *The North West Passage: Being the Record of a Voyage of Exploration of the Ship "Gjoa" 1903–1907*, vol. 1 (New York: E.P. Dutton and Company, 1908), 68–69.

28Helmer Hansen, quoted in S. Bown, *The Last Viking: The Life of Roald Amundsen* (Vancouver: Douglas & McIntyre, 2012), 66.

29Quoted in G. Williams, *Arctic Labyrinth: The Quest for the Northwest Passage* (Berkley: University of California Press, 2010).

30An excellent source on this and other British Northwest Passage expeditions is *Arctic Labyrinth: The Quest for the Northwest Passage* (Berkley: University of California Press, 2010).

31Royal Museums Greenwich, William Edward Parry first North-West Passage expedition 1819–1820. Online resource, accessed 12 March 2023 at rmg.co.uk.

32Quoted in F. Fleming, *Barrow's Boys. A Stirring Story of Daring, Fortitude, and Outright Lunacy* (New York: Grove Press, 2001), e-book.

33R. Amundsen, *The South Pole: An Account of the Norwegian Antarctic Expedition in the "Fram", 1910–1912*, vol. 1 & 2 (Pantianos Classics, 2023), 15

34Polar Worlds Collection. National Maritime Museum and Archives, London.

35R. Sylvain, A Very Special Piece of Paper. Canadian Museum of History (2018).

36O. Beattie & J. Geiger, Frozen in Time: Unlocking the Secrets of the Franklin Expedition (Saskatoon: Western Producer Prairie Books, 1987), 113. Subsequent studies contradict this assessment, by comparing the levels of lead in the remains of Franklin's men with that of British sailors at the cemetery in Antigua: T. Swanston et al., Franklin Expedition Lead Exposure: New Insights from High Resolution Confocal X-ray Fluorescence Imaging of Skeletal Microstructure. *PLoS One*, 13/8 (August 2018).

37B. Z. Horowitz, Polar Poisons: Did Botulism Doom the Franklin Expedition? *Journal of Toxicology: Clinical Toxicology* 41/6 (2003), 841–7.

38R. Amundsen, *The North West Passage: Being the Record of a Voyage of Exploration of the Ship "Gjoa" 1903–1907*, vol. 1 (New York: E.P. Dutton and Company, 1908), 80.

39 On this point, see D. H. Eber, *Encounters on the Passage: Inuit Meet the Explorers* (Toronto: Toronto University Press, 2008) and B. Maddison, *Class and Colonialism in Antarctic Exploration, 1750–1920* (London: Pickering & Chatto, 2014).

40 Good sources on Scott and Shackleton are E. Larson, *An Empire of Ice: Scott, Shackleton, and the Heroic age of Antarctic Science* (New Haven: Yale University Press, 2011) and R. Huntford, *Race for the South Pole: The Expedition Diaries of Scott and Amundsen* (London: Continuum, 2010).

41 R. Amundsen, *The South Pole: An Account of the Norwegian Antarctic Expedition in the "Fram", 1910–1912*, vol. 1 & 2 (Pantianos Classics, 2023), 22

42 R. Huntford, *Race for the South Pole: The Expedition Diaries of Scott and Amundsen* (London: Continuum, 2010).

43 A good discussion can be found in B. *Henderson, True North: Peary, Cook, and the Race to the Pole* (London: W. W. Norton and Company, 2005). A later claim by American airman Charles Bird to have reached the Pole in 1926, shortly before Amundsen and Nobile, is almost certainly false as well. See, D. Rawlins, Byrd's Heroic 1926 Flight and Its Faked Last Leg. *International Journal of Scientific History*, 10 (January 2000): 69–76.

44 S. Bown, *The Last Viking: The Life of Roald Amundsen* (Vancouver: Douglas & McIntyre, 2012), 122.

45 R. Amundsen, *The South Pole: An Account of the Norwegian Antarctic Expedition in the "Fram", 1910–1912*, vol. 1 & 2 (Pantianos Classics, 2023), 118.

46 Quoted in S. Bown, *The Last Viking: The Life of Roald Amundsen* (Vancouver: Douglas & McIntyre, 2012), 154.

47 Quoted in S. Bown, *The Last Viking: The Life of Roald Amundsen* (Vancouver: Douglas & McIntyre, 2012), 154.

48 R. Amundsen, *The South Pole: An Account of the Norwegian Antarctic Expedition in the "Fram", 1910–1912*, vol. 1 & 2 (Pantianos Classics, 2023), ix.

49 R. Amundsen, *The South Pole: An Account of the Norwegian Antarctic Expedition in the "Fram", 1910–1912*, vol. 1 & 2 (Pantianos Classics, 2023), 127

50 R. Amundsen, *The South Pole: An Account of the Norwegian Antarctic Expedition in the "Fram", 1910–1912*, vol. 1 & 2 (Pantianos Classics, 2023), vi.

51 R. Amundsen, *The South Pole: An Account of the Norwegian Antarctic Expedition in the "Fram", 1910–1912*, vol. 1 & 2 (Pantianos Classics, 2023), 133.

[52]R. Amundsen, *The South Pole: An Account of the Norwegian Antarctic Expedition in the "Fram", 1910–1912*, vol. 1 & 2 (Pantianos Classics, 2023), 137.

[53]R. Amundsen, *The South Pole: An Account of the Norwegian Antarctic Expedition in the "Fram", 1910–1912*, vol. 1 & 2 (Pantianos Classics, 2023), 138.

[54]R. Amundsen, *The South Pole: An Account of the Norwegian Antarctic Expedition in the "Fram", 1910–1912*, vol. 1 & 2 (Pantianos Classics, 2023), 153.

[55]F. Nansen, Introduction. In R. Amundsen, *The South Pole: An Account of the Norwegian Antarctic Expedition in the "Fram", 1910–1912*, vol. 1 & 2 (Pantianos Classics, 2023), xi.

[56]R. Amundsen, *My Life as an Explorer* (Garden City, NY: Doubleday, 1927), 66–67.

[57]R. Amundsen, *My Life as an Explorer* (Garden City, NY: Doubleday, 1927), 38.

[58]F. A. Worsley, *Endurance: An Epic of Polar Adventure* (New York: W.W. Norton & co., 1999), 20.

[59]J. Kotter, What Leaders Really Do. *Harvard Business Review* (December, 2001).

[60]R. Owen, *The Fate of Franklin* (London: Hutchinson, 1978), 236.

[61]F. Fleming, *Barrow's Boys. A Stirring Story of Daring, Fortitude, and Outright Lunacy* (New York: Grove Press, 2001), e-book.

[62]See B. Riffenburgh, *Shackleton's Forgotten Expedition: The Voyage of the Nimrod* (New York: Bloomsbury, 2004).

[63]R. Amundsen, *The North West Passage: Being the Record of a Voyage of Exploration of the Ship "Gjoa" 1903–1907*, vol. 1 (New York: E.P. Dutton and Company, 1908), 17.

[64]R. Amundsen, *The South Pole: An Account of the Norwegian Antarctic Expedition in the "Fram", 1910–1912*, vol. 1 & 2 (Pantianos Classics, 2023), 132.

[65]Quoted in S. Bown, *The Last Viking: The Life of Roald Amundsen* (Vancouver: Douglas & McIntyre, 2012).

[66]S. Bown, *The Last Viking: The Life of Roald Amundsen* (Vancouver: Douglas & McIntyre, 2012).

[67]R. Amundsen, *My Life as an Explorer* (Garden City, NY: Doubleday, 1927), 92.

[68]E. Ries, *The Lean Startup: How Constant Innovation Creates Radically Successful Businesses* (London: Portfolio Penguin, 2011).

[69]Quoted in T. Bomann-Larsen, *Roald Amundsen* (London: The History Press, 2006), 544.

[70]R. Amundsen, *The South Pole: An Account of the Norwegian Antarctic Expedition in the "Fram", 1910–1912*, vol. 1 & 2 (Pantianos Classics, 2023), 21.

# Napoleon's Thorn. Toussaint Louverture

[1]The past decade has seen a series of carefully researched books on the life and career of Toussaint Louverture. In addition to various primary sources as cited below, my chapter is based on the three most notable of these recent bibliographies: Madison Bell's *Toussaint Louverture* (New York: Penguin, 2008), Philippe Girard's *Toussaint Louverture: A Revolutionary Life* (New York: Basic Books, 2016) and Sudhir Hazareesingh *Black Spartacus: The Epic Life of Toussaint Louverture* (New York: Penguin, 2021). J. D. Popkin's work on the Haitian Revolution, *A Concise History of the Haitian Revolution* (New York: Wiley-Blackwell, 2012), proved an invaluable source as well. Facts and interpretations not specifically cited in this chapter appear in one or more of these books. Where the authors offer differing opinions, I have noted this in the text or in endnotes.

Additionally, I have relied on various primary sources, many of which are available through the Brown University Haitian Revolution Collection (https://library.brown.edu/haitihistory/7.html). Finally, in linking the Haitian Revolution to broader events and trends in European history, I relied on the broad work of historians working within the global, transnational perspective, including that of Felipe Fernandez Armesto, Howard Spodek and Howard Zinn.

A good discussion of the rationale of capitalizing "Black" and leaving "white" in lower case in references to the social groups can be found in K. A. Appiah, The Case for Capitalizing the B in Black. In *The Atlantic* (June 18, 2020), https://www.theatlantic.com/ideas/archive/2020/06/time-to-capitalize-blackand-white/613159/

[2]P. Girard, *Toussaint Louverture: A Revolutionary Life* (New York: Basic Books, 2016), 151.

[3]P. Girard, *Toussaint Louverture: A Revolutionary Life* (New York: Basic Books, 2016), 150-153.

[4]S. Hazareesingh, *Black Spartacus: The Epic Life of Toussaint Louverture* (New York: Penguin, 2021), 20

[5]P. Girard, *Toussaint Louverture: A Revolutionary Life* (New York: Basic Books, 2016), 152.

[6]P. Girard, *Toussaint Louverture: A Revolutionary Life* (New York: Basic Books, 2016), 151.

[7]R. N. Buckley (ed.), *The Haitian Journal of Lieutenant Howard: York Hussars 1796–1798* (Knoxville: The University of Tennessee Press, 1985), 59–60.

[8]S. Hazareesingh, *Black Spartacus: The Epic Life of Toussaint Louverture* (New York: Penguin, 2021), 309.

[9]R. N. Buckley (ed.), *The Haitian Journal of Lieutenant Howard: York Hussars 1796–1798* (Knoxville: The University of Tennessee Press, 1985), 39.

[10]E. Hobsbawm, *The Age of Revolution: Europe. 1789-1848* (London: Weidenfeld & Nicolson, 1962). A good overview of this revolutionary period, with the glaring exception that it contains no mention of the Haitian Revolution nor Toussaint, is S. Gemie, Revolutions and Revolutionaries: Histories, Concepts and Myths. In *A Companion to Nineteenth-Century Europe. 1789–1914* (Oxford: Blackwell Publishing, 2006).

[11]Remember Haiti. John Carter Brown Library, Brown University, https://www.brown.edu/Facilities/John_Carter_Brown_Library/exhibitions/remember_haiti/revolution.php.

[12]H. Zinn, *A People's History of the United States* (New York: Harper Collins, 2003), 3.

[13]S. E. Morison, *The Oxford History of the American People. Volume One: Prehistory to 1789* (New York: Penguin, 1994), 71.

[14]S. Hazareesingh, *Black Spartacus: The Epic Life of Toussaint Louverture* (New York: Penguin, 2021), 5; J.D. Popkin, *A Concise History of the Haitian Revolution* (New York: Wiley-Blackwell, 2012), 2.

[15]P. Girard, *Toussaint Louverture: A Revolutionary Life* (New York: Basic Books, 2016), 78. See also, M. Parker, *Sugar Barons: Family, Corruption, Empire and War* (London: Windmill, 2012).

[16]M. Bell, *Toussaint Louverture* (New York: Penguin, 2008), Chpt. 1.

[17]S. Hazareesingh, *Black Spartacus: The Epic Life of Toussaint Louverture* (New York: Penguin, 2021), 50.

[18]S. Hazareesingh, *Black Spartacus: The Epic Life of Toussaint Louverture* (New York: Penguin, 2021), 31.

[19]Code Noir. Source Collection: Slavery and the Haitian Revolution, in World History Commons, https://worldhistorycommons.org/source-collection-slavery-and-haitian-revolution.

[20]P. Girard, *Toussaint Louverture: A Revolutionary Life* (New York: Basic Books, 2016), 95.

[21]S. Hazareesingh, *Black Spartacus: The Epic Life of Toussaint Louverture* (New York: Penguin, 2021), 7.

[22] S. Hazareesingh, *Black Spartacus: The Epic Life of Toussaint Louverture* (New York: Penguin, 2021), X.

[23] M. Bell, *Toussaint Louverture* (New York: Penguin, 2008), Chpt. 1.

[24] P. Girard, *Toussaint Louverture: A Revolutionary Life* (New York: Basic Books, 2016), 125.

[25] M. Bell, *Toussaint Louverture* (New York: Penguin, 2008), Chpt. 1.

[26] P. Girard, *Toussaint Louverture: A Revolutionary Life* (New York: Basic Books, 2016), 58.

[27] S. Hazareesingh, *Black Spartacus: The Epic Life of Toussaint Louverture* (New York: Penguin, 2021), 51.

[28] P. Girard, *Toussaint Louverture: A Revolutionary Life* (New York: Basic Books, 2016), 108.

[29] S. Hazareesingh, *Black Spartacus: The Epic Life of Toussaint Louverture* (New York: Penguin, 2021), 54.

[30] S. Hazareesingh, *Black Spartacus: The Epic Life of Toussaint Louverture* (New York: Penguin, 2021), 58.

[31] J. D. Popkin, *A Concise History of the Haitian Revolution* (New York: Wiley-Blackwell, 2012), 56–58.

[32] The Emancipation Proclamation of 29 August 1793. In D. Geggus (ed.), *The Haitian Revolution. A Documentary History* (Cambridge: Hackett Publishing, 2014), 107.

[33] Proclamation of 29 August 1793. In G. Tyson (ed.), *Toussaint L'Ouverture.* (New York: Prentice-Hall 1973), 28–31.

[34] M. Bell, *Toussaint Louverture* (New York: Penguin, 2008), Chpt. 1.

[35] S. Hazareesingh, *Black Spartacus: The Epic Life of Toussaint Louverture* (New York: Penguin, 2021), 77.

[36] S. Hazareesingh, *Black Spartacus: The Epic Life of Toussaint Louverture* (New York: Penguin, 2021), 77.

[37] Quoted in S. Hazareesingh, *Black Spartacus: The Epic Life of Toussaint Louverture* (New York: Penguin, 2021), 90.

[38] Quoted in S. Hazareesingh, *Black Spartacus: The Epic Life of Toussaint Louverture* (New York: Penguin, 2021), 85.

[39] S. Hazareesingh, *Black Spartacus: The Epic Life of Toussaint Louverture* (New York: Penguin, 2021), 147–149.

[40] Grievance List, Source Collection: Slavery and the Haitian Revolution. In World History Commons, https://worldhistorycommons.org/source-collection-slavery-and-the-haitian-revolution.

[41] Original *Discours sur l'État de Saint-Domingue Et sur la Conduite des Agens du Directoire* (Forgotten Books, 2019). English translations as per

S. Hazareesingh, *Black Spartacus: The Epic Life of Toussaint Louverture* (New York: Penguin, 2021), 119–120.

[42]S. Hazareesingh, *Black Spartacus: The Epic Life of Toussaint Louverture* (New York: Penguin, 2021), 120.

[43]D. G. Wright, *Napoleon and Europe* (Harlow: Longman, 1984), 24.

[44]S. Hazareesingh, *Black Spartacus: The Epic Life of Toussaint Louverture* (New York: Penguin, 2021), 213.

[45]D. G. Wright, *Napoleon and Europe* (Harlow: Longman, 1984), 18.

[46]J. Fradera, Chapter Three. The Genealogy of Napoleon's "Special Laws" for the Colonies. In *The Imperial Nation* (Princeton: Princeton University Press, 2018), 74–87.

[47]Toussaint Louverture's Constitution, July 1801. In D. Geggus (ed.), *The Haitian Revolution. A Documentary History* (Cambridge: Hackett Publishing, 2014), 160.

[48]S. Hazareesingh, *Black Spartacus: The Epic Life of Toussaint Louverture* (New York: Penguin, 2021), 19.

[49]Forced Labor Decree, 12 October 1800. In G. Tyson (ed.), *Toussaint L'Ouverture.* (New York: Prentice-Hall 1973), 31.

[50]P. Girard, *Toussaint Louverture: A Revolutionary Life* (New York: Basic Books, 2016), 192.

[51]One such example can be found here, Toussaint letter to Napoleon on the 1801 Constitution. The Louverture Project, accessed 10 May 2021 at http://thelouvertureproject.org/index.php?title=Toussaint_letter_to_Napoléon_on_the_1801_Constitution.

[52]S. Hazareesingh, *Black Spartacus: The Epic Life of Toussaint Louverture* (New York: Penguin, 2021), 301.

[53]S. Hazareesingh, *Black Spartacus: The Epic Life of Toussaint Louverture* (New York: Penguin, 2021), 302–307.

[54]S. Hazareesingh, *Black Spartacus: The Epic Life of Toussaint Louverture* (New York: Penguin, 2021), 309.

[55]S. Hazareesingh, *Black Spartacus: The Epic Life of Toussaint Louverture* (New York: Penguin, 2021), 309.

[56]P. Girard, *Toussaint Louverture: A Revolutionary Life* (New York: Basic Books, 2016), 247.

[57]Toussaint letter to Napoleon from Fort de Joux. The Louverture Project, accessed on 11 May 2021 at http://thelouvertureproject.org/index.php?title=Toussaint_letter_to_Napoléon_from_Fort_de_Joux_(1802).

[58]The Haitian Declaration of Independence. Duke University, https://today.duke.edu/showcase/haitideclaration/declarationstext.htm.

[59]Investigating Haiti's Double Debt. *New York Times* (May 22, 2022), https://www.nytimes.com/2022/05/22/insider/investigating-haitis-double-debt.html.

[60]R. Ashkenas & B. Manville, You don't have to be CEO to be a visionary leader. *Harvard Business Review* (4 April 2019), https://hbr.org/2019/04/you-dont-have-to-be-ceo-to-be-a-visionary-leader.

[61]P. Gilroy, *The Black Atlantic. Modernity and Double Consciousness* (Cambridge: Harvard University Press, 1993), 13.

## "If the women of the English are like her, the men must be like lions." Gertrude Bell

[1]The Gertrude Bell Archive at Newcastle University contains digitized copies of Bell's letters and provided me with a significant source for this chapter. Additionally, recent books examine the life of Bell in detail: G. Howell (ed.), *Gertrude Bell: A Woman in Arabia* (London: Pan, 2015), P. Collins & C. Tripp (eds.), *Gertrude Bell and Iraq: A Life and Legacy* (Oxford: Oxford University Press, 2017), and L. Lukitz, *A Quest in the Middle East: Gertrude Bell and the Making of Modern Iraq* (London: I.B. Taurus, 2019). Letter, Gertrude Bell to Hugh Bell, 8 September 1901. http://gertrudebell.ncl.ac.uk/letter_details.php?letter_id=1268

[2]Letter, Gertrude Bell to Dame Florence Bell, 31 August 1904. http://gertrudebell.ncl.ac.uk/letters.php?year=1904&month=8

[3]G. Howell (ed.), *Gertrude Bell: A Woman in Arabia* (London: Pan, 2015), 30.

[4]P. Collins & C. Tripp, Introduction. In P. Collins & C. Tripp (eds.), *Gertrude Bell and Iraq: A Life and Legacy* (Oxford: Oxford University Press, 2017), 16.

[5]P. Sluglett, Gertrude Bell and the Ottoman Empire. In P. Collins & C. Tripp (eds.), *Gertrude Bell and Iraq: A Life and Legacy* (Oxford: Oxford University Press, 2017), 28.

[6]T. Chalabi, Fragments of a Mirror: The Writing of Gertrude Bell. In P. Collins & C. Tripp (eds.), *Gertrude Bell and Iraq: A Life and Legacy* (Oxford: Oxford University Press, 2017), 163.

[7]G. Howell, *Queen of the Desert: The Extraordinary Life of Gertrude Bell* (London: Pan, 2015), 417.

[8]G. Howell, *Queen of the Desert: The Extraordinary Life of Gertrude Bell* (London: Pan, 2015), 418.

[9]G. Howell, *Queen of the Desert: The Extraordinary Life of Gertrude Bell* (London: Pan, 2015), 416.

[10]L. Lukitz, *A Quest in the Middle East: Gertrude Bell and the Making of Modern Iraq* (London: I.B. Taurus, 2019), 237.

[11]G. Howell, *Queen of the Desert: The Extraordinary Life of Gertrude Bell* (London: Pan, 2015), 419.

[12]Gertrude Bell: The Uncrowned Queen of the Desert. *BBC News*, 30 January 2014. https://www.bbc.com/news/uk-england-tyne-25775990

[13]S. Lloyd, Excavating the Land between the Two Rivers. In J. Sasson (ed.), *Civilisations of the Ancient Near East,* vol. 4 (New York: Hendrickson, 1995), 2732.

[14]G. Howell, *Queen of the Desert: The Extraordinary Life of Gertrude Bell* (London: Pan, 2015), 419.

[15]See also D. G. H., Obituary: Gertrude Lowthian Bell. *The Geographical Journal*, 68/4 (Oct., 1926), 363–368.

[16]Quoted in K. E. Meyer & S. B. Brysac, *Kingmakers: The Invention of the Modern Middle East* (New York: W. W. Norton & Company, 2009). Kindle Edition.

[17]K. E. Meyer & S. B. Brysac, *Kingmakers: The Invention of the Modern Middle East* (New York: W. W. Norton & Company, 2009). Kindle Edition.

[18]*Harvard Business Review*, accessed 12 April 2021 at https://hbr.org/topic/managing-up

[19]J. Barr, *A Line in the Sand: Britain, France and the Struggle that Shaped the Middle East* (London: Simon and Schuster, 2011), 24.

[20]J. Barr, *A Line in the Sand: Britain, France and the Struggle that Shaped the Middle East* (London: Simon and Schuster, 2011), 24.

[21]J. Barr, *A Line in the Sand: Britain, France and the Struggle that Shaped the Middle East* (London: Simon and Schuster, 2011), 25.

[22]J. Barr, *A Line in the Sand: Britain, France and the Struggle that Shaped the Middle East* (London: Simon and Schuster, 2011), 26.

[23]G. Howell (ed.), *Gertrude Bell: A Woman in Arabia* (New York: Penguin, 2015), 156.

[24]J. E. Courtney, In Memoriam: Gertrude Margaret Lowthian Bell. In P. Collins & C. Tripp (eds.), *Gertrude Bell and Iraq: A Life and Legacy* (Oxford: Oxford University Press, 2017), 293.

[25]C. Hitchens, The Woman Who Made Iraq. *The Atlantic* (June 2007), accessed 12 April 2020 at, https://www.theatlantic.com/magazine/archive/2007/06/the-woman-who-made-iraq/305893/

[26]R. Wright, How the Curse of Sykes-Picot Still Haunts the Middle East. *The New Yorker* (30 April 2016), accessed 12 April 2020 at, https://www.newyorker.com/news/news-desk/how-the-curse-of-sykes-picot-still-haunts-the-middle-east

[27]J. Barr, *A Line in the Sand: Britain, France and the Struggle that Shaped the Middle East* (London: Simon and Schuster, 2011), 103.

28G. Howell, *Queen of the Desert: The Extraordinary Life of Gertrude Bell* (London: Pan, 2015), 277.

29G. Howell, *Queen of the Desert: The Extraordinary Life of Gertrude Bell* (London: Pan, 2015), 278.

30G. Howell, *Queen of the Desert: The Extraordinary Life of Gertrude Bell* (London: Pan, 2015), 259.

31G. Howell (ed.), *Gertrude Bell: A Woman in Arabia* (New York: Penguin, 2015), 167.

32G. Howell, *Queen of the Desert: The Extraordinary Life of Gertrude Bell* (London: Pan, 2015), 356.

33G. Howell, *Queen of the Desert: The Extraordinary Life of Gertrude Bell* (London: Pan, 2015), 356.

34H. Berry, Gertrude Bell: Pioneer, Anti-Suffragist, Feminist Icon? In P. Collins & C. Tripp (eds.), *Gertrude Bell and Iraq: A Life and Legacy* (Oxford: Oxford University Press, 2017), 127.

35G. Howell, *Queen of the Desert: The Extraordinary Life of Gertrude Bell* (London: Pan, 2015), 76.

36H. Berry, Gertrude Bell: Pioneer, Anti-Suffragist, Feminist Icon? In P. Collins & C. Tripp (eds.), *Gertrude Bell and Iraq: A Life and Legacy* (Oxford: Oxford University Press, 2017), 151.

37Letter, Gertrude Bell to Dame Florence Bell, 6 September 1917. http://gertrudebell.ncl.ac.uk/letter_details.php?letter_id=257

38J. Buchan, Miss Bell's Lines in the Sand, *The Guardian* (12 March 2003). https://www.theguardian.com/world/2003/mar/12/iraq.jamesbuchan

39C. Hitchens, The Woman Who Made Iraq. *The Atlantic* (June 2007), accessed 12 April 2020 at, https://www.theatlantic.com/magazine/archive/2007/06/the-woman-who-made-iraq/305893/

40R. Stewart, The Queen of the Quagmire. *The New York Review of Books* (25 October 2007). https://www.nybooks.com/articles/2007/10/25/the-queen-of-the-quagmire/

41J. Buchan, Miss Bell's Lines in the Sand. *The Guardian* (12 March 2003). https://www.theguardian.com/world/2003/mar/12/iraq.jamesbuchan

42K. E. Meyer & S. B. Brysac, *Kingmakers: The Invention of the Modern Middle East* (New York: W. W. Norton & Company, 2009. Kindle Edition).

43S. B. Eskander, Gertrude Bell and the Formation of the Iraqi State: The Kurdish Dimension. In P. Collins & C. Tripp (eds.), *Gertrude Bell and Iraq: A Life and Legacy* (Oxford: Oxford University Press, 2017), 215.

44E. Monroe, Gertrude Bell (1868–1926). *Bulletin (British Society for Middle Eastern Studies)*, 7/1 (1980), 3–23

[45]Letter, Gertrude Bell to unknown, 26 May 1900. http://www.gerty.ncl. ac.uk/letter_details.php?letter_id=1199

[46]K. E. Meyer & S. B. Brysac, *Kingmakers: The Invention of the Modern Middle East* (New York: W. W. Norton & Company, 2009. Kindle Edition).

[47]J. Morris, *Farewell the Trumpets* (London: Faber & Faber, 2010), 3.

[48]G. Howell, *Queen of the Desert: The Extraordinary Life of Gertrude Bell* (London: Pan, 2015), 310.

[49]G. Howell, *Queen of the Desert: The Extraordinary Life of Gertrude Bell* (London: Pan, 2015), 314.

[50]K. E. Meyer & S. B. Brysac, *Kingmakers: The Invention of the Modern Middle East* (New York: W. W. Norton & Company, 2009. Kindle Edition).

[51]J. Barr, *A Line in the Sand: Britain, France and the Struggle that Shaped the Middle East* (London: Simon and Schuster, 2011), 105.

[52]Letter, Gertrude Bell to Dame Florence Bell, 10 April 1920. http://www. gerty.ncl.ac.uk/letters.php?year=1920&month=4

[53]Letter, Gertrude Bell to Dame Florence Bell and Sir Hugh Bell, 10 October 1920. http://www.gerty.ncl.ac.uk/letter_details.php?letter_id=427

[54]J. Barr, *A Line in the Sand: Britain, France and the Struggle that Shaped the Middle East* (London: Simon and Schuster, 2011), 105.

[55]K. E. Meyer & S. B. Brysac, *Kingmakers: The Invention of the Modern Middle East* (New York: W. W. Norton & Company, 2009. Kindle Edition).

[56]J. Barr, *A Line in the Sand: Britain, France and the Struggle that Shaped the Middle East* (London: Simon and Schuster, 2011), 111.

[57]J. Barr, *A Line in the Sand: Britain, France and the Struggle that Shaped the Middle East* (London: Simon and Schuster, 2011), 112.

[58]K. E. Meyer & S. B. Brysac, *Kingmakers: The Invention of the Modern Middle East* (New York: W. W. Norton & Company, 2009. Kindle Edition).

[59]G. Howell, *Queen of the Desert: The Extraordinary Life of Gertrude Bell* (London: Pan, 2015), 391.

[60]G. Bell, *Review of the Civil Administration of Mesopotamia* (London: HM Stationery Office, 1920), p 127.

[61]K. E. Meyer & S. B. Brysac, *Kingmakers: The Invention of the Modern Middle East* (New York: W. W. Norton & Company, 2009. Kindle Edition).

[62]M. Yakoubi, Gertrude Bell's Perception of Faisal I of Iraq and the Anglo-Arab Romance. In P. Collins & C. Tripp (eds.), *Gertrude Bell and Iraq: A Life and Legacy* (Oxford: Oxford University Press, 2017), 211.

[63]M. Yakoubi, Gertrude Bell's Perception of Faisal I of Iraq and the Anglo-Arab Romance. In P. Collins & C. Tripp (eds.), *Gertrude Bell and Iraq: A Life and Legacy* (Oxford: Oxford University Press, 2017), 202.

[64]L. Lukitz, *A Quest in the Middle East: Gertrude Bell and the Making of Modern Iraq* (London: I.B. Taurus, 2019), 196.

[65]L. Lukitz, *A Quest in the Middle East: Gertrude Bell and the Making of Modern Iraq* (London: I.B. Taurus, 2019), 185.

[66]L. Lukitz, *A Quest in the Middle East: Gertrude Bell and the Making of Modern Iraq* (London: I.B. Taurus, 2019), 130.

[67]G. Howell, *Queen of the Desert: The Extraordinary Life of Gertrude Bell* (London: Pan, 2015), 451.

[68]Letter, T. E. Shaw (Lawrence) to Sir Hugh Bell, 4 November 1927, in M. Brown, (ed.), *The Letters of T.E. Lawrence: The Years in India 1927–29*.

[69]Letter, Gertrude Bell to Florence Lascelles, 9 April 1905.

[70]L. Lukitz, *A Quest in the Middle East: Gertrude Bell and the Making of Modern Iraq* (London: I.B. Taurus, 2019), 184.

[71]L. Lukitz, *A Quest in the Middle East: Gertrude Bell and the Making of Modern Iraq* (London: I.B. Taurus, 2019), 184.

[72]Letter, Gertrude Bell to Sir Hugh Bell, 1 November 1920. http://gertrude-bell.ncl.ac.uk/letter_details.php?letter_id=431

[73]Introduction. In P. Collins & C. Tripp (eds.), *Gertrude Bell and Iraq: A Life and Legacy* (Oxford: Oxford University Press, 2017), 18.

[74]A. T. Sullivan, Review of *Faisal I of Iraq*, in *Middle East Policy*, 22/1 (March 2015):142–149.

[75]Quoted in C. B. Faught, *Allenby. Making the Modern Middle East* (London: Bloomsbury, 2020), 115.

[76]A. Allawi, *Faisal I of Iraq* (New Haven: Yale University Press, 2014), 79.

[77]A. Allawi, *Faisal I of Iraq* (New Haven: Yale University Press, 2014), xxix.

[78]Letter, Gertrude Bell to Valentine Chirol, 4 February 1921. In G. Howell, *Queen of the Desert: The Extraordinary Life of Gertrude Bell* (London: Pan, 2015), 399.

[79]J. Barr, *A Line in the Sand: Britain, France and the Struggle that Shaped the Middle East* (London: Simon and Schuster, 2011), 35.

[80]J. Barr, *A Line in the Sand: Britain, France and the Struggle that Shaped the Middle East* (London: Simon and Schuster, 2011), 35.

[81]A. T. Sullivan, Review of *Faisal I of Iraq*, in *Middle East Policy*, 22/1 (March 2015):142–149.

[82]Letter, T. E. Shaw (Lawrence) to Sir Hugh Bell, 4 November 1927, in M. Brown (ed.), *The Letters of T.E. Lawrence: The Years in India 1927–29*.

[83]Letter, Gertrude Bell to Charles Doughty-Wylie, 25 March 1915. http://gertrudebell.ncl.ac.uk/letter_details.php?letter_id=1842

# The Myth of the Phoenix and the British Bulldog. Winston Churchill

[1]I became intimately familiar with the Second World War during the writing of my book *Building a Nazi Europe*, for which I conducted research in 19 archival collections across Europe and North America. Additionally, for this chapter I consulted several (though, mercifully, not all) Churchill biographies. Particularly helpful among these were M. Gilbert, *Continue to Pester, Nag, and Bite: Churchill's War Leadership*, The Barbara Frum Lectureship (Toronto: Vintage Canada, 2004), M. Hastings, *Finest Years. Churchill as Warlord, 1940–1945* (New York: Harper Press, 2010), and A. Roberts, *Churchill: Walking with Destiny* (New York: Penguin, 2019). Churchill himself was a prolific writer and his works (always to be taken with a grain of salt) were a boon to me in researching this book, as it has been to others writing about his life.
M. Hastings, *Finest Years. Churchill as Warlord, 1940–1945* (New York: Harper Press, 2010), 69.

[2]J. C. B. Dear & M. R. D. Foot, *The Oxford Companion to World War II* (Oxford: Oxford University Press, 2001), 109.

[3]W. S. Churchill, *The Second World War: Their Finest Hour* (Boston: Houghton Mifflin, 1985), 208–209. See also G. E. Melton, *From Versailles to Mers el-Kebir: The Promise of Anglo-French Naval Cooperation, 1919–40* (Annapolis: Naval Institute Press, 2015).

[4]W. S. Churchill, *The Second World War: Their Finest Hour* (Boston: Houghton Mifflin, 1985), 210.

[5]M. Gilbert, *Continue to Pester, Nag, and Bite : Churchill's War Leadership*, The Barbara Frum Lectureship (Toronto: Vintage Canada, 2004)

[6]Quoted in I. Sebir, Force H to Mers-el-Kébir. *Naval History Magazine*, U.S. Naval Institute (August 2022), accessed 11 March 2023 at https://www.usni.org/magazines/naval-history-magazine/2022/august/force-h-mers-el-kebir.

[7]On this perspective, see, for example, M. Mazower, *Dark Continent. Europe's Twentieth Century* (New York: Vintage, 2000).

[8]Author search in World Catalogue, 30 May 2023, www.worldcat.org.

[9]https://www.pbs.org/wgbh/masterpiece/specialfeatures/world-war-ii-major-events-timeline/

[10]G. Loftus, If you're going through hell, keep going. In *Forbes*, accessed 29 March 2022 at, https://www.forbes.com/sites/geoffloftus/2012/05/09/if-youre-going-through-hell-keep-going-winston-churchill/#423fd178d549

[11]F. Loewenheim, et al., (eds.), *Roosevelt and Churchill. Their Secret Wartime Correspondence* (London: E.P. Dutton, 1975), 20.

[12]I. Kershaw, *Hitler, 1936–45. Nemesis* (New York: W. W. Norton, 2000), 297.

[13]D. Shears, Hitler's D-Day, *The Quarterly Journal of Military History*, 6/4 (Summer 1994).

[14]I. Kershaw, *Hitler, 1936–45. Nemesis* (New York: W. W. Norton, 2000), 303.

[15]A. Tooze, *The Wages of Destruction. The Making and Breaking of the Nazi Economy* (New York: Penguin, 2008), 636; J. C. B. Dear & M. R. D. Foot, *The Oxford Companion to World War II* (Oxford: Oxford University Press, 2001), 667.

[16]W. S. Churchill, *The Second World War: Their Finest Hour* (Boston: Houghton Mifflin, 1985), 204.

[17]D. Edgerton, *Britain's War Machine: Weapons, Resources, and Experts in the Second World War* (Oxford: Oxford University Press, 2011), 14.

[18]Leading Change Without a Burning Platform. *Harvard Business Review* (29 February 2008), accessed 12 May 2021 at, https://hbr.org/2008/02/leading-change-without-a-burni.html

[19]BBC broadcast, 14.7.1940, accessed 10 March 2021 at http://www.winstonchurchill.org/learn/speeches/speeches-of-winston-churchill/1940-finest-hour.

[20]M. Gilbert, *Continue to Pester, Nag, and Bite : Churchill's War Leadership*, The Barbara Frum Lectureship (Toronto: Vintage Canada, 2004), 40.

[21]F.rh.r med K[.] L[.] , 24 December 1943, in Riksarkivet, Stockholm - Arninge (RASA) S.PO Personakter (PA): S.po PA, K[.] L[.]

[22]Quoted in, E. Nideros, Battle of Omdurman: The Last British Cavalry Charge. History Warfare (June 2011), accessed 12 June 2019 at https://warfarehistorynetwork.com/article/battle-of-omdurman-the-last-british-cavalry-charge/.

[23]M. Brown, Cold Steel, Weak Flesh: Mechanism, Masculinity and the Anxieties of Late Victorian Empire. *Cultural and Social History* 14/2 (March 2017): 155–181.

[24]R. Prior & T. Wilson *The Somme* (New Haven: Yale University Press, 2005), 112.

[25]Quoted in M. Eksteins, *Rites of Spring: The Great War and the Birth of the Modern Age* (New York: Mariner Books, 2000), 152–153.

[26]Quoted in J. Keegan, *The First World War* (New York: Vintage, 2012), 364.

[27]The list of works that explore this is extensive. See, for example, R. Paxton, *The Anatomy of Fascism* (New York: Knopf, 2004).

[28] An oft-quoted line from a 1927 speech by Mussolini. It can be found with variations in the translation, including, for example, S. Power, The Original Axis of Evil. *The New York Times* (2 May 2004), accessed 12 March 2022 at, https://www.nytimes.com/2004/05/02/books/the-original-axis-of-evil.html.

[29] International Churchill Society, accessed 31 March 2022 at, https://winstonchurchill.org/resources/speeches/1940-the-finest-hour/the-few/

[30] D. Edgerton, *Britain's War Machine: Weapons, Resources, and Experts in the Second World War* (Oxford: Oxford University Press, 2011), 35

[31] J. C. B. Dear & M. R. D. Foot, *The Oxford Companion to World War II* (Oxford: Oxford University Press, 2001), 225

[32] I. Kershaw, *Hitler, 1936–45. Nemesis* (New York: W. W. Norton, 2000), 148.

[33] A. Beevor, *Second World War* (New York: Little & Brown, 2012), e-book.

[34] Quoted in A. Beevor, *Crete* (New York: Penguin, 2014), e-book.

[35] Quoted in J. Winton, *Voices from the War At Sea 1939–45: Freedom's Battle* Volume 1, (London: Vintage, 2007), 168.

[36] Quoted in B. Gough, Finest Hour 139, Summer 2008. International Churchill Society, accessed 30 May 2023 at https://winstonchurchill.org/publications/finest-hour/finest-hour-139/churchill-proceedings-prince-of-wales-and-repulse-churchills-veiled-threat-reconsidered/.

[37] A. Beevor, *Crete* (New York: Penguin, 2014), e-book.

[38] M. Hastings, Their Wehrmacht was better than out army. In *Washington Post* (5 May 1985).

[39] A. Moorhead, *African Trilogy* (Cassell, 1998), 409

[40] D. Showlter, *Armor and Blood: The Battle of Kursk, The Turning Point of World War II* (New York: Random House, 2013), e-book.

[41] M. Gilbert, *Continue to Pester, Nag, and Bite : Churchill's War Leadership*, The Barbara Frum Lectureship (Toronto: Vintage Canada, 2004).

[42] M. Gilbert, *Continue to Pester, Nag, and Bite : Churchill's War Leadership*, The Barbara Frum Lectureship (Toronto: Vintage Canada, 2004), 12.

[43] M. Gilbert, *Continue to Pester, Nag, and Bite : Churchill's War Leadership*, The Barbara Frum Lectureship (Toronto: Vintage Canada, 2004), 13.

[44] Quoted in M. Gilbert, *Continue to Pester, Nag, and Bite : Churchill's War Leadership*, The Barbara Frum Lectureship (Toronto: Vintage Canada, 2004), 77.

[45] Quoted in M. Hastings, *Finest Years. Churchill as Warlord, 1940–1945* (New York: Harper Press, 2010), 182.

[46] D. Edgerton, *Britain's War Machine: Weapons, Resources, and Experts in the Second World War* (Oxford: Oxford University Press, 2011), 2

[47]International Churchill Society, accessed 12 March 2022 at, https://winstonchurchill.org/resources/speeches/1940-the-finest-hour/war-of-the-unknown-warriors/

[48]Paragraph modified from S. O'Conner and M. Gutmann, Under a Foreign Flag. *Journal of Modern European History* (2016).

[49]Paragraph modified from M. Gutmann, Building a Nazi Europe (Cambridge: Cambridge UP, 2017), 107.

[50]National Churchill Museum, accessed 12 March 2022 at, https://www.nationalchurchillmuseum.org/winston-churchills-broadcast-on-the-soviet-german-war.html

[51]Quoted in M. Hastings, *Finest Years. Churchill as Warlord, 1940–1945* (New York: Harper Press, 2010), 18.

[52]Quoted M. Hastings, *Finest Years. Churchill as Warlord, 1940–1945* (New York: Harper Press, 2010), 177.

[53]Imperial War Museum, Cabinet War Rooms Exhibition, London.

[54]D. Reynolds, *Summits. Six Meetings that Shaped the 20th Century* (New York: Basic Books, 2009), 105

[55]M. Hastings, *Finest Years. Churchill as Warlord, 1940–1945* (New York: Harper Press, 2010), 179

[56]Letter, Churchill to FDR, 12 July 1940, FDR Library, accessed 12 May 2020 at, http://www.fdrlibraryvirtualtour.org/graphics/07-06/7-5-Churchill-to-FDR_12-7-40.pdf

[57]A. Tooze, *The Wages of Destruction. The Making and Breaking of the Nazi Economy* (New York: Penguin, 2008), 641

[58]J. C. B. Dear & M. R. D. Foot, *The Oxford Companion to World War II* (Oxford: Oxford University Press, 2001), 531–533.

[59]E. V. Westrate, *Forward Observer* (Philadelphia: Blakiston, 1944).

[60]R. Overmans, *Deutsche militärische Verluste im Zweiten Weltkrieg* (Oldenbourg, 2000).

[61]https://www.hgwdavie.com/blog/2018/10/6/soviet-casualties

[62]R. Reese, *Why Stalin's Soldiers Fought: The Red Army's Military Effectiveness in World War II* (University of Kansas Press, 2011).

[63]This section is a modified version of M. Gutmann, What we can learn from the D-Day invasion in the age of Brexit and Trump. Swiss Radio and Television, (2019).

[64]Quoted in M. Gutmann, What we can learn from the D-Day invasion in the age of Brexit and Trump. Swiss Radio and Television, (2019).

[65]Letter, President Franklin D. Roosevelt to Winston Churchill, 3 April 1942, in Churchill Exhibitions, Library of Congress, accessed 21 May 2021 at https://www.loc.gov/exhibits/churchill/interactive/_html/wc0163.html.

[66]M. Hastings, *Finest Years. Churchill as Warlord, 1940–1945* (New York: Harper Press, 2010), 299.

[67]A. Beevor, *Second World War* (New York: Little & Brown, 2012), e-book.

[68]The Dieppe raid. Government of Canada, Veteran's Affairs, Factsheet, accessed 21 March 2023 at https://www.veterans.gc.ca/eng/remembrance/classroom/fact-sheets/dieppe.

[69]A. Bevor, *D-Day* (London: Penguin Books, 2009), e-book.

[70]Quoted in A. Roberts, *Churchill: Walking with Destiny* (New York: Penguin, 2019), e-book.

[71]K. Chi Man, T. Yiu Lun *Eastern Fortress: A Military History of Hong Kong, 1840–1970* (Hong Kong: Hong Kong University Press, 2014), 212.

[72]Quoted in A. Beevor, *Second World War* (New York: Little & Brown, 2012), e-book.

[73]Quoted in R. Forsyth, *To Save An Army. The Stalingrad Airlift* (New York: Bloomsbury, 2022), e-book.

[74]Recounted by one of Hitler's technocrats: A. Speer & E. Davidson, *Inside the Third Reich. Memoirs by Albert Speer* (London: Orion, 1970), 258.

[75]I. Kershaw, *Hitler, 1936–45. Nemesis* (New York: W. W. Norton, 2000), 635.

[76]A. Tooze, *The Wages of Destruction. The Making and Breaking of the Nazi Economy* (New York: Penguin, 2008), 582.

[77]A. Tooze, *The Wages of Destruction. The Making and Breaking of the Nazi Economy* (New York: Penguin, 2008), 613.

[78]A. Tooze, *The Wages of Destruction. The Making and Breaking of the Nazi Economy* (New York: Penguin, 2008), 612.

[79]I. Kershaw, *Hitler, 1936–45. Nemesis* (New York: W. W. Norton, 2000).

[80]Though frequently attributed first to Stalin and Russian officials, it appears that the British cartoonist Sidney Strube was the first to make the comparison to a bulldog. See, D.J. Hall, Evolution of a Famous Image. International Churchill Society, accessed 10 May 2021 at https://winstonchurchill.org/publications/finest-hour/finest-hour-106/bulldog-churchill-the-evolution-of-a-famous-image/.

[81]Telegram, Watch and Revolver. Imperial War Museum, Cabinet War Rooms Collection, London.

[82]Quoted in M. Hastings, *Finest Years. Churchill as Warlord, 1940–1945* (New York: Harper Press, 2010), 121.

[83]D. Goleman, What Makes a Leader? IQ and Technical Skills are Important, but Emotional Intelligence is the Sine Qua Non of Leadership. *Harvard Business Review* (February 2004), accessed 21 March 2021 at https://hbr.org/2004/01/what-makes-a-leader?utm_medium=social&utm_campaign=hbr&utm_source=LinkedIn&tpcc=orgsocial_edit.

[84] P. G. Northouse, *Leadership: Theory and Practice* 6th edn. (Thousand Oaks: Sage, 2013), 1654.

[856] A. Marder, *From the Dardanelles to Oran: Studies of the Royal Navy in War and Peace 1915–1940* (Annapolis: US Naval Institute, 2015), 109.

[86] Quoted in A. *Roberts, Churchill: Walking with Destiny* (New York: Penguin, 2019).

[87] B. Bailyn, The Challenge of Modern Historiography. *The American Historical Review*, 87/1 (1982).

## The Story We Tell

[1] It is retold in countless business blogs and teaching material. See, for example, J. Sebenius, Six Habits of Merely Effective Negotiators. *Harvard Business Review* (April 2001), 87–95.

[2] S.L. Beckman, To Frame or Reframe: Where Might Design Thinking Research Go Next? *California Management Review* 62/2, (2020), 144–162.

[3] R. Amundsen, *The North West Passage: Being the Record of a Voyage of Exploration of the Ship "Gjoa", 1903–1907*, vol. 1. (New York: E.P. Dutton and Company, 1908), 64.

[4] K. Marx, *The 18th of Brummaire* (1852), accessed 21 March 2023 at https://www.marxists.org/archive/marx/works/1852/18th-brumaire/

[5] T. Bomann-Larsen, *Roald Amundsen* (London: The History Press, 2006), 546.

[6] R. Sadun, The Myth of the Brilliant Charismatic Leader. *Harvard Business Review* (November 2022), accessed 21 December 2022 at, https://hbr.org/2022/11/the-myth-of-the-brilliant-charismatic-leader.

[7] J. DeNeve, et al., Born to Lead? A Twin Design and Genetic Association Study of Leadership Role Occupancy. *Leaders* Quarterly, 24/1 (2013):45–60.

[8] K. Grint, *Leadership. A Very Short Introduction* (Oxford: Oxford University Press, 2010), 19.

[9] T. Yunkaporta, *Sand Talk: How Indigenous Thinking Can Save the World* (Text Publishing, 2019).

Made in United States
Troutdale, OR
12/30/2024